TALES OF OLD SCHENECTADY

Volume I:
The Formative Years

(Bicentennial Edition)

by
Larry Hart

Old Dorp Books
195 Droms Road
Scotia, N.Y. 12302

By the same author:
The Sacandaga Story
Did I Wake You Up?
Schenectady's Golden Era

First Edition — Manufactured in the United States of America

Published by Old Dorp Books, Scotia, N.Y.
Printed by Benche, Inc., Schenectady, N.Y.
Typeset by Silverline, Amsterdam, N.Y.

To my grandchildren Eddie, Rachael, Jenny and Annie. . .may their tomorrows, as for all the young people of today, be made brighter by what has been learned from the past.

SCHENECTADY, THE GATEWAY

On a valuable piece of property
Across the piney plains;
In the valley of the Mohawk
Lies the gateway to the westward.
Here the Dutch defied the red men
And the restless left their families.
Here the westbound barges gathered
Bound for the inland seas and rivers
While the bargemen cursed and chanted
On the Erie Canal.

Here the dark of night was shattered
By a glow that blazed to floodlight
The homes and highways of a nation
By the man whose dreams meant power,
Not for Steinmetz but his people.

Here the giant locomotives
Breathed their fires,
Tried their whistles,
And, drivers pounding,
Roared out westward —
Thundered southward —
From coast to coast and lake to gulf
They hauled the lifeblood of the nation.

This in brief was our foundation.
This was Schenectady's beginning.
Can we rise to meet the challenge
Or shall our past so dim our future
That, lost in self, we lose our birthright?
I say, we have been great.
We SHALL be great again.

> — *Lauren H. Grandy Jr.*
> *Schenectady 1975*

Table of Contents

SECTION VI RANDOM STORIES OF THE PAST

BIBLIOGRAPHY

Birch, John J. — *As the Fields Ripened* (1960)

Birch, John J. — *The Markers Speak* (1962)

Hanson, Willis T., Jr. — *A History of Schenectady During the Revolution* (1916, reprinted 1974)

Leckie, Robert — *The Wars of America* (1968)

Maddaus, Elsie M. — *Slavery in Saratoga County,* from the Spring 1975 edition of the *Grist Mill*

Pearson, Jonathan A. — *A History of the Schenectady Patent (1883)*

Van Epps, Percy M. — *The Schenectady Patent of 1684 and the Common Lands of Glenville, N.Y.* (1948)

Veeder, Millicent W. — *Door to the Mohawk Valley* (1947)

Vrooman, John J. — *Forts and Firesides of the Mohawk Country* (1943, revised 1951)

Yates, Austin A. — *Schenectady County, N.Y. Its History to the Close of the Nineteenth Century* (1902)

List of Illustrations

Lawrence the Indian statue at the junction of Front, Ferry and Green Streets in Schenectady's historic stockade district was erected in 1887. It marks the site on which the Queen's Fort, a British garrison, was built in 1704. (NYS Dept. of Commerce photo, courtesy of Schenectady County Historical Society.)

PREFACE

One does not have to live in the Schenectady area too long to realize that it is steeped in history. And now that most Americans are getting into the spirit of the nation's Bicentennial celebration, history and historical events have become of greater interest to communities everywhere. It presents a rare opportunity, at least from an historian's standpoint, to dig for as many long ago facts as possible and expose them to public view.

It is because so much history abounds in and around Schenectady, one-time gateway to the west, that one who attempts to tell of it is soon faced with the realization he cannot wrap it up neatly in a single volume without sacrificing the human factor in history. You can "write" history in text book form — giving full attention to dates and places and events — but it makes for dull reading, indeed, if little is told about the people involved in those happenings.

With this in mind, we have resolved to approach the telling of Schenectady's past in peacemeal fashion, one volume at a time in non-hurried pace, with the hope that someday the complete works will represent a composite picture of this area's history and of those who helped make it. Some of the stories are repeated from the weekly series of the Schenectady Gazette column, "Tales of Old Dorp," which we have been pleased to write for the past several years, although most have been embellished with details recently uncovered. We think our readers will agree these stories should not be eliminated from a compilation of local history, even at the expense of being labeled "twice-told tales."

Because this is Volume One and 1976 is the pivotal year of the Bicentennial, primary consideration is given the history of Schenectady's development from a small trading outpost more than three centuries ago and what life was like in this area at the time of the Revolutionary War. Of course, like the founding and the massacre of Schenectady, some accounts will hardly amount to a revelation to most readers because events of such magnitude have been recounted faithfully, almost ritually, through the years. But they should and must be included here as part of the ongoing saga of Schenectady and its people.

In a previous publication, "Schenectady's Golden Era," we covered much of the happenings which occurred in Schenectady between 1880 and 1930 — a period of astounding growth in the community. Included was a detailed account of the development of General Electric, the Schenectady Railway Company, the spectacular careers of men such as Dr. Charles P. Steinmetz and Dr. George R. Lunn and the glittering days of the Roaring Twenties. It is hoped that this and subsequent volumes will fill in the other historic periods of Schenectady's past.

In retrospect, what probably makes Schenectady's past especially intriguing is the fact that in its long history it has been so diversified in all areas of human endeavor. It has lived under three flags — Dutch, English and American (and there could have been a fourth if the French had chosen to hoist their flag the night they had taken over the town). The populace at first was predominantly Dutch, then well sprinkled with English, Scotch and Irish when the New England "Yankees" migrated here before the Revolution; finally, and up to the present, we have a typical American amalgamation of virtually every ethnic group.

The community has passed through numerous phases of commerce and industry; likewise its economy has fluctuated with the turn of these events. One can imagine the amazement of the slow-moving burgher of Dorptown more than two centuries ago were he to be granted a momentary awakening from his long sleep and look upon the fast-paced, automated life in Schenectady and its environs today. Likely as not, he would shake his head disbelievingly and wonder what the human race was coming to.

We have seen startling upsurges in population caused by such momentous happenings as the building of the Erie Canal, the coming of the railroads, electric street cars and automobiles, and the development of industrial plants all along the Mohawk Valley. In more recent years, sprawling farmlands outside the city have been transformed into housing tracts and shopping centers.

In a way, the history of Schenectady parallels the history of America, with the freedom of enterprise and social opportunities showing the way to progress and human achievement; but we are biased enough, out of an unadulterated love for the city of our birth, to believe that it is still a rather special history.

— Larry Hart

July 4, 1975
Schenectady, New York

Section I

THE FORMATIVE YEARS

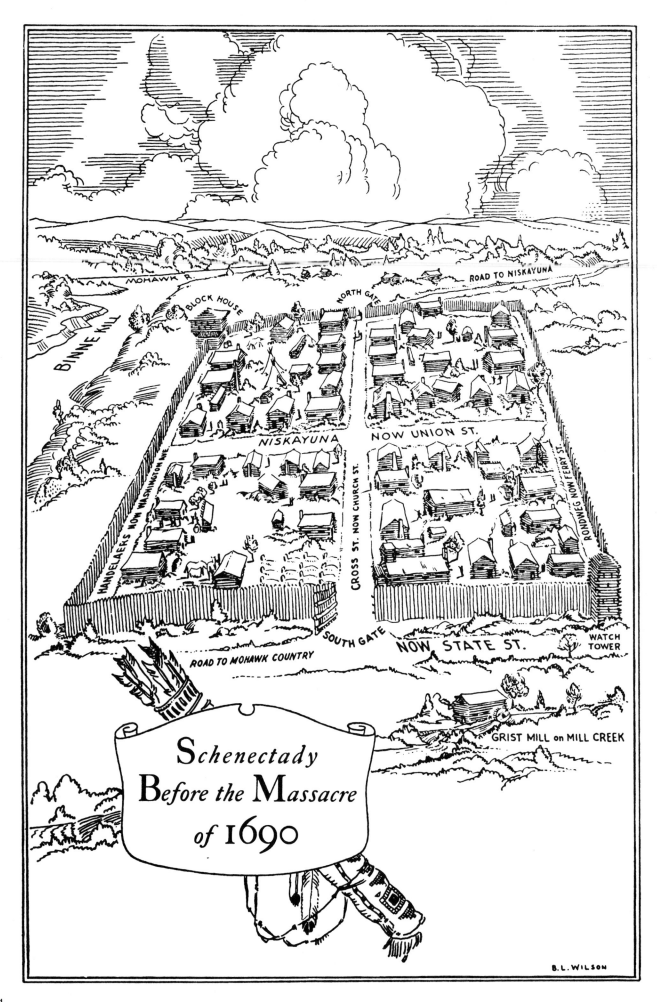

Schenectady Before the Massacre of 1690

The settlement of Schenectady was 52 years in the offing when Henry Hudson, an Englishman engaged by the Dutch West India Company, sailed the Half Moon up the Hudson River in 1609 in search of the Northwest Passage and so blazed a trail for Dutchmen soon to follow. But this was only one area of the magnificent New World then being explored by representatives of Old World powers; besides Holland, the mercantile princes of France, England and Spain were all intensely interested in the lush territory of a virgin continent and ever so anxious to get a colonial foothold on its most promising sectors. Indeed, the Spanish had long established the first white settlement in America at St. Augustine, Fla., in 1565, and the British founded its Jamestown colony in Virginia in 1607.

In succeeding years, many more ships crossed the Atlantic as settlements and forts were built all along the eastern seaboard of America. They came over with farmers, traders, craftsmen, churchmen and slaves, then returned to their home ports loaded with furs, precious metals, lumber and produce for the European market. They found most of the territories inhabited by a strange bronze-skinned race whom the white settlers called savages savages; and yet their presence was viewed as no great stumbling block to colonization. The Indians were uncivilized, but mainly curious and friendly toward the Europeans who came to take over the rich forests and valleys of an unsettled land. These aborigines would, however, later have a marked influence on the fortunes of the visitors who came to their shores to stay.

The stage, then, was set early for confrontation of the European settlers and their Indian allies in America. They vied for territory and riches here, and such intense rivalry often led to open hostility; but worse, they could not prevent their own political and religious squabbles back home from also being fought on the new soil. For more than 150 years in the settlement of America, before it finally became an independent nation and was allowed to look to the west, the British fought the Dutch, the French fought both the Dutch and British, and then the American colonists and their French allies fought the British. And on various sides, we must not forget, the Indians also fought bravely but in some confusion as to who were their friends or enemies.

The Spaniards, who had concentrated on the warmer climes of the Gulf of Mexico and the Caribbean, had no direct bearing on the struggle among the northern colonies. The French were lured to Canada in 1603 but hoped to enlarge their holdings southward. The Dutch chose to settle in what became New York and New Jersey. The English began colonizing in New England and Virginia, but later found reason to take over other settlements in wars with the Dutch and French.

The white man undoubtedly had seen the Mohawk Valley before Arent Van Curler passed through it in 1642 and later wrote that "there lies the most beautiful land that the eye of man ever beheld." If we are to believe tradition, fur traders and bosloopers (woods runners) had roved among the Mohawks and raised families of half breeds by the time the Dutch built Fort Nassau in the vicinity of present day Albany in 1614, and certainly after Fort Orange (Albany) became the first permanent Dutch settlement in North America in 1624. But Van Curler's enthusiasm over a particular region at the throat of the Valley probably waxed not so much from the mere beauty of the place as his assessment of its potential as a settlement and trading post. It is even quite possible that others may have thought of it, but the fact that the white man made no permanent settlement on the Mohawk west of Albany before 1662 could be attributed to the opposition of Albany and the Colonie Rensselaerwyck. To have a fur trading post between them and the Indian castles would be unthinkable.

The settlement of Albany was then called Beverwyck by the Dutch, located alongside Fort Orange. The patroon system had been established by the Dutch West India Company in 1629 to encourage settlement of New Netherland and by the time Van Curler was petitioning for a settlement at Schenectady, the Hollanders and their families were firmly entrenched throughout this territory. The governor and territorial officials held forth from headquarters in New Amsterdam, which had been established on Manhattan Island in 1625.

To complicate matters for the Dutch settlers upstate, including those of Schenectady just after it was founded, Great Britain flexed its muscle and took over Dutch territorial rights in 1664. Charles II gave the erstwhile Colony of New Netherland to the Duke of York and both it and the city of New Amsterdam were renamed New York. Beverwyck was renamed Albany. Almost simultaneous with the takeover, the English promised the Dutch settlers that they would retain their lands and many privileges. The Dutch burghers, just as shrewd as their new authorities, were well aware that the English needed them more than they needed the English but also recognized they had little choice but to remain. Actually, the Mohawk Dutchman knew little about Governor Stuyvesant or lords of the manor, and cared less. He had just begun to settle down to his pipe and "auker of good beere" while building on the Groote Vlachte — and if the British didn't bother him, he'd be well satisfied.

N E

Orhoengene neoni Yogaraskhagh Yondereanayendaghkwa,

Ene Niyoh Raodeweyena,

N E { Onoghfadogeaghtige Yondadderighwanon-doentha,

Siyagonnoghfode Enyondereanayendagh-kwagge,

Yotkade Kapiellhogough ne Karighwadaghkwe-agh Asayea neoni Afe Teftament, neoni Niyadegari-wagge, ne *Kanningahaga Siniyewenoteagh.*

Tehoenvenadenyough *Lawrance Claeffe,* Rowenagaradatsk *William Andrews,* Ronwanha - ugh *Ongweboenvwighne* Rodirighhoeni Raddiyadanorough neoni Ahoenvadigonuyofthagge Thoderighwawaakhogk ne Wahooni Agarighhowanha Niych Raodeweyena Niyadegogh-whenjage.

Eghtferaggwas Eghtjeeagh ne ongwehoonwe, neoni ne fiyodoghwhenjooktannighhoegh etho ahadyeandough.

T H E

Morning and Evening Prayer,

T H E { Litany, Church Catechifm, Family Prayers,

A N D

Several Chapters of the Old and New-Teftament, Tranflated into the *Mahaque Indian* Language,

By *Lawrence Claeffe,* Interpreter to *William Andrews,* Miffionary to the Indians, from the Honourable and Reverend the *Society for the Propogation of the Gofpel in Foreign Parts.*

Ask of me, and I will give thee the Heathen for thine Inheritance, and the Utmoft Parts of the Earth for thy Poffeffion, Pfalm 2. 8.

Printed by *William Bradford* in *New-York,* 1715.

Copy of title pages of a worship booklet printed by the British missionaries in 1715 for their work with the Mohawk Indians. It comprised a morning and evening prayer, the Litany, church catechism, family prayers and several chapters of the old and new testament – all translated into the language of the Mohawks.

By the time the Dutch traders and settlers came up to this part of the country in the 1620's, the Iroquois confederacy was in full command of what is now upstate New York. Five tribes had formed a league about a generation before the invasion of the whites. In the east were the mighty Mohawks, probably most war-like among the Iroquois but soon to prove the staunchest, bravest friends of the Dutch and British settlers. The Oneidas were around what is now Utica, the Onondagas were near Syracuse, the Cayuga tribe lived near the Finger Lakes and the Senecas had their castles in the Genesee Valley in the Western part of our state. The Tuscarora, an Iroquois tribe of North Carolina which had voluntarily moved to New York, was formally admitted into the confederacy about 1715 when it henceforth became known as the League of Six Nations instead of the five nations referred to in earlier records.

From the first, the Iroquois were consistent and bitter enemies of the French, who had shown amity to their traditional foes, the Algonquins. They remained in friendship and trade with first the Dutch and then the English throughout the wars up to the mid-18th century. Without a doubt, the Iroquois greatly hampered French movement from Canada southward and had it not been for the stubborn Iroquois check, the English colonies would have been flanked from behind by the French and the history of their development might have been very different. This must be regarded as a remarkable achievement for a savage people who never put into the field an army greater than 2,000 men.

Through the courage and fortitude of the Jesuit missionaries, the French also enlisted the aid of a band of Mohawks who had been converted to Catholicism by the French priests and moved to the St. Lawrence River near Montreal in an Indian castle they called Caughnawaga. They were as fierce in battle as their Mohawk counterparts to the south, and for many years aided and accompanied the French in sorties downstate in surroundings that were familiar to them. One of these raids was the attack on Schenectady in 1690. Because of their adoption of the Christian faith, the Caughnawaga Mohawks were referred to by Dutch and English settlers as the "Praying Indians."

It was prudent and quite necessary for the Dutch and English settlers to win the friendship of their red-skinned neighbors. They needed assurance that their farms and stockades would not be raided once they had negotiated for either the purchase or gift of land. There was also the expediency of promoting the fur trade. The Indians had the wherewithal to provide a steady and ample source of the skins of beaver (the most valuable in the European market), fox, raccoon, otter, lynx, elk, bear and timber wolf. And it was no pretense that New Netherland was first occupied for the purpose of trade only. Agriculture was secondary, even after the patroon system was established by the Dutch; so intent were the first Hollanders upon the Indian traffic that agriculture was badly neglected and hardly breadstuffs enough for the trading posts were raised.

For a long time, the chief seat of Indian trade was at Fort Orange, where the natives gathered in great numbers with their pelts. Until 1630, the two chartered Dutch companies — the privileged West India Company and the United New Netherland Company — practically had a monopoly of the fur trade in this region. But in 1652, Peter Stuyvesant established new rules for Fort Orange and Beverwyck in which the government claimed municipal rights, excise, taxes and all the privileges of a Dutch governor's seal on the lucrative fur trade. This caused consternation among individual traders and such jealousy and bickering among Albany civil authorities that there probably was no great outcry up-colony when the British took over its administration.

This feeling prevailed when Schenectady was settled in 1662 and on up through 1668 when the Original Patent for Schenectady issued by English Governor Thomas Dongan clarified Schenectady's land and trading rights. The traders at Fort Orange and Beverwyck rankled over the thought that Schenectady burghers to the west were allowed to trade for beaver and forestall the market by sending bosloopers, or runners, up the Mohawk to purchase the natives' pelts. Despite the patent, this and other events caused a bitter feeling to develop between Fort Orange and Schenectady at the time of the 1690 massacre.

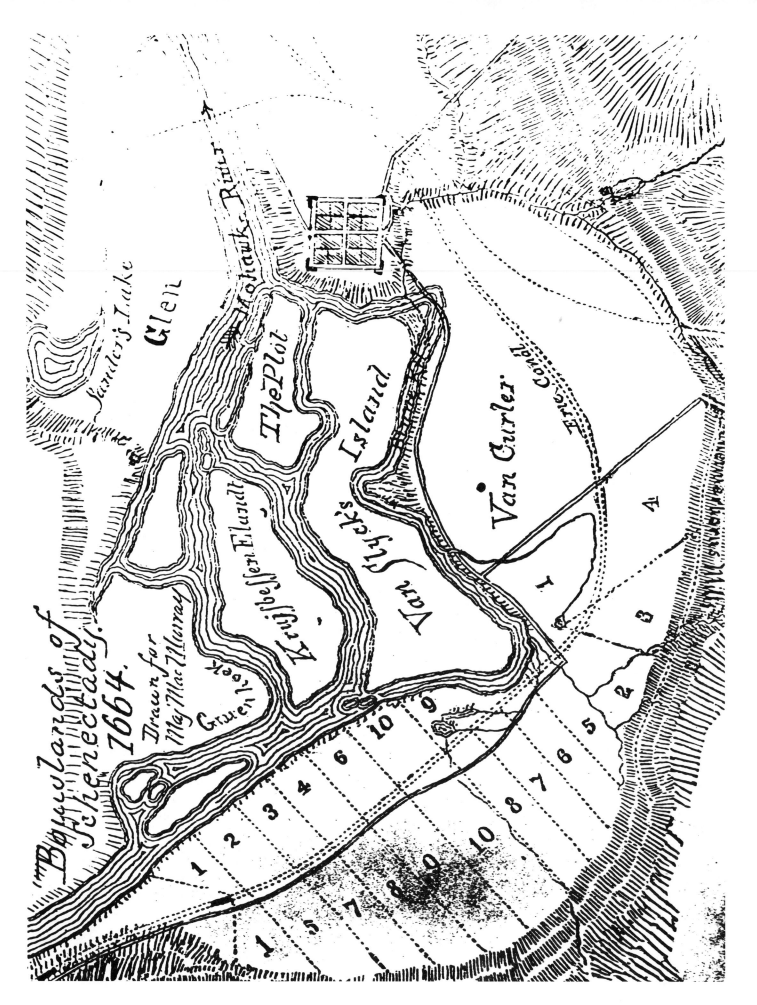

Bouwlandts of Schenectady.
1664.
Drawn for Maj. Mac Murray

Glen
Sander's Lake
Mohawk River
The Plot
Kruijsbessen Elandt
Green Kill
Van Slyck's Island
Van Curler
Erie Canal

18

The Colony of Netherland had a population of about 10,000 persons, most of them Dutch, when Arent Van Curler made formal application in the summer of 1661 to Governor Stuyvesant for permission to settle upon the "Great Flat" which today is occupied almost wholly by the General Electric Co. plant. This much Van Curler had purchased from the Mohawks for a moderate price, but those who wished to settle Schenectady envisioned a much greater territory.

The whites had already invaded the area with the good graces of their Iroquois friends. Alexander Lindsay Glen, a Scotsman to whom the Mohawks were warmly attached, had built a home on the Scotia shore three years before. Bible entries show that Jacques Cornelise Van Slyck, the half-breed son of Cornelise Van Slyck and his Indian wife, and John Teller, a nephew of Glen's wife, also settled here in 1658, the latter in Rotterdam along what is now Schermerhorn Road. But Van Curler, called Corlaer by the Mohawks, had in mind a stockade and farms nearby — something which the officials and traders of Beverwyck and Colonie Rensselaerwyck objected to from the start.

Van Curler was an intelligent businessman who came over from Holland as an agent for his cousin, Killian Van Rensselaer, a jewel merchant in Amsterdam (Holland) who had been granted a great tract of land along the Hudson River by the Dutch West India Company. He lived at Beverwyck and in a short while had a good working knowledge of the fur market but, even more important, a personal conviction that he would strive to locate a settlement for those sturdy, liberty-loving Dutchmen who could no longer endure irksome conditions at Beverwyck and the domination of Fort Orange.

It was no easy task, convincing a stubborn Dutch governor that a new outpost beyond Fort Orange would be in the best interests of the Colony. Stuyvesant was besieged with letters of opposition to the request by up-colony officials and the directors of the trading companies, and for a time he hedged on any commitment to Van Curler and fellow applicants perhaps in the belief that the problem might simply go away without further disturbing the established traders.

Meanwhile, Van Curler and the original proprietors began colonization of the land which the Mohawks called Schonowe (their name for the river flats) by 1662 and the leader of the settlement once more sent off a pleading message to New Amsterdam to give direction to the new settlers so that they could set up a local government and make their holdings secure by law. To this latest entreaty, Beverwyck and

Rensselaerwyck induced Stuyvesant to order that the inhabitants of Schenectady must confine themselves exclusively to agriculture and restrain from all trade with the Indians. Van Curler and the settlers would not agree to this, imploring the Governor in 1663 that, as they had paid for their lands, they should have them without any restriction. Finally, in a directive handed down by Stuyvesant on May 20, 1664, Schenectady was assigned a surveyor by the name of Jacques Cortelyou "to lay out the aforesaid lands in the best manner possible and for the best accommodation of those interested therein, viz: to each man his Share. . ."

* * *

So it was that, after a delay of more than two years, Stuyvesant came to an understanding with the settlers of Schenectady, and the several lots and farms were surveyed and conveyed to them by patents. In August that same year, the Duke of York through his emissary had ousted Stuyvesant and the Dutch companies. It would be not until 1684, when Governor Dongan issued the Original Patent for Schenectady, that the exact territory for the new settlement would be formally acknowledged.

These were the signers to the indenture of 1663 wherein petition was made to have the land surveyed: Arent Van Curler, Alexander Lindsay Glen, Philip Hendrickse Brouwer, Symon Volkertse Veeder, Pieter Adriance Van Woggelum, Teunise Cornelise Swart, Bastian de Winter (attorney for Catalyn De Vos, widow of Arent Bradt who signed the original petition but died before he could come here), Gerrit Bancker, William Teller, Pieter Jacobse Borsboom, Pieter Danielse Van Olinda, Jan Barentse Wemp (Wemple), Jacques Cornelise Van Slyck, Marten Cornelise Van Esselstyn and Harmen Albertse Vedder. They were known thereafter as the 15 original proprietors of Schenectady.

Large tracts of farmland were assigned to the proprietors and their families all along the river flats from beside the Binnekill westward up the valley. The rich alluvial plain, though sometimes subject to flooding, would provide the foodstuffs needed to sustain the settlers and their livestock. Lots also were divided and assigned within the stockade area that was built to ensure more adequate protection against possible incursions by unfriendly Frenchmen or Indians from the north.

Van Curler, the acknowledged leader of the small community, took up residence on his bouwland southwest of the stockade, the largest that was assigned any proprietor because of his efforts to establish the settlement. He and his wife, nee Antonia Slaaghboom, also were given a home lot within the stockade which probably was the whole eastern half of the block now bounded by Washington Avenue, Union, Church and Front Streets, but they never lived there. After the death of Van Curler and his widow, without issue, the lot was divided into four smaller portions and sold.

Schenectady's founder met a tragic death long before the community was attacked and burned by the French and Indians. There was a lull in the wars between England and France in July, 1669, when Van Curler accepted an invitation from De Tracy, the Governor of Canada, to visit Quebec. The Dutch leader was well known and respected by the French in Canada for having arranged the rescue of Frenchmen, mostly Jesuits, from the Mohawks. And probably no man up to that time had so fully won the confidence and esteem of the Iroquois as Van Curler. On his journey northward, he embarked in a canoe with several Indian guides on Lake Champlain and a short while later a severe storm caused the craft to capsize. Van Curler was drowned and his body was never recovered.

Likely as not the stockade which was erected shortly after the 1662 settlement was improved upon after a few years, when the settlers had finished building their homes and getting the farmlands in shape for cultivation. A few lived outside the stockaded village, but most preferred to build their habitations together for greater protection. The original stockade lines were as follows: Starting at State Street at Ferry Street, the east wall ran along the east side of Ferry Street to about where the front gate of St. George's Church now stands, then in a straight line to the north side of Front Street a little beyond Washington Avenue, then southerly and parallel to Washington Avenue to State Street, and lastly along State Street about 28 feet south up to Ferry Street.

It is certain that English authorities were well aware of the fact that Schenectady was an important outpost in that it formed a sort of buffer zone for other settlements to the south and east. At least a blockhouse was soon built in the original stockade, supposedly in the north angle of the bastion at or near the junction of Washington Avenue and Front Street, and small military detachments were regularly garrisoned there. There were two gates — one at the north end of Church Street, called the "north gate," and the other at State Street, the "south gate."

* * *

There was considerable excitement in the Stockade neighborhood in March, 1972, when remains of the original stockade were uncovered and, very likely, the old "north gate" where the French and Indians entered prior to the 1690 massacre.

Employes of the Niagara Mohawk Power Corp. started the whole thing when they ripped open an eight-foot square hole at the intersection of North Church and Front Streets and came upon a row of decayed wood. The company agreed to delay its repair work for another day while two archeologists from the State Museum examined the evidence. They finally agreed it was "definitely an historic stockade" and said it was characteristic of colonial structure, with flat-bottomed logs being used rather than the pointed-end timber used by the Indians. They found a double barricade in the north wall at that point, which led to the surmise that it was the location of the celebrated "north gate" because double walls were customarily built in the area of gates or blockhouses.

It was ascertained from the darkened sections of the rotted wood that the stockade logs were spaced out in trenches about three inches apart and then filled in with compacted soil. It was estimated that the timber used for the wall must have been from 8 to 10 inches in diameter. Also found in the soil were a clay pipe bowl and bits of the stem, a hand-fashioned nail, several Dutch brick, a piece of crockery and parts of bone and teeth, either equine or bovine.

It is known that a mill was built early in the settlement's history just outside the stockade to the southeast in what is today Mill Lane. The First Reformed Protestant Dutch Church was organized by 1680 and a small church was built in 1682 in the public square of the village at which is now the intersection of State, Church and Water Streets. It was constructed through the benevolence of Alexander Lindsay Glen, the original proprietor whose home was just across the river. For this reason, the street which led northward from the church was called Cross Street, changed to Church Street after the massacre. The first pastor of the Dutch Church was Dominie Petrus Tessachermaecker (often written Tessemaker), who came to Schenectady in 1684 but met an untimely death for he was one of the victims of the massacre six years later.

We mentioned that the Dutch Reformed Church was organized by 1680. That is not to say that the early settlers were not without church affiliation or adherence to religious upbringing of the Holland Dutch. Although the official organization of the church is not listed until "about 1680," its unofficial organization more truly dates back to the settlement of Schenectady — when the Dutch brought their religion along with them as surely as they did their supplies and implements.

Hans Janse Eenkluys, an ancient soldier of the Dutch West India Company, is a prime example. As early as 1668 he was an inhabitant of Schenectady, where he continued to live until his death in 1683. In May, 1680, he had made the deacons of the Dutch Reformed Church administrators of his whole estate, but as far back as 1670 church people had given him support while he was ailing. His estate included what came to be known as the Poor Pasture although at first was called Hans Janse's Wey or De Arme Wey. In its original condition, it consisted of 18 morgens (about 36 acres) of the finest Mohawk flats bounded by the river on the north — the extension of Front Street which in later years became part of the American Locomotive plant. It had been Eenkluys' intention to aid the "poor of Schenectady" through his estate to be administered by the church.

In 1795, the church consistory resolved to sell the property but no purchaser was found. However, it was finally disposed of in 1863 at auction for about $11,000 and the funds were directed to be used for the welfare of the poor.

So within the stockade, homes were built and streets laid out in accordance with the surveyor's calculations. Unfortunately, there are no existing records which may give some hint as to what kind of dwellings were erected in the original stockade. Some historical writers through the years have assumed the homes were simple log structures; others have concluded the buildings were of typical Dutch architecture built "of brick brought over from the Netherlands in the holds of the ships as ballast."

However, it is unlikely that the Dutch would have built log cabins. It was just not their nature. It is also improbable that bricks were brought over from the old country. Ships came from Holland when they had paying cargoes, or remained in the Maas or Scheldts until they had one.

Historians in later years have come to the conclusion that our Dutch settlers built their homes of hand-hewn wood, stone or brick, probably a combination of the three. Clay was plentiful in this area and steenbackers, or brickmakers, were here at that time to make their living; even unskilled labor was capable of turning out sun-dried brick. Stone was also abundant, large flat stone which could be laid up for sturdy foundations and walls. And lumber of all kinds was available to every landowner.

The first homes built probably were rather simple but substantial, consisting of one or two main rooms and a garret for sleeping. Stone walls ordinarily were laid up "dry" with mud mortar, and chimneys were usually erected inside the houses, built of stone or brick. In the earliest times, especially when block houses were built, chimneys sometimes were constructed of wood, plastered or daubed with mud. The style of the Dutch houses was that of a building gable end to the street or with a round topped front. Likely as not, there was also a "stoep" on which the Dutch burgher and his wife might sit in the early evening, perhaps watching the setting sun cast a sparkling reflection in the river just beyond Van Slyck

Island. It's a cinch that if a stoop was added, it was scrubbed clean.

Twenty-five years after it was established, Schenectady had grown into a rather respectable village — although its exact size at that point in its history is unknown. Historians have written scads of accounts of the 1690 massacre, including events leading up to it, but when it came to the matter of population and dwellings the result has been absolute confusion. But the writers are hardly to be blamed, except perhaps in some instances of quoting figures from old records as being the ironclad truth. There have been far too many conflicting reports, supposedly from people who had been in the settlement, to hazard what one might call even an "educated guess." The population of 1690 in Schenectady ranged from 200 to 800 persons, while the buildings (which probably in some cases included barns and out buildings) numbered between 50 and 80.

We do know that the village expanded greatly beyond the 15 original proprietors (all of whom did not even come to live here) and that by 1690, the first lots had been divided and sold for more compact building. The only dwellings immediately outside the 10-foot high palisade were said to have been built on the northerly side of State Street extending about up to where Broadway now crosses State. For a happy medium, since a clearcut record is not available, we might say that there were about 300 inhabitants of Schenectady living in about 60 houses in and around the stockade at the time of the massacre.

By now, the village was garrisoned on order of the English authorities even though the Dutch settlers were by nature reticent to ask for "outside" protection. A double stockaded fort at the northwest corner of the stockade was garrisoned by a detachment of 24 men of Capt. Jonathan Bull's Connecticut company under the command of Lt. Enos Talmadge.

In the interim between Schenectady's settlement and the massacre, there were numerous but isolated incidents of killings and scalpings by raiding parties of northern Indians. Although England and France were at an uneasy peace for most of this time, their provinces in America were very much unquiet and suspicious of a sudden outbreak of warfare. For one thing, the intermittent confrontations between the French and the Iroquois were a constant source of irritation to the English provinces. But there was also the haranguing between British and French authorities over who was to blame for the outbreaks of Indian hostility.

The French charged the English with furnishing the Indians with muskets and powder and inciting them to war upon the French and their allies in Canada. The English said the French were audacious in claiming for the French crown the valleys of the St. Lawrence, of the Great Lakes and of the Mississippi on the basis of the exploits of the Jesuits. In 1670, Governor Lovelace wrote that the French pretended "it is no more but to advance the kingdom of Christ when it is to be suspected it is rather the kingdom of his most Christian Majesty."

Meanwhile, the Dutchmen were caught in the middle.

Site of the old north gate of Schenectady's original stockade was uncovered March 1, 1972, during an excavation at Front and North Church Streets by a utility company. Above, state archeologists delve into the past while Niagara Mohawk employes wait to resume their work.

Confusion is generally rampant whenever historical accounts are given of that period in American history when words, proper nouns included, were in conflict with the language inflections of those who settled here, principally the Dutch, English and — to the north — the French. Little wonder that those engaged in genealogy have been led along blind alleys to the point of distraction and utter frustration.

Here in Schenectady, our early history also carries names with Indian derivation, to make the issue more confusing. In fact, as we will relate at the end of this chapter, it is not certain to this day whether the name Schenectady is from the Dutch or Indian.

A good bit of the Holland influence naturally rubbed off on this city which was founded by Dutch settlers in 1662. Many descendants of those early inhabitants still reside here, family names such as Van der Bogart, Wemple (or Wemp), Bradt (or Bratt), Schermerhorn, Vrooman, Veeder, Van Guysling, Van Eps (or Van Epps), Fonda, De Graff, Teller, Barhydt, Clute, Dyckman, Van Patten, Hagedorn, Groot, Marselis, etc. The list would be long, indeed, if all of our city's Dutch lineage was set down.

Throughout the early records, these Dutch names appear: Kil (stream), bouwlandt (farm land), bouwery (house lot), Groote Vlacht (great flat), straat (street), ganse gat (goose pond), dove gat (pool), morgen (Dutch acre), groote schult boek (church papers), Hoek (point of land), te blok huys (the blockhouse), boslooper (bush runner or a trader among the Indians), juffrouw (widow), leeghte (valley), bouwknecht (farm laborer), beuken (beach), Beuke (a Beech tree) and hofstede (country house).

Some Dutch names remain with us to this day. The early surveyors referred to the area of Alplaus as Aal Plaas, or eel place — eel fishery in the river. Woestina is from the Dutch, Woestyne, or wilderness. Binne Kil (the backstream of the Mohawk River at the rear of Washington Avenue now known as Binnekill) meant inner creek and Platte Kil (now known as Plotterkill) was a low, muddy stream.

Confusion also was inherent in the spelling of surnames and Christian names in those days. It seemed that individuals themselves were sometimes guilty of setting down their signatures with varied spelling, but largely it was due to the fact that official details, which naturally involved people's names, were written by many different ethnic groups in the style of their homeland.

For example, the French interpreted English and Dutch spelling much differently and many of the records that have been passed down from the French and Indian wars concerning the New York colony show a variation in proper nouns.

In an account of the burning of Schenectady in 1690, Monsignor De Monsignat referred to Capt. Johnannes Sanders (Sandertse) Glen in what looked in the Frenchman's longhand as "Coudre." This was puzzling to historians. Could he have used an Indian term, one which had not been heard before by the English or Dutch of the area? Rather, it is now speculated that an "n" had been mistaken for a "u" and that he had written "Condre" in a French pronunciation of "Sander."

The French also often referred to the Schenectady settlement as "Corlaer," after the founder, Arent Van Curler, and some Indian tribes later took it up.

The man we know as Alexander Lindsay Glen, one of the first proprietors of Schenectady and who chose to build across the river, has been listed in historical records in many different ways. He often was referred to as Sander Leenderste Glen, probably the result of the Dutch compulsion to call anyone by the name of Alexander as Sander, or Sandy for short; the Leenderste being the Dutch version of Lindsay. It is suspected that the Glen came from the total reference to Alexander, the Lindsay of the Glen near Inverness, Scotland.

The Dutch custom of denoting sons and daughters also resulted in a "se" being attached to the end of a man's name, signifying "son of" and "je" at the end of a girl's name, meaning "daughter of." Thus Janse meant "son of John" and Jannetje meant "daughter of John." For the latter, she might have been named Maria Jannetje, or known in social circles as Maria.

For a full treatment of this custom, let us take the name of Harme Janse Knickerbacker. He was Harme, son of John the Knickerbaker, maker of knickers (or childrens' marbles) or small china ware in general. Or Kleyn Robberse de Steenbacker, who was Kleyn, son of Robert the Steenbaker, maker of bricks.

Surnames were a muddle in those early accounts. It was Bratt or Bradt, Vroman or Vrooman, Veeder or Vedder, Mabee or Mabie. The ill-fated first pastor of the Dutch Reformed Church has been written variously as Dominie Petrus Tesschenmaker, Peter Tessenmacher, Petrus Tessachermaecker, Petrus Tesschenmaecker, and Petrus Thessenmaecher. His successor was Dominie Barnardus Freerman, Barnhardus Freerman or Bernard Freeman.

Christian names also were spelled in different ways and entered into official records in various forms, such as Aques for Jacques, Simon for

Symon, Marie for Maria, etc. Even the name of the founder, Arent Van Curler, appears in many ways. It is pupularly written after the English as above, although the Dutch spelling for the Christian name was Arendt. As mentioned previously, the French preferred "Corlaer" to "Curler."

The Iroquois nation had a hand in the naming of many surrounding communities, perhaps Schenectady included. They called what is now known as Niskayuna by the name of Canastagione and Saratoga by the name of Sarachtoge. The Mohawk tribe became known as the Magua or Maquaa. The Mohawks called themselves Gagnieguahague, but as the tribe was collectively Ganniageari, the She Bear. However, the neighboring Algonquins called them Maqua, the Bear, a name which the English and Dutch accepted. Not too infrequently, the term Maqua appears in records of the 17th and 18th centuries from this area. Usually, during the threat of French sorties, it was: "We have learned from our Maqua scouts that. . ." In early maps, the Mohawk River sometimes was referred to as the Mauquas or Maquas River.

The Maqua Co., a printing and binding firm later taken over by General Electric and which closed only a few years ago, was established in the old Brandywine knitting mills off Altamont Avenue and took its name from the Mohawks who once roamed this area.

As for the naming of Schenectady — well, there we have really opened a can of worms and the reader can take his pick from the hypotheses of historians and linguists who have gone before. You may be right, as each of those who studied the origin believed he was; but then again, there is always the possibility that all of these people looked too hard and too long. Of this we may be reasonably sure — that the word is derived either from the Indian or the Dutch.

It is an unusual name, that is for sure — which is most likely why it has been spelled in so many ways up through the centuries. The last estimate we heard placed the variations at 78, including the earliest versions of the English and French. Suffice to say, Schenectady probably has the distinction of having been the most misspelled city in the land.

Actually the first recorded name in reference to this city was Schonowe, which was written in the Indian deed in 1661 to Van Curler for the flats along the river, called the Groote Vlacht by the Dutch. This probably identical with S'Guan-ho-ha, meaning "the door" in Indian, both in sound and signification.

Strangely enough, the Iroquois first called the settlement of Beverwyck (Beaver Town in Dutch) Schagh-nect-ha-tie signifying the place the natives arrived at by traveling through the pine trees (Pine Bush area). Similarly, the settlement of Schenectady took the name when referred to by people of Albany as ' beyond the pine plains."

There is also a theory that the name comes from a combination of Indian names — first from S'Guan-ho-ha (the door) and then with Hac-ta-tie (without) to make the combined form of S'guan-ho-ha-hac-ta-tie. This abbreviated word might have led to S-Guan-hac-ta-tie, meaning "without the door" and which, in gutteral Indian sounds, could have become Schenectady.

As for the Dutch version, it has been argued that the city's name was taken by a combination of Dutch words — Schoon (beautiful, Achten (valuable) and Deel (portion of land), making the sound Schoonachtendeel which was changed and twisted by the tongues of different nationalities until it finally came out Schenectady. A long shot, perhaps, and yet plausible.

Actual reference to the name Schoonechtendeel appeared in a journal written in Dutch manuscript by two Labadist monks, Jaspar Dankers and Peter Sluyter, called "Voyage to New York and a Tour in Several of the American Colonies, 1679-1680." This is part of the translation from that journal:

"The horses were got ready and we left (from Albany) about 8 o'clock (April 24, 1679) for Schoonechtendeel, a place lying about 24 miles west or northwest of Albany towards the country of the Maquaas. We rode over a fine sandy cart road through a woods of nothing but beautiful greens or fir trees, but a light and barren soil. . .

"This Schoonechtendeel is situated, as we have said, 24 miles west of Fort Albany, toward the country of the Mohawks, upon a good flat, high enough to be free from the overflowing of the water of the river, which sometimes overflows the cultivated lands which lie much lower. . ."

We do know that Governor Stuyvesant wrote Schenectady as we spell it now as early as 1663, only two years after the original patent. But, oh, how it was misused for years after that. In official papers of 1664, the town is designated as Schaneghstede and Schanechstede (the egh and ech being used interchangeably). In 1696, the commander of the fort, Lieutenant Hunt, spelled it Schonactady. In orders of Governor Andross in 1678 was written, "Sconextady prohibited all trade," etc.

Even in 1802, residents who were familiar with the town and its history, drew up a petition which was accompanied by "a list of ye Lands and Income of the township of Schonhectady."

Who knows, really, why and how everyone finally settled on the name we use today? Regardless of the 1802 petition, our guess would be that Schenectady became Schenectady at least by the turn of the 19th century. Perhaps those who signed the petition didn't notice that the person who drew up the document was a poor speller.

Mill Lane, with old cobblestone paving partly covered by blacktop, is one of oldest byways in Schenectady. Plaque on building at extreme left marks the spot of the first mill built in 1666. (Photograph by Ed Schultz)

Plaque affixed to building on Mill Lane, denoting the site of the first mill in Schenectady.

Rare old print from glass negative in 1880s looking northeasterly toward the hill atop which became Summit Avenue and Strong Street. Gerritt S. Veeder's residence is at left and his mill at center. Area is now Broadway.

On the side of a building on Mill Lane, just south of State and Church Street in Schenectady, is a metal plaque which marks the site as the first grist mill to be established in the community. Sweer Teunise Van Velsen, its owner, was also a victim of the 1690 massacre.

Millwrights and mills of years gone by represented an important phase in the economic history of Schenectady. When first settled, farming became an industry of vital necessity to Schenectady's growth, actually more so than the lucrative (and, at first, illegal) fur trade. And the mills were an integral part of the agricultural scene as they later came to be a boon to other needs of society in succeeding generations.

The many streams which coursed down from the hills from the east were conducive to milling of all kinds. Most were dammed up in gullies to ensure constant and substantial power, and it has only been until this century that many of these old mill ponds (such as Brandywine, Fuller's and Veeder's Ponds) have disappeared. There are people today, in fact, who can still relate to their grandchildren how, as youngsters, they cooled off in the summer by swimming "in the old mill pond."

Our first miller, who came over from Holland in the early 1660s and settled first in Beverwyck, is usually referred to in existing records as Sweer Teunise Van Velsen. However, occasionally his name appears simply as Sweer Teunisen or as "alias Van Westbrook." He and his wife, Maritie Myndertse, who was the widow of Jan Barentse Wemp, came to Schenectady in 1666 after he bought the Mill Lane property just outside the stockade. Van Velsen almost at once built the town's first grist mill at that site. His contract with the commonalty stipulated that "no other mill was to be erected as long as he did accommodate the people with good meal."

His first mill was carried away by a flood, but he rebuilt it in 1673 and continued to grind corn and other grain until death stilled his industry. He was killed by the French and Indian attackers, along with his wife and four Negro slaves, at the Van Velsen house next to the mill.

Mill industries were located mainly on the Poentic Kill, Davities Gatt Kill, Long Gatte Kill, Oil Mill or Sweet Hill Creek, Schuylenberg Kill, Sand Kill and Cowhorn Creek. Still well known to Schenectadians is the Cowhorn Creek. It was called Coehorn Kill in the early days of the city because a Dutchman named Coehorn had a mill on the creek.

Another early grist mill was that owned by John Baptist Van Epps, which was located a few yards east of what is now Lafayette Street. He owned all the land roughly bounded by Jay Street, Union Street, Nott Terrace and the north and west sides of Cowhorn Creek as it cut down across present State Street. The mill that Van Epps operated was known at first as Coehorn Mill and later as Dawson's mill and Quackenbos Mill. The road to the site was a lane in the same location as Jay Street is now.

The Schermerhorn Mills were located on Schuylenberg Kill, now on the Broadway hill at Congress Street. There were a grist mill, saw mill, carding mill and minor works. The Schermerhorn mill pond was filled in during October, 1935.

Nearby the old city of more than a century ago, the Veeder grist and saw mills were located at the foot of Pleasant Valley at Broadway. The Sand Kill which ran through the ravine was dammed into a large pond at that point. Upstream in Pleasant Valley was Archibald Craig's firm known as the Schenectady Cotton Co., a brick building nestled in the vale near present Craig Street. The factory included a fulling and coloring plant. For many years, the area was known as Cotton Factory Hollow and the women employed there were called "cotton dolls."

At the head of the ravine was the old Duane grist mill and distillery, which in 1875 became the Schenectady Knitting Mills adjacent to the then Brandywine Pond along Duane Avenue. (the last traces of the pond were removed about a quarter century ago). The building was razed by fire in 1878 and replaced by a brick structure three years later. About 130 persons were employed at the Brandywine mills as the business prospered through the early 1900s. The Maqua printing com-

Veeder's grist and saw mill (later Schenectady Milling Co.) on the Broadway curve near the foot of Pleasant Valley. There was once a pond beside the mill on the right side, nearest the valley.

pany, now defunct, later took over the premises and added another building to the plant.

The extensive Henry Yates manufacturing plants and mill ponds occupied a considerable part of the area just south of the present city limits. There were also the Jonathan Crane milling industries located at the end of Crane Street in what was then known as Mohawksville. Flax, oil, and cordage were manufactured there.

A grist mill was located in the early days in what is now Dakota Street, between Smith and Hamilton Streets, as was another in the area just south of State Street between South Church and South Ferry Streets. In both places were ponds.

Alexander "Sandy" Alexander was a colorful mill owner who established a grist mill about 1800 north of Schenectady at a point called Alexander's Bridge near Craig and at what became known as the Aqueduct when the Erie Canal was constructed. Alexander's mill served all of the people of that area, Rexford included, and his successors ran the business until well past the mid-19th century. Alexander, a native of Scotland, was a partner of David Tomlinson beginning 1790 after having learned the shoemaking trade as an apprentice of Aaron Vedder. The Alexander & Tomlinson store was located on Union and Church Streets opposite the Dutch Reformed Church.

While these were not all of the mills of the Schenectady area during its long history, they were the principal ones — and serve to give some idea of the importance and need of this particular industry.

Millstone from "Sandy" Alexander's grist mill at Craig.

In this unusual view from the Crane Street hill in the early 1880s can be seen the Groote Vlacht or Great Flat in the far background which today is occupied by the General Electric Co. plant here. The Jones Car Works are the buildings in right background. At left center is Congress Street as it meets the Broadway hill, while in left center are the buildings of Schermerhorn Mills.

28

The Dutch settlers who came to America in the 17th century during the massive colonization efforts by the seafaring nations of Europe were made to order for the courage and ruggedness it demanded, if ever any nationality was.

They were frugal, to be sure, having known the value of every square inch of soil reclaimed from the sea. While not particularly outgoing in personality, the Hollander was resolute in his friendship once attained, an attribute which was invaluable to relations with the Indians — who greatly respected honesty in their dealings with the white man. And, lastly, the Dutch were not easily discouraged by setbacks or hard times; they were accustomed to adversity in their homeland.

It was a patriarchal society that the Dutch brought to the New Netherland colony and, specifically, to Schenectady. Marriage was always early and very often happy, but the man strictly ruled the family and the old English law of primogeniture was strictly observed in the Dutch home. The eldest son inherited the greatest share of the family estate, the second son being next in line, and so on. Daughters would inherit real estate only if there were no males born to the family; ordinarily, at the death of her father, a daughter would obtain such effects as he thought she needed, or deserved, for there was no rule in these cases.

The law of primogeniture was generally observed until about the Revolutionary War. The girls, it was assumed, needed no fortune except health and strength for future marriage.

The Dutch churches had their Trouw-boeks or marriage registers in which were recorded the names of the newly betrothed, the date of the ceremony and the presiding minister. A marriage was considered to be a civil contract and could be confirmed (bevestight) either by a magistrate or minister of the Gospel. Due notification of intention of marriage, however, was required before confirmation. The banns were published three Sundays by the minister of the church or by a magistrate in court, after which the marriage could be confirmed on presentation of a certificate (attestatie) of such publication. Occasionally, but not often, wedding ceremonies were performed in private homes.

There does not seem to be much handed down regarding courtship customs in the early Dutch burghs. In all probability, however, the first settlers practiced "bundling" or "Queesten" as inherited from an old European custom in areas remote and unsettled. Call it a matter of convenience or affection, bundling was purely and simply a case of two sweethearts lying in the same bed — without undressing. It was not just a Dutch custom; bundling was done in many places of Europe and in early New England, but it was not looked upon as dishonorable by either the young people or their parents. Only those who intended to be married engaged in the overnight togetherness, usually in the girl's home.

Bundling, it is said, took place in those cases where the lovers lived far apart. After a long day's work and family dinner, it was usually well into the night when a young man came a-courting. The early homes boasted of merely one or two rooms and even light and fuel were deemed luxuries; thus the courting was done in the dark and the young swain returned to his work before daybreak.

Some ministers spoke out against bundling during Sunday sermons, but throughout the 17th century the practice appears to have been defended by the settlers. It was deemed, if you will, a necessity of the times and a part of normal courtship for an engaged couple.

There was a case brought before an Albany magistrate in 1658 in which a young woman's reputation had been assailed because she had "bundled" with her lover. The latter was the principal witness and he testified "when we were visiting together, we slept in the garret," adding that the lady was "perfectly virtuous." Doubtless she was, in her day and generation.

"Old maids" were unknown and widows did not remain without a husband for long unless at a very advanced age. After a year or sometimes less, a "juffrouw" took another husband, a very necessary arrangement for both man and woman in the sparse settlements of the border lands. So very often, through the early records of families who lived in this area in the 17th and 18th centuries, it will be found that a person may have been married three or four times before his or her death. There were many more ways for a person to die young in those days than there are today — and the need for a helpmate was also much more acute.

Dutch funerals retained a curious custom that was brought to the early colonies from the mother land. No woman ever accompanied the deceased to the cemetery; but after the corpse was borne out, remained to eat cake and drink spiced wine with other female members or friends of the family. They retired quietly before the men returned to resume the feast and regale themselves.

The best room in the house was used as the "dead room" where the body was laid out and the wake held afterward. After the funeral took place and the men had left for the burial ground, a table was set by the widow, slaves or hired help. On it was usually placed a quantity of wine, made hot with spice, small sugar cakes including Dote

Kooken or "dead cake," plates of tobacco and a number of clay pipes and a roll of paper done up to light the tobacco. The wine was put up in bottles and encircled by wine glasses. Lighted candles on the table completed the almost festive atmosphere. If there was spiced wine left over, it was taken to sick friends and those who were not able to come to the funeral.

When the coffin was carried out of the house, it was placed upon a bier beside the front door and covered with a pall of black cloth. Usually the sexton of the Dutch church would see that the church bell tolled at this point. The bearers then lifted the bier and carried it upon their shoulders to the grave site, followed only by invited guests.

In those days, and probably on up to the 19th century in the more isolated areas, families often buried their dead in private plots on their own land. These private burial grounds, not only of the Dutch but of most settlers, can still be found on old homesteads scattered throughout the Mohawk Valley — often enclosed by stone or wrought iron fencing and, sadly enough, often covered by weeds and uncared for.

The bier and pall were used in all funeral processions until about the 19th century, the pallbearers continuing to carry the dead from the home to the grave; hence it would not have been convenient in the early days to perform the last rites if the public cemetery was any great distance. The first mention of obtaining a hearse for Schenectady funerals was at a meeting of the Dutch church consistory held April 7, 1800: "Resolved, that a herse be procured as soon as convenient for the use of carrying the dead of this congregation to the burying ground, and also for the use of the public, under such regulations as this board shall afterwards prescribe." On Dec. 3 that same year, was this subsequent reference: "Resolved, that the herse and harness be kept by the sexton in some convenient place as near the burying ground as possible, to be provided by the consistory; and that whenever any of the citizens may want it, application be made to him, and that it be his duty to collect the fees."

Probably the earliest burial ground in the village was on the west side of the first Dutch church building at the junction of State and Church Streets. After about 60 years, the church selected another spot for a cemetery outside the stockade — this time between Front and Green Streets just east of Ferry Street. Shortly after Vale Cemetery was established, the remains of those in the Green Street plot were reinterred in the new cemetery.

It is likely that, according to the Dutchman of the 17th century, the massacre of Schenectady occurred not in 1690 but in 1689. Before the influx of English and Scotch settlers and a general conversion to British law and customs, the Dutch observed New Year's at midnight, March 24; therefore, according to Dutch calculation, the French and Indians laid waste to the town before the start of 1690.

If we seem to have placed particular emphasis on the Dutch Reformed Church in this segment of early Schenectady, it is because the church was so important to the personal affairs of the burgher and was so very much interwoven with the settlement's welfare. Indeed, it is believed that when the stockade was first laid out, provision was made for the church building years before it was built. The Dutch church was the great landowner, loaner of mortgage money and provider of alms for the poor.

The primitive peculiarities of the Dutch as a people — including their Old World customs and beliefs — gradually disappeared until by the time of the Revolutionary War, the citizens of Schenectady had a relatively common mode of life. Colonization, as it progressed into the 18th century, had taken the simple Dutchman from his bouwery on the flats and had brought him in contact with people from many different countries.

From all accounts, our earliest inns or taverns were not so much places of shelter for the weary traveler as a gathering spot for thirsty Dutchmen looking to "whet the whistle" and talk over events of the day. The inns of the carriage trade did not become popular or even necessary until well into the 18th century.

By English law after 1664, barkeeps — or tapsters, as they were known in those days, must apply for a license in order to legally sell the hard stuff. It is from these records that we have the names of those who made their living through the "publick" houses which most set up in the front room of their dwelling. They were not all men, either. In many cases, the widow kept the business after her husband died and proved a natural as an innkeeper.

The two earliest licensed tapsters in Schenectady were (J)Aques Cornelise Gautsh (Van Slyck) and Cornelise Viele, although Douwe Aukes (De Freeze) came over from Holland in 1663 and soon after settled in Schenectady as an innkeeper or victualler (probably in partnership with Viele), acquiring his license a few years later.

Gautsh, who was popularly known as Van Slyck, got his license about a year before Viele — although the latter was the more legitimate innkeeper. Van Slyck, an Indian half-breed whose tribal name was Itsychosaquachha, was respected by both the Dutch and Indian and not long after Schenectady was settled he set up sort of a "roving shop" both inside and outside the stockade. On the other hand, Viele, who came to Schenectady in 1668, built an inn on the south corner of State Street and Mill Lane near Church Street — almost adjacent to the first edifice built by the Dutch Reformed Church. When Viele applied for a license from the English colonial governor, Francis Lovelace, on Jan. 9, 1671, there was this notification in reference to a "Lycence for Cornelyse Cornelyssen Vielen of Schanechtide to tapp strong Beer & Liquors there &c.":

"Whereas Cornelys Cornelyssen Vielen of Schanechtide haveing made this Address to ye commissarys att Albany, desiring hee may have Liberty to tapp strong Beer & Liquors and to keep an Ordinary, in recompence for several services done by him between us & ye Maques, the wh: they have Recommended to mee for my approbation. But in regard there is a Person already there by name Aques Cornelyssen Gautsh (Van Slyck) an indyan, that doeth ye same by Lycence and Appointm' of my Predecessor, Coll: Richard Nicolls, would give noe Determinacon therein:

"And it being likewise represented that ye said Acques hath not sufficient Accommodacon for Strangers wh. ye said Cornelys Cornelyssen Vielen doth promise to bee well provided off ye reliefe of Strangers & Travellers, upon consideracon had thereupon I have Thought fitt to graunt ye Request of ye said Cornelys Cornelyssen Vielen & by these Presents doe give him free Lycence and Liberty to tapp or sell by Retayle strong Beere & Liquors to Strangers & Travellers at Schanechtide, wth this Proviso, That this Lycence now granted shall not take away ye priviledge of ye former Lycence given by my Predecessor to Acques: And that ye said Cornelys Cornelyssen doe keep fitting Accommodacon for men and horses, but does not presume to sell any strong Liquors to ye Indyans to cause any disturbance that way under ye penalty of forfeiting this Lycence & paying such ffine as ye Law shall Require."

Here, the Governor was dealing with two problems: A lively competitiveness between Schenectady's two legal tapsters and the selling of "fire water" to Indians.

The intense rivalry between Van Slyck and Viele, in fact, was not only in supplying Dutchmen with their schnapps but in trying to convince the authorities that one or the other should be a "confidential" liquor salesman to the Iroquois who frequented the area.

Not a little attention, and apparently concern of officialdom, was given the dispensation of strong drink to the Indians by the colonists. The real worry, if we can read between the lines of orders and/or warnings handed down by authorities, was that an intoxicated Indian could not be trusted.

We must remember that the white man in the colonial days still regarded the red man as a savage, even though he may have traded goods and intermarried within the neighboring tribes for many years after he took over land that he had bought for a pittance or given him many years before. Stockades in the outposts were no guarantee of safety should a band of Indians suddenly decide to become unfriendly. Knowing the effect that any distilled or fermented drink had on some "civilized" persons, causing them to become argumentative, boisterous or belligerent, administrators of the colonies and settlements frowned upon the common practice of many colonists of supplying liquor to Indians often for selfish motives. They might ply an eager but unsuspecting brave with a tankard of rum to "seal a deal" of bartered furs, to try to win a friendship on a personal basis and sometimes even to curry tribal favors where Indian maidens were concerned.

As it turned out, the Governor may have seized upon an opportunity to show a humane gesture toward a prominent and believed widow in Schenectady and also settle the argument between Van Slyck and Viele.

It was on Jan. 27, 1673, three and half years after the tragic death of Arent Van Curler, Schenectady's founder and acknowledged leader, that the governor acted favorably on a recommendation by the Court of Albany, Rensselaerwyck and Schenectady that his widow be granted special consideration because of her need. After her husband had perished in a boating accident on Lake Champlain, Antonia Van Curler soon after suffered another calamity. Fire swept the Van Curler bowerel farm on the Groote Vlachte.

Governor Lovelace's order, giving Juffrouw (widow) Van Curler a 14-month period in which to sell "rumm, lead and powder" to the Indians, was as follows:

"Upon ye Request of Antonia Van Curler of Schanechtide presented to His Honor ye Governor, that having not long since received a very great Losse by ffire, there may for her Reliefe bee so farr indulged as to have licence to sell some Rumm to ye Indyans, as also some quantity of Powder and Lead; the Premises being taken into serious consideration, It is ordered that in regard to the very great Losse and Damaged sustayned by the said Antonia Van Curler in having her House, Barnes and Corne destroyed as by her is set forth, as also the Losse of her Husband, Arent Van Curler while hee was employed in his Majesty's Publick Service, Shee, the said Antonia his widdow shall have free Lyberty and Licence for ye space and term of one whole yeare and two Months after the date hereof, That is to say, from the first day of April next untill the 29th day of May wh. shall bee in the yeare of Our Lord 1674, to sell and dispose of to the Indyans or others in and about Schanechtide in Rumme one hundred Anckers and in Lead to the value of two hundred Beavers or 1,000 weight; But for Powder in this conjuncture of time during the Warr, Its thought inconvenient any Extraordinary Liberty should be granted therein."

Attached to the order was the Governor's notation: *'The matter of difference between ye two Tappers (Viele and Van Slyck) at Schanechtide, not thought fitt any order shall be made therein further, this Liberty to the Widdow probably being a mean to defeat both their Expectations."*

We do not know whether the Governor's action quieted the friction between Viele and Van Slyck, but it can be doubted. At any rate, Widow Van Curler just managed to profit by it in her lifetime, for she died two years after getting the permit.

While records agree that Van Slyck and Viele were the first two licensed barkeepers in Schenectady, it is fairly certain that drink was also being dispensed in other quarters in violation of the law which stated that the retailing "of beere and strong waters" was a privilege granted through a license from the Governor on the payment of a certain yearly sum as an excise tax. Innkeepers and tapsters increased as the settlement grew, some of them legitimately qualified to sell drink but many others not. It is interesting to note that Douwe Aukes, who married Maria Viele, grand-daughter of Cornelise Viele, succeeded the latter as proprietor of the State Street inn. Auke's wife, two children and a Negro servant were slain in the 1690 massacre, and his brother-in-law, Arnout Viele, was among the prisoners taken to Canada.

Meanwhile, some whites and also Indian chiefs began to complain about the traffic in liquor both at Albany and Schenectady, and the "disastrous effects" it had upon the Indians. For instance, Col. Peter Schuyler wrote to Governor Dongan in 1687 that "the selling of strong liquor to the Indians is a great hindrance to all designs they take in hand; they stay a drinking continually at Schenectady; if your Ecell: would be pleased to prohibit itt for two or three months it would do very well." Even a half century later, Chief Hendrick of the Mohawks told an Indian Council held in New York on June 12, 1753: "Brother I am going to tell you how many persons we design to drive away from our Lands; Barclay, Pickett's wife who lives just by us and who does us a great deal of Damage by selling us liquors and by that means making us destroy one another."

The winter of 1687 might have been especially bad for those who feared the combination of Indians and rum. It was bitterly cold and a frozen Hudson River closed all communication with New York, a situation which prompted the French to take advantage of helpless border settlements by sending out marauding expeditions. Governor Dongan ordered 200 men and several hundred Indians of the Five Nations to quarter in and about Albany and Schenectady as protective forces. The gathering of large groups of Indians about the village was always a source of irritation to some of the inhabitants, especially when they were treated to drink. This is what prompted Colonel Schuyler to complain to the Governor.

Among the actions taken by a kind of committee of safety (which called itself "the Convention") which convened in Albany on Sept. 4, 1689, was the following:

"Whereas the selling and giving of Strong Drink to ye Indians at this present juncture is founde by Experience Extreame Dangerous inasmuch ye divers Inhabitants of Schenectady and Elsewhere have mad their Complaint that there is no living if ye Indians be not kept from Drinke, Wee doe therefore strikly Prohibite & forbid in the name of King William and queen Mary yt no Inhabitants of the City and County of Albany doe sell or give any Rum, Brandy, Strong Liquor or Beer to any Indian or Indians upon any pretence whatsoever upon ye penalty of Two monthes Imprisonment without Baile or main prise & more over a fine of

five Pounds toties quoties, ye Proofe here of to be made as is Incerted in ye Proclamation Prohibiting ye Selling of Strong Drink dated ye 21st day of May 1689 which is by Proof or Purgation by oath, always Provided yt it shall and may be in ye Power of ye Mayor aldermen & Commonality of ye said Citty if they see cause to give any Smal quality of Rum to any Sachim who come here about Publick Businesse, any Prohibition above in any manner notwithstanding, given att ye City hall of Albany ye 12th day of September, 1689."

The sobriety of their red brothers, however, was not the main concern of the "commies." This was five months before the Schenectady massacre, and word had reached Albany that the French were planning to send out raiding parties to molest the northeastern outposts. The Convention wanted to warn the settlements and urge them to prepare for any attack. Within the minutes was this observation:

"Understanding by ye Commission officers of Schenectady that there is no settlement there how or what way they are to Behave themselfs if ye enemy should come, since they cannot agree amonst themselfs in that particular."

* * *

The magistrates of Schenectady and Rensselaerwyck well before 1680 apparently found it necessary to impose fines and regulations pertaining to the innkeepers — even beyond that of obtaining a license or "spinhuyssedul" (a workhouse certificate). Perhaps some of the places stepped over the bounds of propriety and caused the more sober residents to register complaints. At any rate, this was one of the rules issued by the magistrates:

"...their honors, in the name of his Royal Majesty of Great Britain, expressly notify all tavernkeepers and guests of whatever station they may be, that such guests must depart at the ringing of the bell and the tavernkeepers shall not be allowed to entertain parties, whether directly or indirectly and that neither the tavernkeepers nor the guests shall be able to claim exemption under any cloak whatsoever...except that extraordinary meetings of strangers, domestics and invited guests shall be excluded herefrom, being not liable in this matter, and whoever shall act contrary hereto shall be fined..."

It has been written in several earlier historical accounts of Schenectady that some merrymaking was going on in Aukes' tavern the night of the 1690 massacre. If so, the ringing of the bell must have been delayed past the traditional 11 p.m. closing.

In the minutes of the Common Council of Albany is an account of at least one instance of "white man's violence" due to drink. A court martial was held at Schenectady, Aug. 7, 1691,

The old Arent Bradt house at 7 State St., a fine example of Dutch architecture, is shown at left in this view of the late 1800s. It was once one of Schenectady's early taprooms.

which involved a soldier named George Castleton accused of killing a fellow soldier after a quarrel about some beer. Five Schenectady residents (including Aukes) from within the fort, were called to testify for the prosecution. It seems that during the argument, James Desvallons struck Castleton with a stick; whereupon Castleton drew his sword and plunged it into Desvallons' side, killing him almost instantly. Castleton was convicted of manslaughter, "burnt in the hand and banished from the Province."

In the early 1700s, after construction of the Queen's Fort and reincarnation of Schenectady, many more tapsters received licenses "to draw or sell liquor by retaile" and a number of inns and coffee houses were opened.

Caleb Beck, whose home lot was on the southeast corner of Church and Union Streets (now the site of the Knights of Columbus headquarters), was a new innkeeper at the turn of the 18th century. After he died in 1733, his widow ran the business, even expanding it to include retail trade in groceries and drygoods. Arent Bratt (Bradt), whose father, Andries, was killed in the massacre, was a brewer who opened the Bratt House at 7 State St. and died there in 1765. Bratt, whose mother was the daughter of Cornelise Gautsh Van Slyck, was succeeded in business by his sons, Andries, Johannes and Hermanus. The Bratt House, which was on the site of the present Schenectady YMCA building, apparently was well established as a meeting house by 1751 since records for April of that year show that the Town of Schenectady paid two pounds to Bratt "for troubles in his house and board for councilmen."

⚜ ⚜ ⚜

Jacobus Cromwell, who purchased a house on Front Street from Wouter Vrooman in 1711, was another early innkeeper. The tavern he set up at that address was said to be "a pretentious place" with grounds extending to the river bank. It stood on the site of the present DeGraff House built in 1790 at 25-27 Front St. After Cromwell's death, his widow married David Lewis in 1717, also an innkeeper.

Around the time of the Revolutionary War, probably no inn was as well known in Schenectady as the Clench Tavern, which was located on lower State Street on the eastern portion of the present island park there opposite the downtown YMCA. This will be mentioned again in the account of General Washington's 1782 visit to Schenectady, but in a listing of early Schenectady taverns, Clench's could not very well be omitted.

It was at the Clench Tavern that the St. George Masonic Lodge was organized in 1774, and as the war drew on there was suspicion among the Whig element that Robert Clench was a Tory or at least a Tory sympathizer. The former British solder settled in Schenectady only a few years before and established a respectable inn which he called "The Sign of the Crossed Keys" (although everyone else

called it the Clench Tavern). Clench died in 1781 and, once again, the widow carried on the tavern business. The inn burned in the 1819 fire. A son, Thomas B. Clench, operated taverns on other sites in subsequent years, including the Sharratt House, but left the city in the 1830s.

Then there was the Widow Kendall's place at 10 North Ferry St., still standing. Annie Kendall was the widow of Samuel Fuller, the colonial architect who designed Johnson Hall, St. George's Church and the Campbell Mansion at State and Church Streets. She married George Kendall, a butcher, in 1788 and then decided to open a small shop in the front of the house after her second husband died, a business she conducted until her death in 1833. The Widow Kendall's shop was a rather quiet place where customers were served cakes, beer and probably mead.

It is rather surprising that no real trouble developed during the period leading up to the Revolutionary War, especially when Tory fever began to run high, over the clientele drawn to a tavern on Union Street opposite the present Presbyterian Church parking lot. It was run by Charles Doyle, a Loyalist, from 1762 to 1772 and was a rendezvous for English troops stationed here and other people who were loyal to the crown. No doubt, in the end, Doyle decided it might be prudent to move on.

On the other hand, a favorite gathering place for patriots of the area was the tavern of Reuben Simonds on the west side of Church Street, which he opened after obtaining a license on April 19, 1777. Another Whig stronghold was the William White Tavern, located on the lot adjacent to the Mohawk Club where the Colonial Apartments are today.

In those early days, the local tavern was not only a place to meet and drink with friends, talk politics and personal business. It was also very often a community meeting house where the political leanings of the host dictated the sort of groups which met there.

A remarkable view showing the wood and brick construction of the Dutch dwellings. Again, this is the Arent Bradt house but now in the process of being torn down in December, 1895, after having stood since about 1730. The photographer, incidentally, was Dr. Charles P. Steinmetz, the electrical wizard of GE. The building which replaced the Bradt house was razed in 1924 to make way for the present YMCA center.

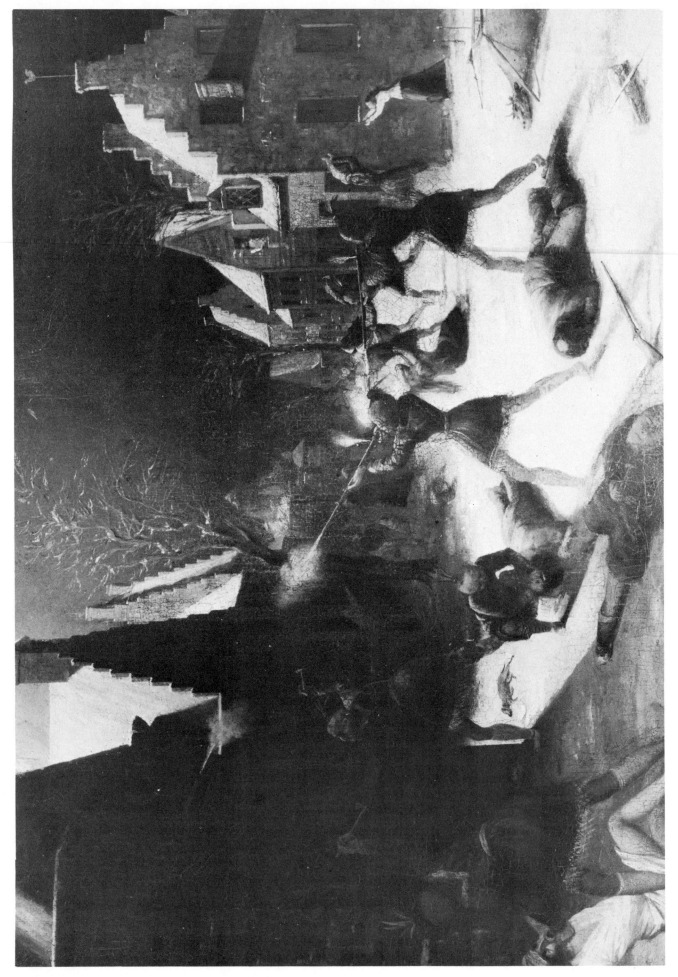

Massacre of Schenectady, from a painting by Samuel H. Sexton in the Schenectady County Historical Society art collection.

The foregoing gave some indication that the young settlement of Schenectady faced an unsure future because of the wrangling and oftentimes territorial greed of the colonizing powers. The reasons were both religious and political, and though the Schenectady inhabitants at first generally had no personal interest in taking sides, they had to be concerned with the side effects.

It suddenly changed in 1689, however, and the Dutch town became both apprehensive and involved in the sequence of events which ultimately led to its destruction at the hands of the enemy from the north.

Back in 1683, the "Charter of Liberties and Privileges," which granted religious freedom to all Christians and suffrage to all freeholders, was drawn up by 17 representatives of the New York colony. It was signed by the Duke of York, but he repudiated it when he became King James II in 1688. Needless to say, the new king was not popular in the colonies.

Two things happened then which affected Schenectady's role in history. James was driven from the throne shortly after he had ascended it and fled to the protection of French King Louis IV. The latter declared war on England, although it was directed chiefly against Holland, whose "Stadholder" had now become King William III of England with his queen, Mary. The war, known as the War of the Grand Alliance but popularly called "King William's War," lasted from 1689 to 1697 — and, naturally, had a profound effect on the colonies across the water. In this area, Schenectady was seething with indignation over the actions of both James and Louis.

When the revolution broke out in England, the majority of the English colonies in America sided with William and Mary. In 1689, Jacob Leisler, a colonist of German birth, led an insurrection against King James and for a time took over the fort at New York City. Leisler, a well-to-do merchant and a deacon of the Dutch Reformed Church in New York City, managed a pseudo appointment as governor of the New York province but was not recognized by the officials in Albany. Most Schenectadians favored Leisler's leadership, not only out of loyalty to Dutch beliefs but because he promised to repeal a recent ban against Schenectady on extended fur trading in the Mohawk Valley.

This set up an even greater animosity between the dorp and Albany. It was alleged that because Albany authorities warned Schenectady three days before the massacre that a watch should be kept against possible attack by the French, the Dutch settlers posted snowmen beside the stockade gates in derision of the anti-Leislers.

As for Leisler, his insurrection was doomed to failure. William and Mary sent over Henry Sloughter as governor in 1691, whereupon Leisler surrendered to the new administration. The latter was shipped to England and, after what was said to have been an unfair trail, was hanged for treason.

It is curious to note that in America at this time, time, the French were far outnumbered by the English colonists. The white population of Canada was only 12,000 while that of the English provinces was more than 200,000, nearly 18-to-1. Had the English and the colonies so willed, they might have crushed Canada and the French out of existence at any time for a century after 1660; but despite the disparity of number, the French were usually the aggressive party, carrying the continuing wars to the enemy's country.

* * *

The fate of Schenectady was sealed in the middle of January, 1690, when 114 Frenchmen and 96 Sault and Algonquin Indians, most of whom had been converted by the Jesuits, started from Montreal to attack English outposts to the south. It was part of the master plan of Count Frontenac, governor of Canada, to fulfill the commission of French King Louis XIV to "build a new empire in America."

They came down across the frozen reaches of the St. Lawrence and over the ice of Lake Champlain and finally, in about six days, down to a point at what is now Fort Edward, where the French officers held council on the plan of attack. It was here that they began to compromise with the Indian leaders on the feasibility of attacking Schenectady instead of the original objective, Fort Orange (Albany).

Another journey of about 17 days down to the Mohawk Valley brought the war party scarcely two miles from the fur-trading post beside the Binnekill on Feb. 8. It was about 4 o'clock in the afternoon and a blizzard came howling down from the northwest, icy winds swirling snow about the would-be attackers as they huddled in a final council near what is now Alplaus.

The French leaders, Lts. Le Moyne de Sainte Helene and Daillebout de Mantet, ordered Indian scouts to cross the Mohawk and see what precautions the Dutchmen had made against enemy attack. The French were well aware that attack warnings had been posted in the valley communities and they did not know how well the Schenectady stockade might be garrisoned.

The Dutchman's fireside on that night of Feb. 8, 1690, glowed with the radiance of humble content. Within the raftered room, its floor and ceiling re-

A scale model of Schenectady as it might have looked at the time of the massacre. The Binnekill is in the background, the north gate of the stockade at right.

flecting Holland cleanliness, he warmed himself before the crackling logs. He was smugly certain that his house was safe from attack – on a night such as this, even the foolhardy Frenchmen would not be expected from the frozen north regions.

The scouting party sent to spy on the objective returned to the Alplaus encampment about 11 p.m. and reported to the French commanders that no one was guarding the stockade; even the north gate facing the river had been left open. This information, and the extreme cold, prompted the decision to attack at once rather than wait until 2 a.m. as originally planned.

The half-frozen invaders crossed the river on the windswept ice and soon were inside the stockade, forming a cordon around the houses that now were quiet with sleep. Suddenly the high-pitched war cries of the warriors split the silence, the signal for a bloody massacre that was to last fully two hours.

Houses were quickly put to the torch and inhabitants who came stumbling out in their night-clothes were shot or tomahawked and their scalps taken by the shrieking Indians. Neither woman nor children were spared, and soon their bodies

lay along the snow-covered streets, illuminated now by the fitful glow of the burning dwellings.

Adam Vrooman, whose house stood on the west corner of Front and Church Streets, fought so desperately that his life and property were spared by the French. It was a tragic stand by the valiant Dutchman, however. His wife and child were killed and his son Barent and a Negro servant were carried away as captives.

About 60 persons were killed outright, including 10 women and 12 children. Some managed to escape from the burning stockade area to seek shelter with families some miles distant. It is said that many of these died of exposure in the bitter cold before they got far.

The ride of Simon Schermerhorn to warn Albany of the French invasion often is cited as a testimony to the stamina of the Dutch settlers. When the massacre started, Simon mounted a horse and managed to escape by the north gate. Though wounded, he made his way through the snow-drifted Niskayuna Road until he reached Albany about 5 o'clock the next morning. Later, a party of Albany militia and Mohawk warriors pursued the northern invaders and killed or captured 15 or more almost within sight of Montreal.

A grim scene greeted the first streaks of dawn as the French rounded up their prisoners and spare horses and supplies to begin the long trek back to Canada. The ruins of the burned homes were steaming mounds beside the blackened chimneys; victims still lay in blood-stained snow where they had been killed or dragged.

A party had been sent across the river early that Sunday morning to the Sanders mansion in Scotia. "Coudre Sander" (John A.) Glen was told that he would have the privilege of choosing his relatives from among the prisoners in return for having been kind to some French captives when they were in the hands of the Mohawks a few years earlier. Glen claimed as many relatives as he dared.

The French and Indians left early in the afternoon with 27 prisoners and 50 good horses.

The utter helplessness of the Schenectady inhabitants during the massacre — many offered no resistance since they had no time even to seize their weapons — was shown by the fact that only two of the enemy were killed and one severely wounded. However, aside from the fact that a long and difficult sortie into the English territory had been accomplished, it is doubtful that French authorities considered the mission a great success.

By capturing Albany, and perhaps destroying it, the French might have succeeded in detaching the Iroquois from the English besides holding the key to the navigation of the Hudson. But it was not done, and now the whole English province was stirred up like a hornet's nest over the carnage wrought at Schenectady.

* * *

The Dutch village which had begun its settlement in 1662 had suffered a setback so severe nearly three decades later that there was some doubt it would be rejuvenated. The uncertainty of future safety of border inhabitants and the utter dejection which prevailed after the massacre raised serious doubts among the survivors as to the expediency of rebuilding the village and cultivating the soil.

They were encouraged, however, by the Albany Convention — which may have combined compassion for their unfortunate neighbors with a realization of the value of a frontier outpost in those troublesome times. The Iroquois, too, helped persuade their friends in Schenectady to stay and rebuild. The Five Nations, in a council held at Albany on May 3, 1690, delivered this statement:

Captain Glen claiming prisoners as his relatives after the 1690 burning of Schenectady, from the painting by Tompkins H. Matteson.

"Brother Corlaer (Schenectady) be no wise discouraged but make your fort strong (as we have our castles) at Schenectady and maintain a garrison there, that your Corne may be preserved and reap your harvest, also send for your wives and children from New York and encourage them that we shall be safe, and fear not. . .The words of Diadorus are ended."

Sometime in the summer of that year, work finally was started on a new stockade much along the same boundries as the first one and it was nearly four years in the making — at least until it could be called a secure enclosure. The friendly Mohawks supported their Albany statement by helping the resettlement, both through labor in erecting the stockade and in providing food to the impoverished outpost.

More care was observed in building the new stockade, as far as fortification was concerned, than apparently went into the first. Blockhouses were erected at the foot of State Street nearby the Binnekill, at State and Ferry Streets, Washington and Front Streets and a fourth about 100 feet north of the present St. George's Church. Meanwhile, more settlers began straggling in — although not in great numbers.

A map of "Fort Schenectady" was made by the Rev. John Miller, chaplain to the British forces stationed in New York, in 1695. It showed a quadrangular triple stockade with a blockhouse at each angle and in each blockhouse "two great guns." It also showed 28 houses within the stockade, along with two large "long houses" inhabited by the Mohawks. The township had been depopulated since the massacre. Records of 1698, for example, listed 50 men, 41 women and 133 children — or a total of 224 persons — living in the area from Niskayuna to the Woestyne.

Queen's Fort, a typical British stronghold, was erected in 1704 at the northeastern extremity of the stockade — now the area marked by the Indian statue at the junction of Front, Ferry and Green Streets. Miller's map of the new stockade indicates two gates — one at the south end of Church Street and the other at the west side on lower State Street. The fact that the north gate was not rebuilt is attributed to a need for concentration of force at the State Street side of the town, which contained a mill, gardens and the roads to the bouwlands and Albany.

So for the decade that followed the massacre and closed out the 17th century, Schenectady and its inhabitants presented an unhappy, but industrious, picture of a settlement determined to rise like a Phoenix out of the ashes.

The Fuller House, which stood from 1792 on the west corner of North Church and Front Streets before it was razed in 1955. This was the site of Adam Vrooman's home where he made such a gallant stand during the 1690 attack upon Schenectady by the French and Indians.

Colonial settlers living in the outposts, as did those of Schenectady, learned early that the musket was as necessary as the plow, that vigilance on the home front was a human quality one must develop in order to stay alive.

Since the coming of the white man, there was probably more fighting than the Indian had ever known. In the Mohawk Valley, there were brief respites of peace while the countries of Europe re-organized their armies and navies before starting another war. Always, this antagonism had an effect on the colonies in America and on the Indian tribes induced to become fighting allies.

After nearly three-quarters of the 17th century had been spent in turmoil, peace came to the colonies in 1697 just in time to close it out, and lasted until 1701 — when England and France were back at war again. Schenectady continued to furnish soldiers to the Englishmen's cause as in previous years as both militiamen and officers responded. But at the same time, no home in the bouwlands was safe from marauders. It was during this latest war between England and France, Queen Anne's War, which was to last until 1713, that the Iroquois were not particularly pressed by the British to help in the fighting and, as a result, drifted about as far as they ever had from "protective custody" of the redcoats and their firepower. A few parties of Mohawks perhaps used this lack of attention — which meant also a lack of firearms, powder and rum — as an excuse to indulge in some deviltry. There were isolated, but tragic, incidents of farmers being ambushed in the field by a few Indians, his grain burned and perhaps even his home being attacked for no apparent reason. The English learned a lesson: If their Indian allies were to be kept in line, they were to be kept occupied.

After the close of the war in 1713, there would not be another English-French confrontation until 1744, but the colonies remained on guard nonetheless. For instance, in 1715, Schenectady township had two military companies of foot soldiers, each comprising about 60 men. Capt. John A. Glen was in charge of one company and Capt. Harme Van Slyck the other.

The Old French War was declared by Louis XV in the spring of 1744 and once more the English colonies were faced with the aggressiveness of the French and their allies from the north. This time, the active aid of the Six Nations was obtained almost at once by the English governor of New York, who met with the sachems of the confederacy at Albany on June 18 that year and "renewed, strengthened and brightened the covenant chain that had so long tied them and the subjects of His Majesty, the great King their father, in mutual ties of friendship."

In Schenectady and Albany, able bodied men kept watch and trained daily for defense against ambuscades by the enemy and for possible sorties into the north country. The French and Sault Indians made sporadic raids on various outposts in the English province, including Stone Arabia, Saratoga, and regions around Schenectady and Albany. The English, including troops from Schenectady and Albany, went on retaliatory incursions to Crown Point and even sectors in the vicinity of Montreal.

The war was nearing its close in 1748 when Schenectady met with the worst loss it had suffered since the 1690 debacle. It was referred to later as the Beukendaal (Beechdale) massacre, but was unlike the 1690 massacre in that it was a stand up and hand-to-hand fight in Indian fashion, in which the whites were the attacking party. The area where the battle occurred is today marked by a stone monument along Sacandaga Road in Glenville, on a curve just above Spring Road.

Monument beside Glenville's Sacandaga Road, marking the site of the Beukendaal battle of July 18, 1748. (Photograph by Ed Schultz.)

The whites did not fare well in the battle. Twenty of their number were killed, several wounded and 13 were taken prisoners back to Canada. Perhaps two of the French Indians were killed but, strangely enough, this report was sketchy in accounts given after the fight.

It was started when, on the morning of July 18, 1748, three men set out to look for some strayed horses. They were Daniel Toll, who built the stone house in that vicinity in 1717, his Negro slave Ryckert and a friend, Dirck Van Vorst. When they ventured into a gully called the Clay Pit (Kley kuil), they came upon the Indian party. Toll was killed instantly, Van Vorst was wounded but Ryckert managed to escape and went for help.

In less than an hour, about 60 volunteers were on the way from Schenectady to Beukendaal. The greater part of these were young men, anxious to take up the fight and "get some Indians." They hastened across the river and up toward the Sacandaga trail, not knowing the French Indians were quietly lying in ambush on either side of the gully.

Nineteen of the Schenectady party were killed and others lay wounded in the brief but desperate combat that followed the surprise swoop of the Indians. Finally, the whites managed to break into a clearing by the Sacandaga trail which led up to the deserted Abram DeGraff house, and here they managed to keep their adversaries at bay until help arrived a short time later. Upon the approach of the Schenectady militia, led by Col. Jacob Glen, the Indians quit their siege and retreated north with their prisoners.

Among the dead were eight soldiers from Connecticut who had been barracked in Schenectady. The bodies were brought into town later in the day and placed in a barn at 10 North Church St. belonging to Abraham Mabee. Relatives then came to claim them. Van Vorst, who was wounded and captured by the Indians when Toll was killed, managed to escape about the time the militia arrived.

The old Abram DeGraff house midway up the hill in Beukendaal where Indians held their first white attackers at bay after the brief but deadly skirmish in the vale. The structure stood for many years, weatherbeaten and unused, until it was razed in the early part of the 20th century when Sacandaga Road was widened.

There was once more a short period of peace in the Valley, but then the European political cauldron began boiling again. Called the Seven Years' War, it started in 1756 with the alliance of France, Austria and Russia on one side and Great Britain and Prussia on the other. It was waged on three continents — Europe, India and America — but when it began a year early on the American soil, the war was referred to as the French and Indian War. The battles in Canada and the English colonies were many and fierce, and much blood would be spilled before the end of hostilities in 1763, but that war formed a cohesiveness and provided a military training for American colonists which would make them a formidable force in an-other decade.

When it was all over, France had lost all her American possessions and would never again be fighting on that continent as a colonial sponsor. Great Britain, on the other hand, had now acquired a world empire on which the sun never set and her triumph gave the newly enthroned King George III a confidence that the glories of English military accomplishment endowed the king with new power and prestige. In America, the colonies had a new concept of their own power and place in the British empire. It was clear, by 1763, that a future clash was inevitable although it is doubtful many Americans were aware that it would be as drastic as a revolution.

Scene of the mid-18th century battle. The fighting took place in the gully in left background. Sacandaga Road is at right in this view looking toward Scotia. (Photograph by Ed Schultz.)

The etching on this old gravestone denotes it was erected to the memory of John Mabee (Mabie) who died Nov. 24, 1796. He was the grandson of Jan Mabie, owner of the historic house still standing in Rotterdam Junction. The slate marker, measuring 16 by 31 inches, was uncovered on the Glenville side of the river in November, 1970, during excavation for the reconstruction of Route 5.

Most Schenectadians are aware of it, but there should be little harm in reminding how fortunate we are to have such a historical gem as the Stockade district in our midst. While the fire of 1819 swept away much of the early Dutch architecture, and more old homes were destroyed in the fire of 1861, there remains within the area of the original stockade such a continuous array of 18th century buildings in top-notch condition as to make visitors green with envy.

A stroll around the staid, picturesque neighborhood at the lower northwest end of the city is a walk into history. Many of the quaint dwellings have small metallic markers affixed to the front (permissable only after exhaustive research and verification of a historic markers committee). They give the date of construction and the name of the original owner.

Since many of these homes were around long before the Revolutionary War, we have the unusual happenstance of relating stories of that period and being able to add, "The building is still standing."

We have discussed the 1782 visit of General Washington to Schenectady and his having gone to the house of Col. John Glen. That brick structure, built about 1740, is at 58 Washington Avenue, nearest State Street. Daniel Campbell's home, built in 1762, is at the corner of State and Church Streets, now the headquarters of our Chamber of Commerce. The Abraham Oothout house, where the price control committee occasionally met in 1779, is at 27 Washington Ave. across the street from the historical society. The birthplace of Joseph C. Yates, built by Col. Christopher Yates before the Revolutionary War, is still at 26 Front St. The Governor Yates house at 17 Front St. was built about 1760.

Then there are the Abraham Yates house at 109 Union St., a fine example of early Dutch architecture, and the Hendrick Brouwer house at 14 North Church St., both built about 1700; the Johannes Teller house at 121 Front St., built about 1740 with an unusual gambrel roof; the Adam Vrooman house at 119 Front St., built about 1720; the Abraham Fonda house at 29 Front St. and the Isaac Vrooman house at 31 Front St., both erected in the early 1750s in typical early Dutch style. But they are but a few of the many old homes in the four-block area which make it a delight to visit — especially during the annual walkabouts sponsored jointly by the Stockade Association and the Schenectady County Historical Society.

At the junction of Front, Green and North Ferry Streets is the Indian monument which marks the northeastern extremity and blockhouse of the Queen's Fort that was built by 1705 after the massacre. The statue was placed at that site in 1887 and in recent years has come to be known as Lawrence the Indian, after the Christian Mohawk who was a great friend to Schenectadians and was one of the most persistent trackers of the retreating French and Indians after the 1690 raid. There are other markers in the area, such as the point where Symon Schermerhorn began his ride from the North gate to Albany during the massacre and across the street, at the west corner of Front and Church Streets, where Adam Vrooman made his valiant stand against the attackers.

We cannot forget the three old and stately churches of the Stockade which figured strongly in activities and events through the years. On the corner of Union and Church Streets, where the Liberty pole and flag marked the defiance of local patriots against English rule, stands the First (Dutch) Reformed Church, its sixth edifice since the church was founded in 1680. Just around the corner on Ferry Street is St. George's Episcopal Church, the main portion of which is the same building erected after 1759 with financial assistance from Sir William Johnson. Adjoining courtyards, but fronting on Union Street, is the First Presbyterian Church, built in 1809. The church

The Abraham Yates House at 109 Union St., built early in the 18th century, as it looked about 1900. It and the Hendrick Brouwer House around the corner at 14 North Church St., are reputed to be the oldest dwellings in the city.

A view up North Church Street about the turn of this century with Front Street in background, the location of the north gate in the original stockade. The Hendrick Brouwer House is at right.

cemeteries of both St. George's and First Presbyterian contain grave markers bearing the names of some of our earliest citizens.

Just outside the city are homes as old and older than those in the Stockade. Across the river is the Glen-Sanders house, built at least by 1713 by Capt. John A. Glen, son of Alexander Lindsay Glen, who built the first house in the Mohawk Valley adjacent to that site in 1659. Diagonally opposite it, fronting on Mohawk Avenue, is the Abraham Glen house, built in 1730 by Abraham Glen, the ninth child of John A. Glen. Farther up Scotia's main thoroughfare, at 511 Mohawk Ave. is the Maalwyck house, built by Karel Hanson Toll shortly after he acquired the property in 1712. In Rotterdam, there is the Bradt (Bratt) house on Schermerhorn Road, built by Arent Bradt, grandson of the original proprietor, about 1736. And in Rotterdam Junction stands probably the oldest dwelling extant in the Mohawk Valley, the Mabie house, which was built by Daniel Janse Van Antwerp soon after he bought the land in 1670. It is something to consider that this house was standing at the time of the Schenectady massacre.

The Bradt House on Schermerhorn Road in Rotterdam, built about 1736 by Arent Bradt.

The 18th century home of Christopher Yates, one of Schenectady's pro-revolutionary figures and the father of Joseph C. Yates, the city's first mayor, as it looks today at 26 Front St. (Photograph by Ed Schultz.)

The east side of the historic Glen-Sanders house in Scotia, the rear section being built before the front portion was erected by 1713. The present dwelling was built by John A. Glen, son of the earlier proprietor, Alexander Lindsay Glen, who built the first home in the valley near that site on the Mohawk shoreline in 1658. This is a 1900 view, but the structure is probably in much better condition today under custody of its newest owners, Dr. and Mrs. Dolph G. Ebeling.

The Hendrick Brouwer house at 14 North Church St., part of which is claimed to have existed since about 1670. At least, there is little doubt that it is one of the oldest houses in the city. Brouwer, a fur trader, died here in 1707.

A 1960 view of the Jan Mabie House in Rotterdam Junction, probably the oldest dwelling extant in the Mohawk Valley. It was built by Daniel Janse Van Antwerp soon after he bought the land in 1670.

Section II

SCHENECTADY
AND THE
REVOLUTIONARY
WAR

When city workmen tore up a four-inch covering of blacktop on Front Street in June, 1972, in preparation for resurfacing, the old brick paving was uncovered. Howard Bray, left, and Louis Valentino are shown admiring the workmanship. (Gazette photo by Sid Brown.)

A city's development can be traced through the naming, even the contour and layout design, of its streets much the same as furniture or architecture is classified according to period styling. And when one is considering a city as old as Schenectady, those streets tell interesting stories.

Growing out of the hub of its development in 1661-62, Schenectady spread its history over a span of five notable eras. The first comprised the years between 1661 and the burning and massacre of the small settlement by French and Indians in 1690. The second epoch lasted until the great disaster and the loss of shipping commerce by the fire of 1819, destroying a great part of the city including the wharves along the Binnekill. The third era began with the Erie Canal in 1825 and continued through a long, lethargic period until the new awakening in the 1880s. The fourth era was one of revitalization as the city gained mature industrial strength. The fifth period, which began shortly after World War II, saw a shift in population to suburban living until currently the five towns have grown to more than half of the county's population of about 160,000 persons.

This present period has also seen a rather extensive though sporadic effort on the part of the city toward urban redevelopment, a project which not only has removed entire blocks of housing blights but streets as well.

As a start, let's go back 200 years. What were the streets of Schenectady like in 1775? To begin with, there were not many of them, only a few principal thoroughfares located within the big stockade which was in the shape of a parallelogram. Today it would roughly enclose that portion south of State Street between the river and Erie Boulevard, then from Wall Street over to College Street and from College Street back down to the river.

For one thing, they were nothing that would gladden the heart of any present day civil engineer or maintenance man by today's standards. They were plain dirt carriage roads, often rutted and sometimes muddy with occasional flagstone crosswalks for the convenience (?) of pedestrians. Paving with gravel from surrounding quarries did not take place until after 1799 and most streets in the stockade section were so put in order by 1804. These streets were then filled with the shops of the merchants, taverns or small grog shops, and a few artisan establishments (blacksmiths, brickmakers, carpenters, tailors, etc.)

Cobblestones followed in the 1820s with material obtained mostly from rifts in the Mohawk River at the head of Frog Alley (now Washington Avenue between State and Erie Boulevard). They

remained thus until about 1895 when State Street and a few offshoots were paved with Hanson (granite) blocks. As late as 1845, State Street was unpaved — just a dirt lane — from Maiden Lane (now North Broadway from the Woolworth store) eastward. About the only remaining evidence of cobblestone paving is on Mill lane, a narrow alley which runs between South Ferry Street and State Street at Church Street. Only a few years ago, the steep cobblestoned surface of Lottridge Street, which extends from Nott Terrace up along the Vale Cemetery to Close Street, was paved with asphalt. Patches of the granite block are still visible through the blacktopping on Broadway between Woolworth and Imperial stores. Many of the so-called side streets of the city were paved with brick, both red and yellow variety, and are often uncovered whenever an asphalt repaving job is undertaken.

Rotterdam Street did not come into existence until the beginning of the 19th century. Before that time, a road up the river left the south end of Church Street at State and followed Water Street to the line of the Binnekill, and from there westward along the former bank of the stream. It was called the River Road. The erosion of the bank of the Binnekill by floods gradually pushed the road back until finally Rotterdam Street — actually an extension of Washington Avenue — was developed farther inland. The area of Rotterdam Street, from State Street to the canal, was called Frog Alley. About the turn of the 20th century it became part of Washington Avenue.

The street names of Schenectady, some developed even before the start of the American rebellion, are indicative of the spirit of the times — a spirit caught up in the motto of the Schenectady militia: "Liberty or Death." There were streets like Washington, Lafayette, Franklin, Liberty, Jay, Clinton, Jefferson and Monroe. Of course, they were not all originally named thus, but future generations were to memorialize the spirit of the Revolution.

When speaking of 1775, we are referring principally to the Stockade section of Schenectady, which is now a living historic past. The streets of the original stockade section (bounded roughly by State, Ferry, Front and Washington) have managed to maintain their quaint and narrow contours, meandering ever so slightly in places to follow the original lines set by the whims of the early builders or the shorelines of the river. Contrast these, if you will, to the checkerboard streets laid out in the uptown areas by developers during the turn of the 20th century.

Union Street in the early times was Niskayuna

Street but was changed after 1795 in honor of the newly formed Union College.

State Street was Albany Street, but after the 1690 massacre it was changed to Martelaer's (Martyr's) Street, then finally to State.

Washington Avenue was first called Handelaer's (Trader's) Street, but after the massacre it was changed to Lion Street — no doubt by influence of the British authorities. It was renamed Washington Street at the close of the Revolutionary War in honor of the victorious commander-in-chief. Still later, it became Washington Avenue.

Ferry Street was at first Rondweg Street, later changed to Ferry because a ferry boat operated at a point at the river end of the street before 1808.

Front Street, fronting the river to the north, was once Boswegh Street.

Wall Street, opened in 1803, was so named because it once followed the east perimeter of the city stockade that had been rebuilt during the Revolution from the present location of the railroad overpass on State Street north to North Street.

Green Street was Cow Street, so called because the burghers herded their cows through a lane past the old cemetery to the pastures beyond.

Church Street was originally Cross Street and was renamed after the massacre.

That essentially made up the streets of Schenectady settlement in 1775, aside from a few alleys and lanes outside the stockade which led to grist mills and trading posts.

Schenectady got its city charter in 1798 and on the following July 8 our first mayor Joseph C. Yates, and the new Common Council decreed that new city streets be developed beyond the Stockade area. The ugly wooden pallisades had been torn down after the close of the war and now, for the first time since its settlement, Schenectady was an open community ready to expand to the south and east. New streets would facilitate that eventuality.

Governor's Lane, once a pathway used by batteaux builders to get down to the waterfront from Front Street, became one of these new streets. College Street was once part of Wall Street but was renamed in honor of Union College after

An early photograph, probably in the 1870s, of the intersection of Front Street (from foreground to left), Green Street (right background) and Ferry Street (at right center) where once stood the Queen's Fort. The Indian statue was erected in 1887 in the small enclosure in center. Note the cobblestone paving.

1804. The curve near the end of College Street was once called Elbow Street because of its shape.

Barrett Street, first called Montgomery Street, opened in 1793, followed a year later by White Street — later to be renamed Clinton Street. An early pathway was Long Lane, between what is now State and Union. It became Maiden Lane after 1800, was changed to Center Street in 1854 and in recent years has become a part of Broadway.

Jay Street, a rather narrow thoroughfare but one important to the development of the "uptown" area just beginning to grow east of the former stockade line on the eastern extremity, was laid out in the late 1790s extending from Union Street to State Street. In time, this would become a busy mercantile strip and in 1880 was chosen as a site for a city hall constructed two years later and which was replaced in 1931 by the present city hall. Franklin Street, originally built from White (Clinton) Street to Maiden Lane (Broadway) was opened about 1820. Jay Street, by the way, was named after John Jay, second governor of our state, who was in office at the time it was developed.

Pine Street was once a lengthy thoroughfare, extending easterly through the yards of the Schenectady Locomotive Works in the mid-1880s, crossing the college brook, then called Symon Groot's Kill, on through the college grounds to Nott Street.

One of the first big streets, however, to be cut through uptown Schenectady after the war was Liberty Street, from Ferry to Jay Street, completed in 1802. The citizens erected a lofty Liberty pole on the northeast corner of Liberty and Ferry Streets to celebrate its opening. It must have been a durable pole because it wasn't until June 6, 1867, that the Evening Star reported it was to be taken down because "it is deemed unsafe to allow it to stand any longer." In 1854, Liberty Street was extended to the College Terrace (later Nott Terrace) and a few years later beyond Old Niskayuna Road which cut over from Union Street in the vicinity of the college president's house to Prospect Street.

It was this same year, 1854, that Lafayette Street was extended from Liberty to Union Street, which was then mostly pasture land with a few scattered outbuildings. During the excavation and grading, workmen began uncovering the remains of about 65 men who had died during the Revolutionary War. Along with the bones were found an assortment of bayonets, sabres, uniform coat buttons and shoe buckles. This was the burial site for the general hospital of the Northern Department and the Continental Barracks built in 1776 on orders from General Washington and which was used until 1780 by troops either stationed here or passing through.

The remains of the American soldiers were re-interred with military honors in a vault on the side of the ravine in the then new Vale Cemetery. In the fall of 1879, the Green Street Cemetery (which had been maintained by the First Reformed Church) also was cleared and the remains of early Schenectady citizens were solemnly removed to the Vale on the State Street side.

Moyston Street, atop State Street hill nearly opposite the Gardner monument works, was originally called Reed's Lane after the first resident of that section. That was even before the development of Vale Cemetery in the 1850s. However, when the side streets off "upper" State Street were being laid out about the turn of this century, it was called Moyston Street because the old Moyston farm covered part of that area.

It was not until 1939, incidentally, that Liberty Street was extended clear into Church Street. One of the few buildings to be taken down in this project was the Timeson & Fronk funeral chapel at 15 South Church Street. The street extension was done in conjunction with the city's installation of a new storm sewer from Nott Terrace and diversion of the Cowhorn Creek into the river next to the Western Gateway Bridge.

Dr. Eliphalet Nott, esteemed president of Union College from 1804-1866, was thought enough of by Schenectady citizenry to have two thoroughfares named after him — Nott Street and Nott Terrace. The Rev. Dirck (Theodore) Romeyn, pastor of the First Reformed Church from 1785 until his death in 1804, was a moving force in the founding of Union College. Romeyn Street was named after him, but that street north of Union Street became part of Barrett Street in 1934 to simplify things.

Jackson Place, near Union's campus, was named after Prof. Isaac W. Jackson, who developed Jackson's Gardens. Smith Street was laid out in 1836, named after Peter Smith who owned a foundry at what is now the southeast corner of Broadway and Smith Streets. Hamilton Street is believed to have been named after Henry Hamilton, one of the owners of the Bowery lands along the summit of the hill and which were deeded to the city in 1842. The street was accepted by Common Council in 1851 and real estate development began in 1857. Veeder Avenue was named after Gerritt S. Veeder, owner of the Sand Kill mill located before the Revolutionary War near the Old Albany Road in the area of what is now Pulaski Plaza and former site of the old state armory. Development of that avenue began about 1861 even though a few scattered buildings existed there before that date.

It has been a long time since the Hamilton Hill area as we know it today has been called the Bowery Woods or Bowery Hill, from the Dutch name for the higher lands lying between Albany Street, Veeder Avenue and Paige Street. It probably got its name from its green cover of trees, mostly pitch pine which grew tall and stately from that point eastward to Albany in the colonial days.

A gang of laborers pauses for a photograph in the late 1800s while laying block stone along what was then called South Centre Street (now Broadway) between Smith and Hamilton Streets. A southerly view, looking away from State Street.

The hill was sandy with a deep underlay of clay exposed on a high face along lower Veeder Avenue.

Summit Avenue marked the north boundary of the hill. From it, Hamilton Street provided the only cross-connection to downtown. In the days until just after the Civil War, when housing began to be developed in that section, boys played Indian and made forts on the Bowery Hill.

In 1901 there was much talk of plans to put through a road from Nott Street to Union Street along what was then a lane called Central Avenue. There were some objections to the proposal, mostly that the area between the college pasture and the locomotive works would be spoiled by a street and houses. In its center was a small pond. However, the road was developed in time and it was named Seward Place in honor of Secretary of State William B. Seward, a Union College alumnus.

One last glance at the "old" section of Schenectady and you will see the influence of leading figures in our earlier state and national history — streets named after James Monroe, John Jay, DeWitt Clinton, Joseph C. Yates, Thomas Jefferson and the Marquis de Lafayette.

Erie Boulevard, of course, was so named after the canal which followed it course before the

boulevard was formally opened in the spring of 1925 — exactly a century after the Erie Canal began operations.

Some street names were changed before the turn of the century. Jay Street north of Union was once Fonda Street, Eastern Avenue was East Liberty Street, Summit Avenue was Ramsay Avenue (after Henry Ramsay, city engineer), State Street east of Crescent Park was East Avenue, and finally, Center Street became Broadway its entire length. That portion of Broadway from Weaver Street leading up the hill to Bellevue was once Villa Road.

Campbell Avenue, which became part of the city when Bellevue (and Mont Pleasant) were annexed in 1901, was named after Colonel David Campbell and son John, whose large estate lay at the western end of that section.

Shortly after the founding of the Edison Machine Works in Schenectady in 1886, the names of people prominent in the new industry began to crop upon Schenectady maps — people such as Thomas A. Edison, John Kruesi, Samuel Insull, William Turner and E.W. Rice, Jr. Prominent citizens of the day, some successful businessmen and others in public service, also were perpetuated at least in memory by having new city thoroughfares named after them. Some of these names represent the "Who's Who" of Schenectady families of the mid-19th century: Fuller, Furman, Veeder, Craig, Maxon, Stanford, Barney, Daggett, Landon, Duane, Crane, Hulett, Paige, Van Guysling, DeForest, DeGraff, Rosa, DeCamp, Ingersoll, Mynderse, Van Voast, Schermerhorn and Campbell.

As previously mentioned, Seward Place was named after William B. Seward. Not long after, in the early 1900s when the streets atop Hamilton Hill were being developed in the new housing sections, Lincoln and Grant were included in the honored list of Civil War renown.

Other U.S. presidents so honored included Arthur, Harrison, Cleveland, Jackson, Johnson, Garfield, Roosevelt, Wilson, Jefferson, Coolidge, Van Buren, Adams, McKinley, Madison, Monroe, Fillmore, Hoover and, of course, Washington.

Shortly after World War I, as Woodlawn was being settled, street namers turned to colleges: Vassar, Cornell, Harvard, Brown, Rutgers, Yale, Princeton, Fordham and Dartmouth. And there were birds to inspire other street names — Hawk, Eagle, Swan — and states — Michigan, Delaware and Pennsylvania.

So they go on and on. New housing developments outside the city have acquired streets or boulevards named for contemporary heroes of history, such as Eisenhower, MacArthur, Lindbergh, Roosevelt, Truman and Kennedy. They become the outer reaches of American history, bringing us up to date.

But the next time you stroll down a Schenectady street, new or old, reflect a moment on how it got its name.

Photograph by William H. Peckham of the 1880s showing the parklike Bowery Hill in what today is the area between Veeder Avenue and Summit Avenue. This section was formerly known as Paige Hill, as the Paige and Mumford families had summer homes on the brow of the summit prior to the 1880s.

57

THE MOHAWK MERCURY.

SCHENECTADY, *(on the Banks of the Mohawk)* PRINTED BY *WYCKOFF & BROKAW,* CORNER OF STATE & WASHINGTON STREETS.

[PRICE 12s. PER ANN.] MONDAY, FEBRUARY 9, 1795. [No. 9.]

FOR SALE,

A Yoke of likely young OXEN, cheap for CASH. Enquire of the Printers.
Schenectady, Feb. 2. 8

SEEDS.

FRESH *GARDEN SEEDS*, for ſale by ROBERT H. WENDELL; at his ſtore, next door to the Land-Office, among which are the following:

CABBAGE.	
Savoy,	Onion,
Drumhead,	Parſley,
Imperial,	Scarlet Beet,
Large Scots,	Scarlet Radiſh,
Sugar Loaf,	Parſnep and
Red,	Carrot,

And a variety of other Seeds, all of which are warranted genuine, and of laſt year's growth. 7
Schenectady, January 23. 3w

TAKE NOTICE!

WHEREAS by the 7th ſection of an act paſſed the 5th day of April, 1790, it is enacted, "That every perſon who ſhall at any time thereafter, cut or otherwiſe deſtroy or carry away from and out of the common lands of the town of Schenectady, any hickory, oak, maple, beach or aſh tree, growing thereon, of a leſs ſize than ſix inches diameter at the ſtump, ſhall forfeit and pay the ſum of five ſhillings for every ſuch offence. That every perſon, who ſhall at any time thereafter, in any of the ſaid common lands, cut down any tree, with intent to make ſtaves thereof, or ſhall cut down any tree and ſhall not carry away every part of ſuch tree fit for fuel, excepting all kinds of pine trees, and ſuch as may be applied to building and fencing, and opening of roads, every perſon ſo offending, ſhall for every ſuch offence forfeit and pay the ſum of twenty ſhillings." In, order therefore, to prevent future waſte and deſtruction of the wood on the premiſes above mentioned, we the ſubſcribers, in virtue of the power to us given, do hereby notify our intentions of ſtrictly adhering to the above recited act, in proſecuting all perſons who ſhall hereafter make themſelves liable to any of the penalties therein ſpecified.

ARENT S. VEEDER,
BERNARDUS F. SCHERMERHORN,
SIMON DEGRAFF,
JOHN VAN PATTEN.

Schenectady, Jan. 30, 1795.

WE the TRUSTEES of the town of Schenectady, do approve of the preceding notice, and are determined to aſſiſt the above named perſons to put the act of the Legiſlature in force.

JOHN SANDERS,
ABRAHAM FONDA,
NICHOLAS VAN PATTEN,
HARMANUS BRAT,
NICHOLAS VEEDER,
GERRIT S. VEEDER, jun.
ABRAHAM OOTHOUT,
ABRAHAM WEMPLE,
ISAAC VROOMAM,
JOHN GLEN,
8 NICHOLAS VANDE VOLGEN.

NAIL MANUFACTORY.

THE ſubſcriber, at his Nail Manufactory, in New Ferry-ſtreet, near the Engliſh Church, in Schenectady, reſpectfully informs his cuſtomers and the public, that he has brought his manufactory to very great perfection, and the Nails of all ſizes which he makes are equal if not ſuperior to thoſe imported; and are ſold at as reaſonable rates as heretofore, notwithſtaning the great riſe of nail rods. He has on hand a large quantity of nails of every ſize, and will receive with eſteem and thankfulneſs the cuſtom and favors of the public.

SEBASTIAN OLSAVER

FOR THE MOHAWK MERCURY.

Meſſrs. Printers,

I often reflect upon the folly of many who are diſſatiſfied with their own ſtate, and envy the condition of others; if my reflections on this ſubject ſhall be judged worthy of a place in the Mercury, you are at liberty to inſert them.

MR. POPE, who was not only the greateſt poet of his age, but was alſo well acquainted with the uncertain enjoyment of the many gilded pleaſures ſo warmly purſued by man, and with the many pains and diſappointments incident to human nature, in ſome of his writings has theſe lines:—

"*Aſk what others feel, what others think,*
"*All pleaſures ſicken, and all glories ſink,*
"*Each has his ſhare, and who would more obtain,*
"*Shall find, the pleaſure pays not half the pain.*"

Many learned men who have undertaken the taſk of reconciling mankind to their preſent ſtate, and of relieving the diſcontent produced by the various diſtribution of fortune, very frequently remind us that we judge too haſtily of good and evil, that we only view the ſuperficies of human life, and determine concerning the whole by a knowledge of a ſmall part. Theſe writers further obſerve, it frequently happens that grief, fear, anxiety and deſire lie hid under the golden roſe of proſperity, and that the gloom of diſtreſs is often cheered by the ſecret rays of hope and comfort; as in the natural world the bog is often covered with flowers, and the mine is concealed in the barren crag. I do not mean to intimate that the lots of life are equal, yet it cannot be denied that every one has its pleaſures, and its anxieties—that misfortunes and bleſſings operate differently on different minds, and no man can judge with preciſion from his own ſenſations, what another would feel in like circumſtances. If we were to form our ideas of things by the repreſentation every one makes of his own condition, we ſhould be led to conſider the world as the abode of miſery and ſorrow, for the mouth of almoſt every one is filled with the relation of his own difficulties. If, on the other hand, we judge of every man's fortune by the account given of it by others, we ſhall conclude that we are placed in the regions of Elyſium, overſpread with the luxuriance of plenty, and in the full enjoyment of felicity.

We are either born with ſuch diſſimilitude of temper and inclination, or receive our opinions from the ſtate of life in which we live, that the griefs or cares of one part of mankind ſeem to the other hypocriſy, affectation or folly. Every claſs of ſociety has its particular cant of lamentation, which is regarded by none but themſelves; and every part of life has its pains, which thoſe, who do not feel, will not commiſerate.

An event that alarms half the commercial world, that aſſembles the trading companies in committees, that threatens the deſtruction of commerce at large, is read by the farmer with mere indifference; the ſoft paſſion of love, which fills the young breaſt with inceſſant returns of hope and fear, and ſteals away the night and day from every other pleaſure and employment, is regarded by them, whoſe paſſions time has extinguiſhed, as a trifling amuſement, which can properly excite neither joy or ſorrow. The man who never had any other wiſh than to fill his cheſt with money, or who never entered a company but to make a bargain, would be of their wiſhes. At firſt view, we ſhould ſuppoſe that female happineſs is never diſturbed by anxiety and diſappointment. A ſolitary philoſopher would imagine that the ladies are exempt from care and ſorrow; for what can interrupt the content of thoſe, upon whom one age has labored after another to confer honors, and increaſe their felicity: thoſe to whom all rudeneſs is injury, and inſult is cowardiſe; whoſe eye commands the brave, and whoſe ſmile ſoftens the auſtere; whom the ſailor travels to adorn, the ſoldier bleeds to defend, and the poet ſpends his days to celebrate, and who claim tribute from every art and ſociety. Surely amongſt theſe favorites of nature, unacquainted with toil and danger, felicity muſt have fixed her reſidence, that they can never aſſemble but to pleaſure, or retire but to peace.

Such would be the thoughts of every man who ſhall hover at a diſtance around the world, and know it only by ſpeculation: But experience will ſoon diſcover how eaſily thoſe are diſguſted who have been made nice by luxury, and tender by indulgence: He will ſoon ſee to how many dangers power is expoſed, which has no other guard than beauty; and how eaſily that tranquility is moleſted, which can be ſoothed only by the ſongs of vanity. There are ſome ſtrokes which the envy of fate ſeems to aim immediately at the Fair: Lap-dogs will ſometimes be ſick—the fineſt brocades are liable to receive ſtains—the neateſt muſlins may be torn.—One lady may take more attention of the gentlemen than another, and all diſtinctions of dreſs may be obliterated by a general mourning. Such is the ſtate of every age, every ſex and every condition of life; all have their cares, either from nature or folly: and whoever finds an inclination to envy another, ſhould remember, that he knows not the real condition which he deſires to obtain, and that by indulgence he may leſſen that happineſs, which he thinks already too ſparingly beſtowed.

Y.

Schenectady, Jan. 26, 1795.

FOR THE MOHAWK MERCURY.

Meſſrs. PRINTERS,

HAVING ſeen a very lengthy piece with ſome hard name to it, in your two laſt papers, abuſing the ladies at a moſt ſhameful rate. I am ſurpriſed that none of them has entered the field of battle with him; but I ſuppoſe the poor women are much like myſelf, afraid to ſhew their bad ſpelling, compoſition, &c. Want of proper education, lays them under theſe difficulties; but when we meet with any that have had theſe advantages, they ſurpaſs the men as much as the light of the ſun outſhines that of the moon.

It ſeems the author of that ſcurrilous piece, to ſhew his great learning, has quoted ſome few names of infamous characters of idolatrous nations, from ancient hiſtory; probably the bad example was ſhewn them by the men:—and I dare venture to affirm, that if he had taken half the pains to ſcrape up bad characters from among the men, he could find twice as many; for my part, I own myſelf at a loſs to follow him thro thoſe old books, therefore muſt leave the lad to ſome abler pen.

I have in my youthful days learned to read the bible and teſtament, and ſince to write a little and fiddle a little, which is the very extent of my education; and by what I have ſeen in that old book, and diſcovered by my own experience ley with the ſerpent before ſhe yielded, but Adam, no ſooner than the apple was preſented, ſnapp'd at it without ceremony: next comes Cain—he ſlew his brother; after that Joſeph's brethren ſold him for a ſlave, and were about taking his life; Pharoah ſlew the Iſraelitiſh infants; David ſlew a faithful ſervant for the ſake of his wife; Herod ſlew the innocents; the Jewiſh rulers crucified our Saviour——Theſe were all of the male kind. On the other hand, the Egyptian midwives, contrary to the king's command, ſaved the infants doomed to die; Queen Eſther ventured her life for the ſafety of her nation; Judith did the ſame; Suſanna reſiſted at the riſk of her life the ſnare laid for her innocence: many others might be mentioned who have ſhone as bright in hiſtory as any of the male kind ever did. But to come nearer home, we hear of Queen Elizabeth reigning well; and even the Empreſs of Ruſſia has done more good to her people than any of their former kings ever did: although I do not think ſhe is the beſt of women, I believe ſhe is full as good as the king of Pruſſia. But, to come nearer home ſtill, need it be told what the women in New York did for our priſoners there, when the men endeavored by poiſon, cold and hunger to deſtroy them?

Ceaſe then *gentle railer*, to traduce the characters of women: think what your mother has done for you, and bluſh to be told, that after all the pains ſhe has taken to nurſe and educate you, the firſt fruit of your production, that has made its appearance, is the defamation of her ſex.—A noble mind indeed, if you mean to mend the world by abuſing it! Have you ever read the travels of the famous LEDYARD? Hear what encomiums he beſtows on females—not only among civilized nations, but among ſavages. My own experience convinces me, that there is more friendſhip and gratitude to be met with amongſt women than men: And if any of the ladies have reſolution enough to ſhake this *Male Inhabitant of Johnſtown* in a blanket, I ſhall not be backward to lend a hand, ſhould he be too heavy!

Be not ſurpriſed, Meſſrs. Printers, at my zeal in the cauſe of women: my ſituation in life (which is travelling thro the country ſelling knicknacks) gives me an opportunity of experiencing their friendſhip. I am fearful I have wearied your patience, but am in hopes the cauſe I have endeavored to defend, will plead my excuſe. Pray make ſuch corrections as you may deem neceſſary, and you will much oblige the Ladies and your Friend,

A PEDLAR.

Schenectady, Jan. 28.

PARIS, October 18.

Another convoy of five waggons loaded with ſilver, part of the contributions from the Low Countries, is arrived at the national treaſury. Warm debates took place in the Convention on the 17th, on the fate of all the conquered countries.

BERLIN, October 28.

From appearances, the events of the 10th of this month will be followed by the moſt fatal conſequences to the cauſe of Poliſh liberty; their laſt hope to put a ſtop to the farther progreſs of the Ruſſians to Warſaw, ſeems to have vaniſhed away.

The body of troops commanded by Dombrowſki and Madalinſki was ſurrounded and entirely cut off.

Prince Joſeph Poniatowſki, who had

Front page of oldest known issue of Schenectady's first newspaper, "The Mohawk Mercury." This was issue No. 9, printed on Monday, Feb. 9, 1795.

It was a red letter day in Schenectady the afternoon of Monday Dec. 15, 1794. President George Washington was just completing the first year of his second term of office and in Schenectady, as in all communities of the 13 states, there was eager anticipation for the dawning of a new century which posed an exciting challenge to the newfound nation. What better time, then, for the city to have its first newspaper?

Cornelius P. Wyckoff and Abraham Brokaw formed a partnership as co-publishers of The Mohawk Mercury and on that December day, the hand presses ground out 300 copies of its first edition. It was of course printed on rag paper and when folded once consisted of four pages approximately 12 by 24 inches. Most was local news and advertising, but there were stories out of Washington less than a month old and a few European items nearly four months in the reporting. It all depended on the speed of ships and horses.

It is interesting to note that in the early days of the Mercury, subscriptions apparently were collected by the postoffice if the papers were to be delivered by post riders. The charge for the weekly when it began in 1794 was 12 shillings a year plus postage.

In 1800, Schenectady's first postmaster, Joseph Shurtleff, announced that "receivers of newspapers must pay quarter postage in advance." This was shortly after post riders threatened suit for non-payment of newspapers delivered by mail.

The earliest known issue of The Mohawk Mercury is its ninth, dated Monday, Feb. 9, 1795. Original copies of this edition are in the archives of both the American Antiquarian Society at Worchester, Mass., and the Harvard University Library. Reproductions of each of the four pages of this now priceless publication are among the archives of the City History Center.

Above its dateline, the Mercury proudly boasted it was printed "on the banks of the Mohawk." Indeed it was, since the plant is believed to have been located at the corner of State Street and Washington Avenue (the present site of the Furman Building or Alexandra Apartments at 1 State St.) The wood framed Dutch gable structure was built about 1730 and was torn down in December, 1895.

In its last half century of existence, the building was occupied by wagon maker James Simpson on one side and a private school on the other. It also served as an early postoffice.

The publishers parted company with the issue of Feb. 8, 1795. Brokaw left but Wyckoff stayed on as editor and publisher until he left Schenectady in March, 1798. He was succeeded by John L. Steven-son, who soon made several changes. He moved the newspaper offices to State and Ferry Streets and, as of Jan. 6, 1799, changed the newspaper's name to The Schenectady Gazette and again nearly three years later to the more comprehensive title of The Western Spectator and Schenectady Weekly Advertiser.

From then on, although some of the publications seemed to lack both interest and subscribers and therefore folded in a year or two, Schenectady was never without at least one local newspaper.

A few of the early ones, that is before 1850, were The Western Budget, The Mohawk Advertiser, Schenectady Cabinet, Freedom's Sentinel, The Mohawk Sentinel, The Protestant Sentinel, The Reflector and Schenectady Democrat, The Schenectady and Saratoga Standard, The Wreath and Freeman's Banner.

The latter part of the 19th century saw fewer newspapers begin publication for the simple reason that they lasted longer. By now, the page sizes were similar to, if not larger than, today's average newspaper. They published daily and ground out (about the time of the Civil War) nearly 4,000 copies on mechanical flat presses.

The Schenectady Evening Star began in 1857 and the Schenectady Daily Union in 1865. The two merged in 1912 to become the Schenectady Union-Star and operated as a daily under that name until 1969 when it was bought by the Hearst Newspapers and published in Albany under the name Knickerbocker News-Union Star.

The Schenectady Weekly Gazette began in 1869. The Schenectady Gazette started out as an evening paper in 1893 but, under the new ownership of Gerardus Smith, became a morning paper in 1895 and has been so ever since.

Incidentally, the Gazette is credited with hiring the first press photographer in Schenectady about 1900. Up to this time, photographs had been used sparingly because the engravings were costly and not perfected sufficiently to replace the reliable old steel etchings. But the reproduction of photographs definitely was coming into its own, and Mr. Smith purchased a bulky Graphlex camera with that in mind.

The first photographer was Russell R. Beyer Jr. the grandson of J.W. Beyer, who for years had been a Schenectady hatter, and the son of Russell Beyer, Schenectady furrier. Young Beyer had some amateur experience with the lens box and eagerly accepted the chance to work for the Gazette in a professional capacity.

"His shots were few and far between," recalled the late William B. Efner, who worked for the Gazette and later became city historian. "The day of full-scale photo reporting had not arrived, but he was the first in the game and it was a beginning."

In 1911, when Dr. George R. Lunn decided to run for Schenectady mayor as a Socialist candidate, he and the Socialist Party began publishing a weekly at 156-60 Barrett St. known as The Citizen. Lunn was its publisher and editor, while Hawley B. Van Vechten was managing editor and business manager. When Lunn split with the Socialists in 1917 and went over to the Democratic Party, he also severed connection with the newspaper and it was taken over by Herbert M. Merrill. Van Vechten continued as managing editor. The publication ran into hard times in the early 1930s and finally folded.

Scotia has had several newspapers. The Scotia News Weekly was published in the 1920s at 312 Mohawk Ave. by Angus Seamans. George Churchill founded the Scotia Journal, then Kenneth Parkis took it over, suspending it briefly but publishing for most of the 1930s. Herbert Moore began publishing the Mohawk Tribune at 217 Mohawk Ave. in 1948 but it did not last long. The Scotia-Glenville Journal is currently published.

John English tried his hand as a newspaper publisher during the Depression Thirties, editing a Democratic-oriented weekly called the Schenectady Sun that was printed for Sunday distribution. However, the venture was doomed to failure and the publication went under in a short time.

Over the years there have been a number of ethnic publications in Schenectady – Jewish, Polish, Italian and German – some of them being printed in the language that most of the new immigrant subscribers solely comprehended. However, those that published a number of years gradually printed both in the European and English languages, some going over entirely to English.

Ettore Mancuso was editor and publisher of The Record, an Italian-American weekly published at 415-17 Liberty St. from 1925 until the early 1930s. Another Italian weekly, The New American, had a brief tenure in the mid-Thirties.

A Polish paper, Gazeta Tygodniowa, was printed weekly at 233 Broadway by Kasimir Ogonowski.

A German weekly newspaper, The Schenectady Herold-Journal, was published at 151 Barrett St. from 1911 until 1965. The late Oswald E. Heck, father of the late Assembly Speaker Oswald D. Heck, was editor and president, while the late Thomas Unseld Jr. was treasurer and in charge of printing.

For its comparative small size in 1794, Schenectady was not too far behind the times in establishing its first newspaper. The first daily newspaper in America, as a matter of fact, was not started until 1774 with the founding of The American Daily Advertiser. Next came the New York Daily Advertiser in 1785. During the Revolutionary period, news-hungry citizens got their printed information from about 30 papers which were published more or less regularly in various sections of the colonies. Once The Mohawk Mercury hit the streets, Schenectady never has been without a news publication.

Early print of the building at the northeast corner of State Street and Washington Avenue where Schenectady's first newspaper, "The Mohawk Mercury," was published. The Alexandra Apartment building at 1 State St. is now located on the corner, opposite the entrance to the Western Gateway Bridge. At the time the above picture was made, about 1870, the building was occupied by James Simpson, carriage and sleigh maker.

60

Chapter 13

SLAVERY. . .NORTH AND SOUTH

Slavery in the north has long been dealt with lightly by historians, although it decidedly existed in the American colonies many years before the sunny south turned to slave labor to build its cotton and tobacco empire. We of the north have been taught through generations of textbook enlightenment to believe that the southern states constituted the slave territory of America, that the U.S. abolished the slave trade as early as 1808 but was unable to stamp out involuntary serfdom until slaves were freed only after a bitter and bloody Civil War. All of which is only partially true. The fact is that black slaves were kept in most of the original colonies by white families who could afford them; their existence, however, was usually acknowledged in reference, not to slaves, but rather "domestic servants" or "household workers."

White slavery, of course, existed in ancient world history as captives in war, whole families of them, were subjected to servitude by the victors. Slaves built the great pyramids of Egypt and slaves were used as servants and turned into gladiators by the Romans to entertain the populace in arenas in fights to the death. Serfdom was an integral part of feudalism and lived on in many countries long after feudalism had passed away. It was the Portuguese, however, who were the first to introduce the African slave to Europe after pushing down the west African coast in the 15th century. Portuguese ships carried slaves to Spain, and after the New World was discovered, descendants of these Spanish slaves were brought to Haiti to work the mines. In later years, the great ship companies of Europe bid against one another for the fortune which lay in the African slave trade.

With the settlement of North America, the demand for slave labor soon passed from the West Indies to the colonies and became so great it is estimated that between 1680 and 1786 more than two million blacks were brought into the West Indies and the English colonies. It is said that slavery was introduced in the territory that is now New York State as early as 1624 by the Dutch through the West India Company, eager to settle and develop this fertile new land.

Thus slavery was well entrenched in the New World long before the makers of the U.S. Constitution met in Philadelphia to decree that all men are created equal and are entitled to inalienable rights. Involuntary servitude was far from being approved in principle by the most eminent of the fathers of the American Union. George Washington, who had a number of black servants among his household at Mount Vernon, provided in his will for the emancipation of his own slaves. He once remarked to

Thomas Jefferson that it was "among my first wishes to see some plan adopted by which slavery in my country might be abolished by law." John Adams vigorously expressed his abhorrence of slave-holding and said that "every measure of prudence ought to be assumed for the eventual total extirpation of slavery from the United States."

Benjamin Franklin had earlier declared his outright objection to any form of slavery and Madison, Hamilton and Patrick Henry all reprobated the practice. Jefferson, recognizing the inconsistency of the rights of man while slavery existed, said "I tremble for my country when I reflect that God is just."

At the Philadelphia convention in 1787, where the Constitution was drafted, the sentiments of the delegates were against slavery, but South Carolina and Georgia insisted on its recognition as a condition of their joining the Union. However, the words "slave" and "slavery" were excluded from the final document because, as Madison said, they "did not choose to admit the right of property in man" in direct terms; and it was at the same time provided that Congress might interdict the foreign slave trade after the expiration of 20 years.

It should be pointed out that either before or shortly after the formation of the Union the northern states — beginning with Vermont in 1777 and ending with New Jersey in 1804 — either abolished slavery or adopted measures to end the slave trade.

When the party of French and Indians fell upon the town they called Corlaer (Schenectady) that fateful February night of 1690, it was as a reluctant second choice that they chose to attack the Dutch settlers rather than their more hated enemies, the English, at Fort Orange. It should be noted that this early Dutch community also had its share of "domestic servants." Of the 62 persons reported killed in the massacre, at least 15 of them were blacks, obviously slave help and probably living in the garrets of the household. Several were among the 27 prisoners taken back to Canada.

Described in "ye list of persons killed" in the massacre were notations such as "Sweer Teunise (Van Velsen) shot and burnt. His wife killed and burnt. Antje Jans, daughter of Jan Spoor, killed and burnt. Four Negroes of the said Sweer Teunise the same death. Enos Talmadge, lieutenant of Capt. Bull, killed and burnt. All in one house." There were also other references to slaves: "Maria Viele, wife of Douwe Aukes and her two children killed, and his Negro woman Francyn. . .shot" and "Meese Vrooman and Bartholomeus Vrooman, killed and burnt. Two Negroes of Hend. Meese the same death."

In the house across the river, Captain Glen prepared to defend his house and household, including "his servants and some Indians," until he was given assurance by the French officers that no harm would come to them.

In the early churches of this area, upper galleries were commonly set aside for the Negro servants of the congregation. It is said that ordinarily the slaves were well treated and that many were given their freedom by their master. The slave had some legal rights — which included a right to limited religious instruction, security and support in old age and sickness.

But no matter how humanely the servants were treated, either by their Dutch or English masters in the early history of this section, the fact remained that they were still in bondage, suffering the accompanying indignities of being allowed to "live together" when it was convenient and also being separated for the same reason. An advertisement in the Albany Gazette in the early 1700s, for example, stated "a likely Negro wench for sale." There were rewards for apprentices or slaves listed as one cent compared to $20 for the recovery of a missing horse.

Some slaves probably wanted to escape but the fear of punishment if caught usually was enough to stop them from trying. Blacks who had been fleeing to Canada after the Revolution were warned that they would be killed by the authorities if found traveling 40 miles away from Albany.

* * *

Slaves as a property, and thus part of an estate, frequently were mentioned in litigation.

Take the case of Mrs. Gerrit Bancker, born Elizabeth Van Eps, daughter of Dirk Van Eps. Her husband was one of the original proprietors of Schenectady but never actually settled here. After his death in 1690, Mrs. Bancker moved to New York and became a successful businesswoman in her four remaining years of life. In the surrogate's inventory of her effects was listed ". . .in Colonie, Rensselaerwyck, a bouwer, two houses, barn, orchard, hofstede, negro slaves. . ."

On June 28, 1692, a suit against the estate of the late Sweer Teunise Van Velsen, the mill owner who was killed in the massacre, was brought by Baata Clute. She was the wife of Johannes Clute, held in Canada as a prisoner of the French, and was managing her husband's affairs in Schenectady.

Sander Glen and Barent Wemp were cited as administrators of Van Velsen's estate before the Court of Albany, demanding of them "9 pounds, 6 shillings and sixpence for ye remaining pay of a negro named Jacob sold by Old John Cloet (Clute) to Sweer Teunise. . ."

Records show that the sale of the 24-year-old black was negotiated on April 3, 1678, when Captain Jan Clute (uncle of Johannes Clute) turned over the slave to Van Velsen for whom the latter promised to pay "100 good whole beaver skins @ eight guilders a piece." Apparently, Van Velsen had reneged on the balance of the terms agreed upon.

The Committee of Safety at Schenectady late in 1775 organized a patrol or watch by virtue of a resolution of the Continental Congress that each community take such steps to tighten security. In Schenectady, it was to consist of two men "to go round thrue all the Streets in the Towne every hour." It is probable that the watch house for the required sentry was the old Dutch Church which stood at the intersection of State, Church and Water Streets and was unused after the new church was built at Union Street. From the committee records, it is apparent that there was a concern for "slaves on the loose." When the watch was organized, this resolution also was made:

". . .that the Town Wach be very delegent in apprehending all Negroes that may be found to run on the Street after ten OClock, that if they take any of them up to confine them in the Wach House till next morning and then their owners may release them on paying ten Shillings to the Watch for Each Negro or Els they are to receive thirty lashes on their naked back and also that the said Wach be very Delegent in apprehending such places that Negroes may be combined together and take them in Confinement and inflict the above punishment on them, and the owner of such house where Negroes may be found together Shall pay a fine of forty Shillings to the Officer of the Wach, which fine Shall be recovered by warrent from the Chairman of this or any future Committee."

However, it was not too long after the colonists won their independence and the freedom of a new state progressed, the idea of slavery began to gnaw at the conscience of householders who still indulged in the practice. Before the dawn of the 19th century, churches and statesmen were railing against slavery in the north as a great evil and an inconsistency with the principles of the Declaration of Independence. Gradually, as the slaveholders were convinced by the pressure of such arguments and also by the coolness of some of their neighbors, slavery in New York State lost its hold. By 1825, it is doubtful that anyone in this area was beholding to the whims of owner and master; at least the records do not show any.

Slavery was not a local problem, just as it was never a political issue in New York State. Its abolition was sought by both the Federalists and Democratic-Republicans. It was a thorny issue, nevertheless, which permeated the young nation and which one day would have to be settled.

The Friends Meeting House erected in 1807 at Quaker Street by the Society of Friends which organized there about 1790. The Quakers there as well as in Charlton assisted the Underground Railway in helping fugitive slaves escape to Canada.

The election of Abraham Lincoln in 1860 presaged the beginning of the Civil War in which the slavery question was a dominant issue right along with that of the rights of states to decide such matters. By now the north was overwhelmingly behind the rising sentiment to end human bondage, whereas the south opposed it as a death knell to its agricultural and industrial economy. President Lincoln's Emancipation Proclamation issued Sept. 22, 1862, promised freedom to some three million slaves of the Confederacy if their masters "still were in rebellion" on the coming New Year's Day, an act which greatly intensified the efforts of abolitionists to spirit slaves from out of the southland.

The so-called Underground Railroad, which was the system set up to aid fugitive slaves to escape from their masters and elude pursuit, had actually been active since the 1820s and New York figured largely in the movement. There was always the fear, both by the slaves and the abolitionists, that should the fugitives remain in the northern states they might be picked up by groups of men who profited by returning them to the plantation owners. Thus, being next to the Canadian border where many slaves ultimately were taken to wait out the end of the war, New York State was the last link to assured freedom. (The story of Moses Viney, who escaped from slavery in the south and finally settled in Schenectady, is recounted elsewhere in this volume. His experience relates directly to the danger of fugitives being returned to their masters).

For the people of the north, it was a complete turnabout from the once accepted practice of slavery as a normal part of life to involvement in guaranteeing freedom for all. The prominent areas of Schenectady which most actively took part in the Underground Railway were the Quaker (Society of Friends) settlements at Quaker Street and Charlton, and Ballston Spa. Runaways were kept in houses designated as temporary hideaways where they were furnished food, shelter and sometimes sick care. They were eventually turned over to intermediaries who shunted the slaves to more northerly quarters, often in canvas covered wagons and in the dead of night so that unfriendly eyes might not be alerted.

The Emancipation Proclamation did not apply to the border states which were not in rebellion, and of course it could not be enforced in territory held by the Confederate troops. However, the slaves were freed as soon as the Union armies captured a region. The remaining slaves in the United States finally were given absolute freedom from bondage by the 13th Amendment, (ratified Dec. 18, 1865) which decreed that "neither slavery nor involuntary servitude, except as a punishment for crime whereof the party shall have been duly convicted, shall exist within the United States, or any place subject to their jurisdiction."

There were no more slaves in America, and yet the century that followed saw slow progress in the ending of discrimination against blacks or even a half-hearted attempt at integration of humans despite the color of one's skin.

The Deep South was claimed by the northerners to be the more prejudicial against blacks, Yankees being quick to cite the south's long history of lynchings, the "Jim Crow" sections in public transportation and strict segregation between whites and blacks in the school systems. But when desegregation finally began to make inroads across the nation, many northerners were rather astonished to learn that they, too, had not been treating their black brethren much better. The ghettos were as bad and often worse in the big cities above the old Mason-Dixon line, Negroes were sadly shortchanged in educational and job opportunities, and white northerners were just as flabbergasted as southerners over the mere thought of their sons and daughters mixing freely with black youths at social gatherings. If the favorite repartee of the southerner, whenever the topic of integration arose, was "How would you like your daughter to marry a Negro?" then that of the northerner might have been "The coloreds are all right. . .in their place."

Generations of Negroes born of ex-slaves grew up in America conscious of a stigma which set them apart from white society, both in the north as well as other parts of the country. For example, the Schenectady city directories which began publishing in the early 1800s always specified whether a resident was a "colored" and this practice ensued until the 1880s. And local newspapers, until the post-World War II period, regularly carried news stories pointedly denoting that the subject was a black; i.e., "John Smith, 20, Negro, of 144 South St., etc."

Blacks excelled in sports throughout the first half of this century, but with the exception of boxing they never made the big time. The color line would not permit it. In entertainment and music, there were, indeed, many Negro stars — but, as in other endeavors, there always existed a social barrier which they were not expected, or permitted, to cross. Until perhaps 30 years ago, segregation was generally accepted by both whites and blacks as an unwritten law, a way of life, and few attempted to change it.

And that's how the blacks enjoyed their freedom for the greater part of the century following the Civil War.

Perhaps it was the perseverance of such black leaders as Dr. Martin Luther King Jr., and the courage of thousands of civil rights workers, both black and white, that finally caused America to see what an injustice was being done to the black minority. Many gave their lives to the cause, including Dr. King and Medgar Evers, the first black to enter the University of Mississippi. By 1955, things began to change. The U.S. Supreme Court, on May 31 that year, reaffirmed the principle of public education without racial discrimination and said all provisions of federal, state and local law must honor that principle. The confrontation in Little Rock, Ark., at Central High School, previously an all-white school, soon followed, in September, 1957, after President Eisenhower sent federal troops to enforce the court's integration order. In 1964, President Johnson signed the Civil Rights Act which banned racial or religious discrimination in many areas, including public accommodations. The U.S. military branches, which had heretofore practiced segregation in the ranks, also banned the practice and even began to move black officers up to top brass.

Discrimination in voter registration, one of the scourages of racial prejudice which civil rights demonstrators sought to eliminate in anti-violent demonstrations two decades ago, has largely vanished. Negro leaders were encouraged to seek office and today blacks are mayors of some of our largest cities, some have been governor and many are state and federal lawmakers. Even the idea of a black someday becoming president of the United States does not now seem preposterous, as it would have when the civil rights movement began three decades ago.

Thus, on the occasion of America's celebration of its 200th birthday, one might be inclined to point with pride at the tremendous strides made over the past quarter century toward the elimination of a vexing social problem which has for so long been contradictory to the underlying principles of the Land of the Free. At the same time, one might regret that it all took so long — nearly a century to obliterate slavery within the new nation and another hundred years to enact and enforce laws guaranteeing civil rights.

To be entirely candid, none of us today should be too shocked over the fact that many of our forebears of the colonial days went along with the practice of slavery when we consider that so many generations to follow did relatively nothing to right the wrong of racial discrimination. That is all the more reason why America's Bicentennial should also be a period of rededication as well as celebration. It is not enough to say we believe in the principles on which this nation was founded; we must guard them jealously and see that they are not transgressed.

For a start, there are these words penned by Thomas Jefferson in the text of the Declaration of Independence: "We hold these truths to be self-evident, that all men are created equal, that they are endowed by their Creator with certain unalienable Rights, that among these are Life, Liberty and the pursuit of Happiness."

Moses Viney, an ex-slave from the South, escaped from bondage and settled in Schenectady where he lived a long and happy life.

Historic and picturesque St. George's Episcopal Church on North Ferry Street, from an old photograph before extensive alterations in 1953. It is the city's second oldest church, designed by Samuel Fuller and constructed between 1759 and 1763. Sir William Johnson was a benefactor of the church, had a private pew there and attended occasionally.

The people of mid-18th century Schenectady owed a great deal to Sir William Johnson, a man most democratic in his manner of living and in his dealings with both the white settlers and the red men of this area. We are reminded of his influence in Indian and crown affairs, which ultimately benefited Schenectady.

Born in Ireland in 1715, he came to America when but 23 years old to manage an estate of several thousand acres that had come into the possession of his uncle, Admiral Peter Warren of the Royal Navy. Here he made his first home, in an area known as Warren's Bush, located along the south bank of the Mohawk River in the town of Florida, opposite the present Amsterdam. It was not long before he became known for his friendship and fairness with the Mohawk Indians who said of him after long acquaintance, "He never deceived us."

He lived at Warren's Bush about five years and about 1740 bought a large tract of land for himself on the north side of the river, extending westerly from present Amsterdam. One of the mansions he built was Johnson Hall, which today is a well-visited historic site in Johnstown. He was made Commissioner of Indian Affairs and used his influence to protect the Indians from exploitation by the whites. He also was instrumental in preventing an alliance between the Iroquois and the western Indian Chief Pontiac during the French and Indian War. It is said that had the six nations of this vicinity joined in such an alliance against the white settlements, as Pontiac proposed, Schenectady, Albany and most of the settlements in this area would have been destroyed.

It was Sir William who in 1748, as commander of the Albany County Militia (of which Schenectady was then a part), renamed the lake which Father Jogues had earlier christened Lake Saint Sacrament for the day on which he discovered it. Sir William renamed it Lake George in honor of His Majesty King George of England.

The advent of the Revolutionary War found Schenectady opposed to the tax acts imposed upon the colonies by the British Parliament but still very much a friend of, and in turn befriended by, Sir William Johnson. The local gentry had not forgotten Sir William's appeals to the crown and influence with the Indians on their behalf.

Sir William employed masterful strategy and diplomacy on two fronts — with the mother country and the Iroquois — to see that Schenectady was not maltreated in those uncertain, tense and threatening days of the early 1770s. He was loyal to the crown but yet worked until his dying day to promote peace for both the Indians and the white citizens of this area. He could not believe there would be justification in senseless bloodshed over the "misunderstanding" between the colonies and England, that the whole thing would be resolved peaceably given time. He was particularly concerned that the Iroquois might be drawn into the controversy by being convinced that they should take sides and join raiding parties.

He was thus engaged with a council with the Indians, about 600 of them, at Johnson Hall on July 11, 1774, in spite of illness. His death that day was dramatic in its suddenness.

He was seized with spasms of pain after nearly two hours of conference with the sachems of the Iroquois nations, and was carried indoors where he died two hours later of "a suffocation" (according to Guy Johnson.) His physician later diagnosed it as a "stoppage of the gall-duct."

Sir William Johnson, from a copy of a painting on glass among the possessions of the Montgomery County Historical Society.

General William North of Duanesburg, chief of Baron Steuben's staff during the Revolutionary War. He became the first chairman of Schenectady County's Board of Supervisors in 1809.

Chapter 15

THE DIVIDING LINE. . .WHIG OR TORY

Whig or Tory, patriot or loyalist. . .it was not all that simple as it became evident by 1770 that the American colonies were heading toward a confrontation with Great Britain over the question of sovereignty.

In Schenectady, for example, the townsfolk were no longer a solid bloc of Dutch burghers as a century before; rather, there was a goodly smattering of many nationalities, some who had only recently come over from England, Scotland and Ireland. There were many Britons, and a few Germans, who had served in the British forces in the recent wars and were now mustered out of the service and married with women of local families. They had settled in Schenectady, had children of their own and were respected businessmen of the community.

Is it any wonder that when the specter of a revolution against the King and Parliament cast its shadow over the American soil that many individuals were torn between allegiance to the crown and to their newfound home? Was there no gray area in which a man or woman born under the union jack might find themselves befuddled as to which cause to support wholeheartedly? We must keep in mind that the colonies were not yet united to fight a common battle against what some descendants of early settlers called "tyranny and oppression" by the mother country. That would not come for another six years, and only until then did the issue emerge crystal clear — either one was for the United States or for Great Britain, for a republic or dominion.

For more than a century, many of the colonists had fought with the British against the French as those two major powers waged what seemed an unending struggle for control of the New World. By the time the Revolutionary War became inevitable, there came an agonizing decision to loyal subjects whether to renounce their upbringing and fight for an uncertain freedom or to again pull up roots and head for loyalist strongholds to the south, west or north. For a time, some couldn't make up their minds and led rather tortured lives, being accused by patriot neighbors of being outright Tories or else simply waiting to see what would happen so that they could take sides with the victors.

In the early 1770s, as the Continental Congress began to assume increasing powers not delegated to it, the citizens reacted in different ways so that labels were attached long before war finally came. The more radical protagonists in the revolutionary movement, most of whom quickly joined the Sons of Liberty, pronounced themselves Whigs and applauded the congressional dictums. But there were those who, while opposed to revolution, thought there must be another solution to the problem. They were not satisfied with the pretensions of Parliament; neither did they believe America would be best served by despotic committees interpreting laws made in Philadelphia. Many of the latter group were immediately tagged as Tories, when they should more properly have been called loyalists — they opposed strict British domination of domestic affairs and wanted some kind of a change enacted, short of cutting all ties with the mother country. The Tories were staunchly faithful to the crown and would brook no colonial insolence to its authority.

It was a time, most certainly, which must have been trying for the people of the colonies. If they decided to remain loyal to the crown, having experienced no great dissatisfaction with the way things were run, they would become outcasts among antagonists. On the other hand, there were families who would be split by a willingness to fight for a new republic, successful businessmen might be cut off from a livelihood and many political leaders faced treasonable charges should they pursue the course advocated by the patriots.

George Washington, who wasted no time in making his decision, was a British subject for most of his life. He had been a country gentleman and lived in a life style befitting his station. He had also spent the greater part of a quarter century fighting and commanding on behalf of the British territorial rights in the American colonies. It was not until Martin Van Buren, born Dec. 5, 1782, was sworn into office as the eighth U.S. president in 1837, that anyone but a former British subject became the chief executive.

In Schenectady, Daniel Campbell perhaps best typified the erstwhile respectable businessman who walked that fine line between Whig and Tory leanings throughout most of the war. A native-born Irishman, he came to the upstate settlement in 1754 at the age of 23 and at the outbreak of the Revolution had garnered wealth and renown through his success as a shrewd but honest trader. He built the house, now on the northeast corner of State and Church Streets, in 1762 after plans by Samuel Fuller, and established himself as one of the foremost "up-country" Indian traders. In the years preceding the revolution, most of Campbell's friends were among that class of Englishmen who remained loyalists — including Sir William Johnson, who was a close personal friend and often a guest in Campbell's home while in Schenectady.

Throughout the minutes of the Schenectady Committee of Safety are sprinkled entries which tell of that group's suspicions of Campbell's up-

Portraits of Daniel Campbell (1730-1802) and his wife, Engeltjie Bradt Campbell (-1812) from paintings by Thomas McIlworth now in the Winterthur Museum collection. Campbell's loyalty to the crown got him in trouble locally, but he finally succumbed to pressure to take the Oath of Allegiance.

Above, a mid-19th century view of the Daniel Campbell residence at State Street (in foreground) and Church Street (at left). Below, as it looks today at the same location.

state trading and its close watch on all of his activities. He was often refused permission to take special business trips, especially those up near the Canadian border and on several occasions was fined for not reporting back to the committee in the specified time or for having refused to accept Continental currency. However, although he was given close committee attention, it is interesting to note that up through 1777 Campbell was accorded polite consideration and continued access to much of his trading territory.

Beginning mid-1777, the Schenectady committee hardened its attitude toward the man who had been adamant in refusing to take the Oath of Allegiance and served Campbell and a few others notice that they must so swear if they wished to continue living here. On Aug. 1, 1778, notice finally was given to "Daniel Campbell, James Ellice, John Visgar (and others) to appear on Friday the 14th day of August instant in the Court House in the City of Albany with 14 days provisions for themselves and such of their families as they chuse (sic) should accompany them (persons capable of bearing arms excepted). They are also expected if they think proper to take with them all their clothing and household furniture. The charges of Transportation to the Enemies lines is to be defrayed by themselves."

Still, Campbell fought the extradiction order and exerted every possible means to have his case made an exception to the rule. He maintained he would respect local rules while conducting his business, but was steadfast in his convictions regarding the oath. But by May, 1779, Campbell saw that he had no alternative if he wanted to stay in Schenectady. He took the Oath of Allegiance and the King lost another loyal subject to the new republic.

Campbell died Aug. 16, 1802, and left his widow, Angelica, a daughter of Arent Bratt (Bradt), a descendant of one of the original proprietors. She remained a respected citizen of Schenectady and was particularly generous toward her old church, St. George's Episcopal Church, which Sir William Johnson helped build in 1759. She died in 1812, and was placed beside the remains of her husband in a vault at St. George's.

While Daniel Campbell may have been the most stubborn holdout against the patriots' cause, there were other prominent citizens of this area who procrastinated before taking firm, positive action in its behalf.

John and Henry Glen, both of whom lived in Schenectady, were prime examples. They were descendants of Alexander Lindsay Glen, one of the original proprietors, and thus were in the circle of friends which had long supported the King and colonization. They also had a strong affinity for the beauty of this land and the promise of a good life in its fertile valleys. This was why they fought

Christopher Yates, chairman of Schenectady's committee of safety during the Revolutionary War.

in the British militia to repulse the French invaders. . .and why they eventually turned against the crown and vigorously joined fellow Americans to establish a republic.

In 1771, the Glens bitterly assailed their Schenectady neighbors for countermanding British regulations to the point of organizing a Sons of Liberty group here, something which had been done earlier in New York and Albany. Others were critical, too.

On Jan. 26, 1771, a letter signed by John (Johannes) Sanders (who lived across the river) and Johathan B. Van Eps was sent to Sir William Johnson, reporting that inhabitants and freeholders of Schenectady had put up a Liberty Pole which they said was well bound with "iron barrs" 20 feet above the ground in about the center of town and had spiked it with "a great many Iron Nales" with a flag at the top with "the words wrote on each side (Liberty)."

The letter said the pole had stood about three days without being molested and added the writers' opinion that any molesting of the pole would be "the worst Trouble that Ever Has Yet Been in Our Town."

The next day, John Glen wrote to his brother Henry, who was in Albany, to say the pole was "put up in the street near the Church" (Union and Church Streets) and that "they will repent it much which I believe they already do. Chris (Christopher) Yates is one of the Heads but I think the Pole would be a good monument at his Great Grandfather's Burying Place. But we don't mind the Pole one morsal. I am of opinion the King's Attorney will Lay hold of them."

This was the first indication that Schenectady patriots had erected a Liberty pole and flag. The records show nothing of what happened to it for the next three years, but it is surmised that it came down.

Then a letter from Henry Glen on Jan. 12, 1774, reported that he and John Visgar (the same individual reprimanded with Daniel Campbell by the Committee of Safety) and John Glen, all justices of the peace for the County of Albany (which then included Schenectady) went to the Dutch Church where about 50 people had assembled "in an unlawful manner" with such weapons as axes, crowbars and pitch forks to raise "a Pole called by them Liberty Pole in the King's Highway and to Determent of the Subjects of Said Town." The letter reported that the justices commanded silence and read the King's proclamation concerning rioting and ordered the persons to disperse.

Glen's letter noted that the townspeople refused to leave and that the justices an hour later repeated the reading of the proclamation. However, the crowd raised the pole in defiance of the edict. The letter listed persons who had assembled in a "Riotous manner."

We must mention here that in May, 1956, while a ditch was being dug for a new sewer line at the intersection of Union and Church Streets, workmen uncovered what the late City Historian William B. Efner believed was the supporting base of the old Liberty Pole. He made a sketch of the stone foundation, generally conical in shape. (It was the practice of the Sons of Liberty to remove the pole whenever word was received that British soldiers were on the way to destroy it, covering up the base with a stone cap.) The location of the base was at a spot 17 feet south of the present southerly curb line of Union Street and a like distance east of the west curb of Church Street.

It is also believed that a tattered, discolored flag now on display at the Schenectady County Historical Society is the original Liberty Flag flown on those "unlawful occasions" in Schenectady 200 years ago. Now sealed behind glass, the flag is a dull yellowish-brown with the letters "Liberty" in white silk sewn across both sides — just as Sanders and Van Eps described. It is thought the original color of the cloth was blue.

The transformation of John and Henry Glen from loyal British subjects to intense revolutionists must have been sudden — or perhaps it was the turn of events after the Battle of Lexington which inspired many who were either loyalists or neutralists to take up the cause of liberty for America. At any rate, as the war got underway and the Continental Army was organized out of local militia into a united fighting force, Col. John Glen was made quartermaster general for the northern department of the army and Col. Henry Glen his deputy. These were responsible positions, the overseeing of gathering and expediting supplies for military operations in northeastern New York.

Christopher Yates continued a great patriot, organizing and leading the local Committee of Safety with the vigor that he had served in the French and Indian War. He built the house at 26 Front St. (still standing but later remodeled in the Victorian style) before the revolution and it was here that his son, Joseph C., one of a family of 10 children whose mother was Janetje Bratt, was born on Nov. 9, 1768. Joseph, who became a prominent lawyer, was Schenectady's first mayor and New York State's eighth governor. Christopher Yates, a colonel in charge of a fatigue regiment during the Revolutionary War, died in his Front Street home in 1785 at age 48.

At a meeting of the Freeholders of the Town of Schenectady, held May 6, 1775, in the Clench Tavern, the following were unanimously chosen to act as a Committee of Correspondence for the safety and protection of the township: Rinier Minderse (Mynderse), James Wilson, Hugh Mitchell, Henry Glen, Harmanus Wendell, John Sanders, Abraham Oothout, Tobyus Tens Eyck, John Roseboom and Christopher Yates. Sanders and Ten Eyck refused to serve, so Cornelius Cuyler and Jacobus Teller were selected to take their places.

Henry Glen was also chosen as one of 11 members to go to New York "to meet in General Congress on the 22nd instant." At another meeting on Nov. 11, 1775, Glen was elected one of five to represent "this City and County in Provincial Congress."

John Sanders, probably like Daniel Campbell, James Ellice, John Visgar and some others, apparently could not bring himself to renounce allegiance to the crown although he could not desert his home and the people he had known all of his life. It was as though he was certain his neighbors would eventually see the error of their ways and go back to living normal lives as British subjects. There is no evidence that he connived to aid the British at any time during the war, all the more reason to suspect that his real sentiments were for the welfare of the people of his community — as had been his ancestors before him. Sanders, son-in-law of Col. Jacob Glen, purchased the Scotia property from John Glen in April, 1765.

We can be thankful for the fact that the Glen-Sanders house in Scotia became a sort of depository of historical artifacts. During the ownership of Jacob Glen, for example, the mansion was used as a place of safe keeping for the military records of the time, as well as treaties, land patents and other state papers. At one time, even the public papers of Sir William Johnson, Indian commissioner for the crown, were kept there. Charles P. Sanders, in later years, was an eminent local historian and it was he who uncovered and turned over to public authorities the minutes of the meetings of the Sons of Liberty and the priceless Liberty flag mentioned earlier.

St. George's Episcopal Church, affiliated with the Church of England in religious doctrine, suffered greatly during the Revolutionary War. The populace was rapidly taking sides by 1775 and those who fully supported the struggle for independence took umbrage at continuance of services at St. George's. The Rev. John Doty, St. George's rector, was a Tory as were many of his congregation. Finally, in July, 1776, rather than hold service and not pray for the King, he was compelled to close the church doors.

Father Doty was summoned before the Committee of Safety on a charge of plotting against the State. He pleaded "not guilty" to the charge but admitted he was loyal to England, whereupon he was sentenced to jail in Albany. Soon after, Father Doty obtained a release and returned to Schenectady, where he remained until after the Battle of Saratoga. It was clearly evident by now that England was in for a long struggle against the rebellious colonies since she had not gained a quick victory. Father Doty must have seen the handwriting on the wall. At least, in October, 1777, he obtained permission to move with his family to Canada where he died in 1841.

During practically the entire course of the war, St. George's Church remained idle and the building was vandalized by those who considered it a symbol of the enemy. For a time, because of its proximity to the Queen's Fort, the church was used as a barracks.

In retrospect, one might understand the tolerance and, for a time, patience exhibited by local patriots toward their neighbors who were reluctant to "join the cause" in those Revolutionary War times; more so, in fact, than the situation nearly a century later when so-called Copperheads abounded here. On the one hand, those who were still loyalists by 1775 were saying that they had been satisfied with the status quo and did not wish to change it, trusting in the mother country to treat all subjects judiciously. We had no formal government then, only a declaration of independence. On the other hand, the bands of anti-Union people in the Schenectady area during the Civil War had joined the rebellion of the Confederates against the U.S. government. Suffice to say, the Copperheads did not enjoy the same understanding by the local populace as did the Tories. It was, in modern parlance, a whole new ball game.

List of persons charged with raising a Liberty pole in Schenectady, written Jan. 12, 1774, by Henry Glen.

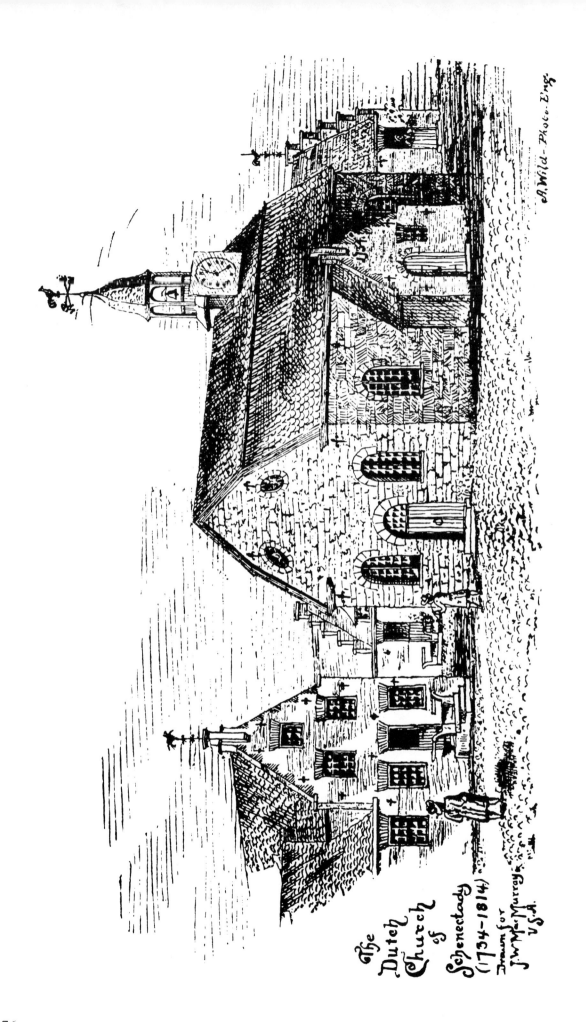

The Dutch Church of Schenectady (1734–1814) Drawn for J.W. McMurray, U.S.A.

A. Wild - Photo. Eng.

The third edifice of the First Reformed Church of Schenectady, built at the present junction of Church and Union Streets and dedicated Jan. 13, 1734. It was here that the Sons of Liberty gathered to raise the first Liberty flag in 1771 and where General Washington worshipped during his 1782 visit to Schenectady. The building was replaced in 1814 by a new church built on the present site.

Committees, committees, committees. They were in abundance in most every settlement of America during the Revolutionary War days as officials encouraged private citizens to look after such matters as safety, protection and correspondence — to keep a watch on how well a place was cooperating with the war effort to the extent that suspected laggards should be spied upon or even confronted with evidence that they were not supporting the cause.

A price control committee was one of these, and its story of operations in Schenectady is as old as the nation. It came into being soon after the Declaration of Independence was signed and the Articles of Confederation were enacted, because communities everywhere in the nation were having monetary problems. The military expenses and the scarcity of some goods and services, coupled with the issuance of new paper currency — the value of which was not yet stable — led to an era of inflated prices.

Following a directive from the General Committee of Albany, some leading citizens of Schenectady met on June 16, 1779, and elected a committee of nine men to represent the District of Albany and to hold regular hearings on the regulation of prices and its enforcement. The minutes of Dirk Van Ingen, clerk (original and copies published in 1876 and 1924 for the Centennial and Sesquicentennial of the American Revolution are preserved at the Schenectady County Historical Society and Union College's Schaffer Library) record the June to August, 1779, activities of the price control committee "to prevent extortioners from pursuing such evil practices, as have been too long made rife of, and must unless immediately prevented, end in the destruction of our country."

A list of names of committee members includes: Abraham Oothout, chairman; James Cuyler, later chairman; Lancaster Conner, James Shuter, Albert Mabie, Myndert Wemple, Jacobus Teller, Dirk Van Ingen, William White, John Roseboom and Col. Abraham Wemple.

The committee soon became active, because complaints of price gouging poured in after the word was out that someone would listen to the aggrieved citizen. Such commodities as West Indian brown sugar, tea, mohair, indigo, serge, buttons, striped linen, yeast and cattle were said, in many instances, to be sold at higher than the regulated prices. Then the committee would summon both buyer and seller to hear both sides. The seller would often claim ignorance of the rules, after which he would make the proper apologies with promises of future compliance with the price restrictions.

They did not get off that easily, however. Sellers were made to refund excess payments and pay fines, and their names as well as the buyers' were printed in public notices. Occasionally, Col. Abraham Wemple would dispatch the militia to escort a transgressor who failed to appear upon notification before the committee. It is recorded that in one such case, the tradesman "appeared too much in liquor" to take the oath and was ordered to appear later, when sober.

There was also a case on record which showed that there was not unanimous accord among Schenectady citizens in 1779 for the committee and its price regulations. One day, John Rent was carrying a package under his arm and happened to pass by the stoop of Dirk Van Ingen (the committee clerk) who was entertaining his neighbors, Abraham Truax and John Van Slice. Van Ingen asked Rent what he was carrying, and the latter replied, "Tea." Van Ingen then inquired as to the price paid and Rent's knowledge of the price regulations. Whereupon the highly incensed tea toter exclaimed he "did not regard the Committee nor their laws, if he had ever so much goods he would buy and sell as he pleased, and before he would sell it at the regulated price, he would rather throw it into the river." The account did not indicate whether Van Ingen pressed charges or, quite possibly, decided to let the matter drop where Rent had left it.

No hard specie was to be used in exchange by this period of the war; only the new Continental paper currency was to be accepted for goods and services. Barter, except for salt, was not allowed. One of the first duties of the price committee was to name a special group of citizens to receive subscriptions for orders of salt, the great necessity and scarcity of which encouraged excessive prices. In conjunction with other districts, the committee arranged to import sufficient amounts of salt for all persons of the area at the sum of 30 pounds per bushel, or the prime cost plus the necessary expenses of its shipment. Each subscriber agreed to pay or made deposits with his order. Those who felt "well disposed toward the poor and willing to assist them" were asked to help the committee in providing salt to the poor by gifts for this purpose with their own remittance and orders.

In order to arrive at what the committee deemed a fair price for certain commodities, various tradesmen and craftsmen (for instance, weavers and carpenters) were asked to testify before the committee to evaluate articles under review. Importers appeared with vouchers, asking indulgences for price increases, allowing for their additional costs and conveyance charges.

The minutes record an amusing aspect of the committee's function. If a member arrived at a meeting more than 15 minutes late and could not give a reasonable explanation for his tardiness, he was required to pay the price of "a bowl of toddy for each such neglect."

Home of Abraham Oothout, chairman of the price control committee in Schenectady during the Revolutionary War. The building, located at 27 Washington Ave., is directly across the street from the Schenectady County Historical Society.

The approximate 2,500 persons living in and adjacent to the village of Schenectady at the time of the Revolutionary War were busy souls, interested of course in the affairs of state but yet vitally concerned with their personal affairs. The people of the Valley had lived with strife — the taking up of arms and the protection of their homes and families — for well over a century, so the advent of the Revolutionary War did not represent a drastic change in their life style. The cause may have stirred greater emotion within the various families, but the necessity of earning a living still prevailed.

Schenectady in 1770 was much different from that of a century before. No longer was it a Dutch town, made up principally of fur traders, a few craftsmen and farmers. It was now an amalgamation of Dutch, Irish, Scotch, English and a few German. Many worked the fields to the west and south, growing edible produce and broom corn for the new broom-making industry that had just been established. Artisans were aplenty — brickmakers, broom makers, carpenters, boat builders, tailors and millers included — and professional men brought the practice of law and medicine into full sway. The women were keeping house and bringing up large families.

In architecture, the gambrel roof was rapidly supplanting the old Holland peaked roof style although there were a number of Dutch gables among the some 300 houses within the large stockaded area. The law was patterned after the British; it was strict and local magistrates held to the letter of that law. Public stocks and a whipping post at Church and State Streets were used if the conviction called for a sentence stricter than a monetary fine or less severe than banishment from the community.

The style of dress varied according to station in life. The working class, still regarded as an English version of "commoners," wore simple but well-fitted clothing in rather sombre hues. The men, clean shaven with long hair tied in a queue, had cotton shirts with bloused sleeves, knee-length pants and knitted or handmade cotton stockings. Their dress jackets were waist-length and for cold weather they wore wool overjackets and hats of numerous styles, ranging from the wool "Liberty" cap to the broad-brimmed straw skimmer. The women's apparel was brighter, although the average housewife spent the day in a plain linen or cotton dress, covered by an apron, and with her hair wound closely about the head topped with a dainty lawn cap or mopcap. Petticoats were often embroidered and wadded. Corsets were made of heavy linen, canvas or brocade and laced in back; the stays were shaped in long vertical lines of whalebone to produce the required look with the

Men's hats (from top left clockwise): knitted Liberty Cap, usually red or blue with "Liberty" embroidered on front; Canadian Cap, trimmed in fox or raccoon, with or without tail; round hat, sometimes turned up on left side; artisan cap, usually made of linen.

Women's hats (from top left clockwise): round-eared cap, with attached lace and ribbon; a variation of same, called the "dormeuse," fitted with stiff material; simple straw hat; mop cap, most popular of the times, made out of a circle of cloth shirred with a ribbon.

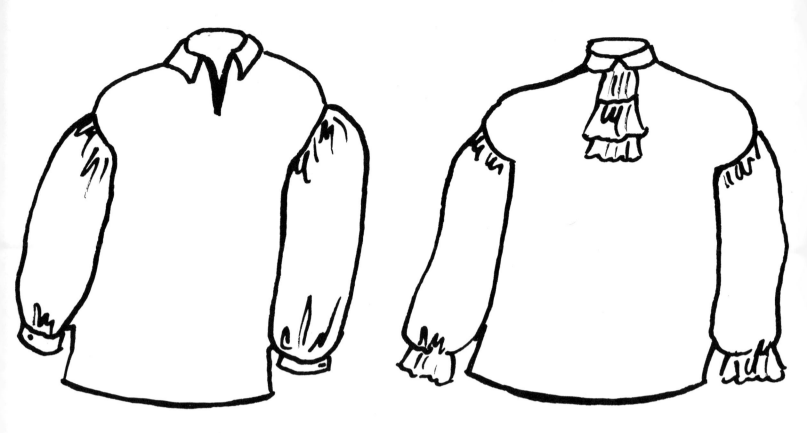

Commoner's shirt

Dress shirt

bosom pushed up high. Triangular shawls sometimes were worn on the streets. Buttons were made of bone, pewter, wood or cloth covered. Women's shoes, the same as the men's, were thin-soled leather slippers often with cloth or canvas uppers. Children's clothing was loose so that it could be handed down to younger members of the family.

The more prosperous tradesmen or professional men and their families were garbed in much grander attire. Baldness was unfashionable in the 18th century, so those aristocratic gentlemen who dressed befitting their respectability usually wore a wig, dressed with powder and styled for special occasions. They were a splendid sight with wide-skirted, flaring tailed coats, a black cocked hat, silver-buckled leather shoes and stockings neatly tied with a ribbon at the knee. Their ladies were also gorgeous in full-figured silk and satin gowns, laced wrist bands and petite fans, mostly of Japanese or Chinese influence.

Some beautiful furniture was purchased by local well-to-do families through houses in Boston and New York. The Glens, for example, early began a family collection of tasteful furnishings, some of cherry and mahogany, made by the best cabinet-makers of England and France and, occasionally, of the colonies. Much of the imported furniture was fancy and tapered in graceful lines, the wood predominantly walnut and mahogany. In colonial times, pine was the favorite choice of American craftsmen and it made up the quantity of hutches, benches, tables, chairs and bedsteads that were used to furnish the average home in the colonies. Colonial cabinetmakers often crafted European styles in their native woods, but the warm, rustic pine gave the American-made furniture a fresh, distinctive look.

Industry had come to Schenectady by the time rumblings of a revolutionary movement in America began to echo in the valleys of the Hudson and Mohawk. Broom corn was found to grow with vigor and substance along the river flats and Schenectady was launched into the broom-making business which it held prominently until after the Civil War. The boatbuilders who came here from Holland, Scotland and England had already established boat yards along the Binnekill in a wide sector called the Strand. The bateaux, long boats that could be either paddled or poled along the river, were first produced, but the pride of the Schenectady yards from Revolutionary War days until the big fire of 1819 was the Durham boat. The rather large craft was broad, flat-bottomed and straight-sided with easy lines at bow and stern. She was decked fore and aft along the gunwhales, with a hold for cargo, covered from the weather if necessary by canvas tarpaulins. A mast was stepped near the bow and was equipped with square sails. Not only did the Schenectady boatbuilders serve the mercantile trade well before and after the

Revolution, but literally proved lifesavers for the young American navy in upstate lake battles during the war. The principal boatbuilders of Schenectady were the Van Slycks, Marselises, Veeders and Peeks.

The latest news was hard to come by in those days (Schenectady would not have its first newspaper until 1794) but get it they did, in a number of ways. Couriers came by horseback or boat, broadsides were printed or handwritten and distributed in the streets, often attached to posts or public notice boards. Town criers, with their bell-ringing and periodic announcements, sometimes were sent out to spread special news. And those who gathered in the public houses rubbed elbows with men of the militia who always had tidbits of information to impress the civilians, much of it the sort of camp rumors which frequently made the rounds of the military.

Working Class Couple

Drawn for Eaves Costume Co., Inc. by Winn Morton

Affluent Couple

81

Nicholas Veeder, who at his death in 1862 was the last surviving Revolutionary War veteran of this area, is shown before his "fort" on what is now Scotia's Halcyon Street. Note the display of muskets. Directly in back of Nick is the Liberty flag now in the historical society's archives.

The Seven Years' War, called the French and Indian War within the American colonies, was hardly over in 1763 when a period of blessed peace brought prosperity and changes to the areas that had been colonized for a century or more. Schenectady was no exception.

The Yankee from New England came over from the Berkshires and Green Mountains imbued with the proverbial ingenuity — but also possessing capital and large families. Schenectady was no longer a frontier town and yet was considered the gateway to the west, a likely industrial and commercial center which attracted those with energy, imagination and ambition. It was really the first opportunity the little town had a chance to grow in its hundred years of existence, and now it was about to take advantage of it.

Storage and forwarding houses were built by the wealthy trade merchants, boatbuilding yards sprang up along the river shore and, besides the mills and agriculture outside the stockade perimeter, in-town businesses made Old Dorp a busy place indeed.

However, peace and prosperity were destined to be brief. The sound that came from distant shores was the drum beat of another seven years' war — one that was to split households and neighbors before it was over. America was becoming a tax-ridden land, beholding to the whims of Parliament and a power-hungry King George III; already there were men in the colonies declaring they were ready to shed their British citizenship and calling for a birth of freedom and liberty for the united colonies.

As a fortress against enemy attack, Schenectady was fairly well prepared. Its stockade had been renewed during the French and Indian War and a garrison called the New Queen's Fort stood in a clearing at Ferry and Front Streets. Its eastern blockhouse is marked today by the Indian monument. The fort was built of heavy wooden timbers set on a stone wall, total height about 12 feet. It was about 100 feet on all sides, its south bastion being across Ferry Street in the vicinity of St. George's Episcopal Church.

Schenectady's role in the outset of the Revolutionary War was to secure itself against attack. Companies of militia were formed. They were not always trained men and their leader was usually one of experience in the recent years, but not necessarily qualified to be an officer.

Probably Schenectady was typical of most American communities when on April 19, 1775, the shot at Lexington heard around the world alerted the colonies that war was at hand, that there was no turning back. There was no American army at first and no united people with unmixed fervor. The Continental Congress even failed to support General Washington's plea for a regular army with enlistments for three years or the duration of the war. The militia, or minutemen, were looked upon as the bulwark of American defense in the primary stage of the war — but, in truth, they were only ill-trained civilians who could leave the field any time they wished to go back home and sit on the sidelines to await "local emergencies." And there was no united action. When men talked of serving their "country," they really meant their "colony" or home province. It was this way during the wars against the French and it would take at least a year before the people or the Congress would recognize the folly of trying to resist the well trained and organized British troops in such haphazard fashion.

This is not to say the people of Schenectady shirked their duty once the war started; they were just no different from the colonists of other provinces. The clearcut issues and the ramifications of an all-out war with the mother country had not yet crystalized. This would occur midway through 1776 when, after a series of military disasters, Congress relented and gave Washington the power he needed to organize and direct a Continental Army. Swiftly, he issued an order to give $10 bounties for enlistments and sent officers home with orders to raise new regiments. Those raised in Schenectady and vicinity were officially known as Albany regiments since Schenectady was then part of Albany County.

What of the Indians of the celebrated Six Nations during the Revolutionary War? Large portions of the Oneidas and Tuscaroras favored the colonies and for their safety and availability were transferred to Schenectady to lodge first in barracks and then in flimsy huts built on the outskirts of town. Most of the Onondagas, Cayugas and Senecas, the most numerous and westerly tribes, remained loyal to England and became an awful scourge to frontier settlements in the Schoharie and Mohawk valleys after moving to Canada and enlisting with British forces. Meanwhile, rum and gun powder having greatly diminished their numbers, the once powerful Mohawks had virtually ceased to exist as a separate tribe.

Schenectady held an important position, situated as it was at the door to the Mohawk Valley. It and the Schoharie country to the south performed a vital role as granaries for the Continental Army during the war. Schenectady also was a gathering point for wagon trains which rolled northward to battle points and its boatbuilders were invaluable to the colonial cause. During the summer of 1776, for example, about 30 ship carpenters left their homes in Albany and Schenectady and set out for Skenesboro on Lake Champlain. There they joined Benedict Arnold and in an improvised boatyard in the wilderness helped build the first American war fleet.

As it turned out, there were no battlefields in the Schenectady district during the Revolutionary War, no raids on the lovely hill slopes and smiling vales here. But Schenectady militiamen and regulars did play a part in surrounding battles. Many local soldiers fought at Fort Edward, Fort Schuyler, Bemis Heights, Saratoga and Fort Stanwix. Tryon (Montgomery) County feared raids by Sir John Johnson and his followers, and Schenectady and Albany detachments responded in 1780 with men and supplies. There was considerable alarm in 1778 by the raids of Walter Butler, the celebrated Tory of the valley, and Sir John with his Indian allies in Cherry Valley and Cobleskill. Schenectady militiamen marched to those communities, but arrived only in time to help bury the dead.

Even closer to home, the settlement of Ballston Lake was attacked the night of Oct. 16, 1780, by a party of Tories and Indians led by a Scot named John Munro. He had been a loyalist who lived previously in Schenectady and Albany, then took refuge in Canada when the war began, receiving a British commission as major. About 200 Schenectady militiamen had been sent to garrison the Ballston fort just before the attack because advance information of the impending raid reached Schenectady a few days previous. But Munro did not attack the fort at Ballston, rather taking Capt. James Gordon, commander of the Ballston militia, and about 22 of his neighbors captive. After firing some farm dwellings and barns, Munro's forces and the captives left under the darkness of night. The militia did not pursue the attackers for fear that the captives would be killed if a rescue was attempted along the trail.

The very next day a raid was carried out by Sir John Johnson's forces in the Schoharie Valley. They passed the upper fort, about five miles southwest of Middleburg, setting fire to buildings along the way. The attackers decided against testing the strength of the middle fort, in the present village of Middleburg, and so went on burning and pillaging their way to the lower fort in Schoharie village. This was the stone church which stands today as the Old Stone Fort and at the time had a palisade and two blockhouses with two small cannon. Once again, Sir John opted to avoid a confrontation but burned most of the structures in the area. About a hundred people were killed or carried into captivity.

Because of the vast number of troops, including injured men, which began passing through Schenectady after the war spread into the New York colony, General Washington issued a directive through Gen. Philip Schuyler that a barracks and infirmary should be erected in the area. The site chosen was the present southwest corner of Union and Lafayette Streets and by November, 1776, the facility was ready for accommodation of 600 men. A burying ground was laid out in the rear of the barracks about halfway between Union and Liberty Streets and those men who died from wounds or sickness were interred there. The barracks were last used by the Continental Army in 1780.

In 1854, when the city was extending Lafayette Street to Union, the remains of many of the Revolutionary War dead were uncovered and immediate arrangements were made to have them transferred for honorary burial in the new Vale Cemetery a few blocks away. The diary of Abram O. Veeder of Scotia alludes to the occasion, an eyewitness account of the transferral of the soldiers' remains. The "old man" mentioned was Abram's father, Nicholas G. Veeder, the last surviving Revolutionary soldier in the county who was buried in the Scotia Reformed Church Cemetery at his death in 1862. The diary read:

"Nov. 28, 1854. Old soldiers dug up to be reburied in the city. Old man sent for to attend the ceremony.

"Nov. 30, 1854. In morning I and old man made ready to go to town to attend a funeral of 65 Continental soldiers that were dug up in Lafayette Street continued. Their bones were placed in a big coffin. We went with one horse wagon in a cold hard west wind. We went to Bankers, then I took horse to John Hemstreet's tavern and I was about city and the old man in a covered carriage. They went to State Street on the hill, put coffin before the dead house. The soldiers fired three volleys over the coffin then came down the road to the city in a terrible west wind and amid flying dust and cold — one could hardly see or walk — to Cane's tavern. I drank brandy and then I and old man came to John Hemstreet's tavern, thence home. Larry Gill rode home with us."

The German Methodist Church was built on the site of the barracks in 1870 and from 1957 until 1975 was used by the Senior Citizens Center. No matter what happens to the old church, the site is definitely a historic site harking back to the Revolutionary War.

The Old Stone Fort in Schoharie, once a church, then a fortress and now a museum.

On display at the Schenectady County Historical Society are, from left, a portrait of Christopher Yates, one of Schenectady's first organizers of freedom fighters; a replica of the Liberty flag, white lettering upon a blue field; and the original 1771 Liberty flag, now encased in glass.

G. Washington.

General George Washington, from an engraving by Currier & Ives.

Shortly after mid-day on June 30, 1782, an excited crowd of Schenectadians had gathered at the east entrance to the town (approximately the present junction of State Street and Erie Boulevard), ready to give a rousing welcome to General George Washington and hopefully to receive his assurance that peace was really at hand.

Lord Cornwallis, having been cut off from the sea, had surrendered his sword and his troops to the Continentals the previous October and all further resistance by the English seemed fruitless, and yet – no armistice had been signed, leaving the uneasy possibility that the British could refortify pockets of resistance with a massive naval maneuver. Peace . . . it was at hand with such tantalizing reality, still without a certainty which might call for all-out celebration.

General Washington, as a matter of fact, was not on his latest visitation to the upstate outposts to bask in the glory of his most recent and quite overwhelming victory. He made it plain, when he accepted an invitation from Gen. Philip Schuyler in May, 1782, to visit the latter's Albany home, that he would combine social amenities with an opportunity to inspect all fortifications in the area. The commander was all too aware that hostilities might yet break out and he wanted to be certain everyone was on the alert.

Time hung heavily on the American commander-in-chief at this point of the war. Not only was there the fear of renewed warfare (the King's troops still occupied New York City) but there now existed a danger of widespread desertion of war-weary soldiers from the Continental forces. After Yorktown, many of the American soldiers were seething over the fact that they had not been paid for months and began to blame the public for ingratitude and neglect. They ached to get back home with their own families and now were grumbling in the camps that they were merely marking time until the formal peace signing. Further, Washington had just rebuked a group of officers for suggesting that the army stood ready to set him up as king of an American monarchy. "Such ideas," he had said, "I view with abhorrence and reprehend with severity."

So it was likely he looked forward to a journey up-country from his Newburgh headquarters for a change of scenery and a momentary relief from tension.

"I am setting out for Albany on a visit to my posts. My stay will not exceed eight or ten days," he wrote to one of his subordinates.

* * *

He had been greeted in Albany on June 27 and was honored at a dinner that evening. On June 29 he visited the Saratoga Battlefield and Crown Point, then stayed that night at the home of General Van Schaick north of Albany. It was Sunday, shortly after the noon hour, that Washington and an Albany delegation rode over the post road to Schenectady, met part way by about 60 representatives of the city headed by Col. Henry Glen, deputy quartermaster general of the Mohawk Valley sector. And it was this impressive group which approached Schenectady, coming down the Albany road slope which was just east of the city gate.

Just outside the palisade gate was a group of about 100 Tuscarora and Oneida Indians who had been quartered that month in and about Schenectady for their own protection against possible recrimination by others of the Iroquois nation who might still harbor a pro-British feeling. The General greeted them with hand-waving and words of recognition, for he had been their host some little time earlier at Newburgh.

Washington dismounted near the gate and from there walked along our present State Street, hat under arm and waving to the townspeople gathered on either side of the road. A burst of gunfire announced his arrival.

Although he had been in Schenectady seven years earlier (at which time he consulted with local authorities and stayed overnight at the home of Col. John Glen, quartermaster general for this sector, the brick structure still standing at 58 Washington Ave.), there were many who had never seen the General — and he had become practically the symbol of liberty since those resolute days of 1775. Some were amazed that he was so tall, six-foot-two, and were quick to observe that he moved with exceeding grace, with long and even steps. His grayish-brown hair was hidden beneath a white powdered wig. Those who were close to him as he strode down State Street saw not only that his eyes were gray but that his face bore slight traces of the small pox he had contracted while in Barbados in 1752. For a man who had just turned 50, which was well into maturity in those days, Washington impressed his Schenectady admirers as a fine physical specimen.

There was an inspection of the fort and barracks at Ferry and Front Streets, and a conference with local military officials. Then the entourage went over to the Sign of the Crossed Keys for dinner. The tavern, located across from the present downtown YMCA, was run by the widow of Robert Clench who took over the business after her husband died the previous October and was buried in St. George's Church cemetery. It is probable that Washington requested the dinner be held there, even though local patriots suspected the

Clenches were of Tory leaning. Clench had been a good friend of Washington, serving as a drum major in the British army during the Indian wars and at one time being an aide to Washington.

As in any ceremonial dinner, there were speeches by local dignitaries and the guest of honor, toasts and compliments passed about. It is likely that General Washington spoke confidently of ultimate victory, while cautioning that everyone must do his part to attain it.

There is no absolute record of what took place for the remainder of Washington's visit here, but apparently he spent the night at the home of Colonel Glen and in the morning attended a worship service at the Dutch Reformed Church before returning to Albany. Prior to taking leave of Schenectady, however, he wrote two letters in praise of his hosts. The first was to the magistrates and military officers of the town:

"Gentlemen — I request you to accept my warmest thanks for your affectionate address.

"In a cause so just and righteous as ours, we have every reason to hope the Divine Providence will still continue to crown our arms with success, and finally compel our enemies to grant us that peace, upon equitable terms, which we so ardently desire.

"May you and the good people of this Town, in the meantime, be protected from every insidious or open foe, and may the complicated blessings of Peace soon reward your arduous struggles for the establishment of the freedom and independence of our common Country."

The second he addressed to the ministers, elders and deacons of the "Reformed Protestant Dutch Church of Schenectady":

"Gentlemen — I sincerely thank you for your congratulations on my arrival in this place.

"Whilst I join in adoring that Supreme Being to Whom alone can be attributed the signal success of our arms, I cannot but express my gratitude to you, gentlemen, for so distinguished a testimony of your regard.

"May the same Providence that has in so remarkable a manner evinced the justice of our cause, lead us to a speedy and honorable peace; and may its attendant blessings soon restore this once flourishing place to its former prosperity."

* * *

All that summer of 1782, on into the winter and the spring of 1783, the uncertainty of a final peace with the mother country persisted. It was an incongruous situation. Diplomats were unable to negotiate satisfactory terms of peace, yet the fighting had stopped and British officers had expressed their disposition to wind up military affairs and leave New York. Everyone, it seemed, longed for peace and was waiting for someone else to declare its arrival.

Washington himself probably decided it was time to prod the peacemakers when he set April 19, 1783 — the eighth anniversary of the Battle of Lexington — as the date of formal cessation of hostilities with England. But it was not until Sept. 3 that year that the Treaty of Paris was signed, declaring formal peace among the warring nations. France, England and the United States had all finally agreed to terms which embarked the New World on a course which had not been envisaged a century and a half before.

The triumph of American revolutionaries was culminated in November when Washington entered New York City, welcomed by fireworks, cheering throngs and waving flags. It was on this occasion that he bid farewell to his retiring officers at Fraunces Tavern and toasted their health, resigning his own commission at Annapolis a month later.

On a September afternoon in 1783, when news came to Schenectady that the war was formally ended, the townspeople celebrated wildly in the streets, taverns and in their homes. John Baptist Clute, a young schoolmaster, rounded up a band of patriots to wind up the jubilation "with a bang." They retrieved an old French cannon and dragged it through the streets of the town up to an easterly summit. While part of the group lit huge bonfires of pine knots, Clute and some others filled the cannon with powder, applied a spark and the ancient field piece roared its salute to peace.

Since that day, the hill from which the signal was given has been known as Victory Hill, and the street leading to the prospect was named Victory Avenue. The cannon on display in Rotundo (Riverside) Park today is believed to be the one fired by Clute and his fellow celebrants.

David Daggett, a lawyer, built his home atop Victory Hill after the Civil War, and it became Daggett Terrace.

* * *

In 1786, three years before he became the new nation's first president, George Washington again visited Schenectady during what amounted to a goodwill tour of former military bastions. Again, there are meagre accounts of the occasion, stating merely that he visited with local dignitaries for a brief time before continuing his journey.

News of the ex-President's death on Dec. 12, 1799 — only 17 days before the start of a new century and only two years after he had returned to the life of a private citizen — was received with much sorrow when it reached Schenectady three days later. On Dec. 24, the Schenectady Board of Aldermen, most of whom were Revolutionary War veterans, ordered the bells of the city to be tolled from 2 to 4 p.m. and the members voted to wear black arm bands for six weeks out of respect to "Gen'l. George Washington, the departed parent of the country."

The John Glen house, still standing at 58 Washington Ave. near State Street, the home of Col. John Glen, quartermaster general for this sector during the Revolutionary War. General Washington is said to have visited here and stayed overnight on at least one occasion while in Schenectady. The house was remodeled several times in the ensuing years.

Joseph C. Yates as he looked in 1823 as governor of New York State, from a full length painting which hangs in City Hall, New York City. Artist was John Vanderlyn. Son of Christopher Yates, Joseph became Schenectady's first mayor when the city was incorporated in 1798.

We who today celebrate the anniversary of our nation's beginning two centuries ago can appreciate the immensity of what confronted the people and their government after independence had been won. If we think we have problems today trying to cope with this business of living — and that includes paying taxes, balancing the family budget, criticizing our legislators and politicians in general, worrying about rising prices and the economy, wondering what world affairs are coming to — we have only to consider what things were like in 1790 to realize we are not so bad off.

The people had themselves a federal government that was a fledgling, untried republic cast suddenly among the world family of nations with the primary task of proving the quality of its membership. Its laws were not yet firmed up past the basic concepts of the Declaration of Independence and the Constitution with its Bill of Rights. It had no national monetary system and the new states were already jealous of their rights in the new union. George Washington had just started his first term of office as the country's first president and the capitol from New York was moved to Philadelphia. Indeed, there were those who still maintained, albeit in confidence for the most part, that the country was better off when it was under the authority and protection of Great Britain with all the benefits to be accrued from tradition and world power.

All things considered, that final decade of the 18th century may have been the most important to America's history than any other; certainly the times must have been both exciting and tenuous for its people. It was a make or break proposition for them and their government, not only for their subsistence as a nation but to prove to the world that a democracy of united states could work. Never before had there been a national government quite like that which Washington was asked to organize in 1789. The 13 states had been, in fact, independent republics during the Revolution but now that they were to be merged as a whole, the question presented itself as to exactly what the new Constitution meant or how far in practice it would limit the independence of the states.

One can imagine the wonderment, the uncertainty of the day as George Washington took the oath as president in New York City, the first capital of the new government, and gathered about him the best advisers available to chart a course for the United States of America. So much remained, including boundary issues left over from the war, before the United States could become master in its own house — and to Washington's everlasting credit, the bulk of it was accomplished during his two terms of office.

He died 17 days before the dawn of 1800, but he lived to see many of his dreams and goals realized.

"It was no easy task to be the first occupant of a mistrusted office under a dubious Constitution," wrote Clinton Rossiter. "He fulfilled the hopes of the friends of the Constitution and spiked the fears of its critics."

Incidentally, Washington never did reside in the executive mansion in Washington, D.C., even though he was instrumental in locating the site for the new federal city on the Potomac River early in his administration. He lived a year in New York City, then moved to Philadelphia where the capital would be located for 10 years while the City of Washington was being laid out according to the plans prepared by Maj. Pierre Charles L'Enfant, a French engineer who had fought in the American Revolution. John Adams was the first to move into the original White House in November, 1800, while it was partially finished. (The place was reconstructed after the British burned the house Aug. 24, 1814, during the War of 1812.)

The U.S. monetary system was in an atrocious state when the new government began operations, in fact there was so little confidence in Continental currency that people traded in goods whenever possible much the same as they had done in the previous century. The only "sound money" in circulation up to the Revolution were metallic coins — mostly British, French and Spanish — but the Continental Congress had done its best to discourage exchange of "hard specie" during the war in favor of distribution of its paper money. During the war, literally carloads of paper money were issued by the states and Congress, and the country was flooded with notes "not worth a Continental" as the saying went.

Neither was there a banking system in existence by the time Washington took office. There were issues of individual notes, but nearly all of them became subject to depreciation with the result that there was a widespread distrust of paper money. However, in 1791, a plan for a United States bank devised by Alexander Hamilton was approved by Congress. President Washington signed the National Bank Charter that same year and the way was paved for a creditable banking system in America. In May of 1802, the currency in Schenectady was changed from pounds (the "York pound," worth about $2.50) to dollars as the influence of the U.S. bank and its accreditation in principal cities of America put local banking on a sound footing. The Mohawk Bank, established in 1807, was the first bona fide banking institution here.

When New York, as the other colonies, ceased to be a province of the British empire at the close of the Revolutionary War, many laws and legal customs of the mother country became obsolete. Federal and state laws were being established and it would be some time before the average citizen could interpret their meaning. Community governments were writing and enacting new sets of rules for lawful conduct of the populace and litigation in the courts. In Schenectady, for example, the old rule of primogeniture was phased out and it caused quite a furor before it was settled by an act of the State Legislature in 1798.

Up to 1790, when the rule was challenged, claims were that the common lands belonged legally to the eldest sons and heirs of the first settlers and trustees or to their assigns, only from 25 to 30 of whom were living in the township at the time. But shortly after, the number of claimants to the common lands was greatly increased and, as a recognition of rights, they insisted these lands should be leased to them on durable leases and at a nominal rent of from 50 cents to $7.50 per 100 acres. It is said that in 1797 there were nearly 500 families in the township, all descendants of the first settlers, who claimed that various lands belonged to them and not to the "latecomers" who had become citizens long subsequent to their forebears. By the same token, these insistent claims and demands of the "descendants" infuriated the others, resulting in a rash of petitions and protests, the appointment of committees, conferences and consultations with legal authorities.

The act passed in 1798 by the state set up a system for adjustment of claims and appointed a commission consisting of Zephaniah Platt, Peter Cantine and Derick Lane, who finally determined the legality of the claims and closed their accounts in August that year. In effect, the common lands of the township now passed to a corporation consisting of the mayor, aldermen and commonalty of Schenectady. It was a radical departure from the law which had existed since Schenectady's beginning. The surviving trustees had thus become divested voluntarily of all right and claim over the common lands, but no sale or transfer of the common lands could be made "unless two-thirds of the number of aldermen and assistants of said City shall give their assent to such sale."

The territory of Schenectady was divided into four wards. The two wards of the city included the territory to the east line of the patent, Union Street and the Niskayuna Road being the dividing line. Rotterdam made the third ward and Glenville the fourth ward. This was the alignment which existed in 1809 when Schenectady County was formed and the first Board of Supervisors was organized to include the townships of Duanesburg,

David Boyd, first cashier of the Mohawk Bank when it opened in 1807 at 10 North Church St., and Schenectady mayor, 1826-27.

Niskayuna and Princetown. Those elected to serve were Maus Schermerhorn, first and second wards; Alexander McMichael, third war; James Boyd, fourth ward; William North (board chairman), Duanesburg; Lawrence Vrooman, Niskayuna, and Alexander Murray, Princetown.

❊ ❊ ❊

A heavy primitive forest covered large areas inland from the river near Schenectady in sections now referred to as Glenville, Niskayuna and Rotterdam. There was a quantity of pine, beech, elm, birch and maple besides the sturdy white oak, so frequently used for the framework of barns by the farmers whose land adjoined the area of the Commons — from which timber might be taken by inhabitants for firewood or construction. These areas were slowly growing in population by 1790, but it was still considered fairly "wild" country. Wolves, panthers and other predatory animals infested the Common Lands as late as the 1820s, and there was for some years after the Revolutionary War a danger of a surprise attack by roving bands of Indians who were dissatisfied with efforts by both the U.S. and Canada to restrict them to small isolated regions.

In about the year 1784, a small group of St. Regis Indians swooped upon a farm home on the present Sacandaga Road, about 10 miles from Schenectady, where they killed and scalped its owner, Joseph Gonzalus, shot and killed his oldest son Emmanuel and took his second son Joseph as a captive to Canada. Word of such attacks spread quickly and the townspeople were outraged, yet it was next to impossible to organize any sort of counter attack against such a will-o'-the-wisp enemy. Those living in outlying sections simply had to secure their homes as best they could.

It so happened that a few weeks after the Gonzalus attack, an incident occurred one night in the Adam Conde home located in the same Glenville area which indicated what rugged lives these people led in rural areas. After serving in the Albany County Militia throughout most of the Revolutionary War, Adam got title to a small tract of land along the Sacandaga Road and built a home there for his family. One night, his wife Catalina sat reading her Bible by candlelight while he slept in the back of the room. Their three boys, John, Peter and Cornelius, were in their beds in the garret. Suddenly, Catalina was startled by a wild scream outside their door and she quickly wakened her husband, "Indians, Adam!" He jumped up, grabbing his gun which he always kept at the head of his bed, and at this moment another scream was heard. "Not Indians, it's a panther!" exclaimed Adam.

Cautiously unbarring the upper half of the outer door, Adam opened it slightly and peered out in the gloom. He could make out the dark form of an animal pacing around his log pig pen, where his pigs were kept each night for safety and so they would not wander off. Adam aimed his muzzle-loading rifle as best he could and fired. He was certain that he had hit the creature from the startled leap and scream, but it ran off. The family learned that on the early morning after this escapade a large panther was shot and killed while prowling around the out-buildings of nearby settlers, so they believed it to be the same that had startled them.

* * *

Travel in the post-Revolution period was difficult but brisk. This was before the toll roads were opened after 1804 which made it easier for families to ride in carriages in comparative comfort for 20 or 30 miles. In 1790, the sole reliance was on the old post roads which often were muddy, rutty and even sometimes blocked by fallen trees, but stage coaches were in great demand despite inconvenience and discomfort. In the spring of 1793, Moses Beal of Schenectady started a stage coach line for the accommodation of passengers from Albany to Schenectady, Johnstown and Canajoharie, once a week. The fare

was three cents a mile. Shortly after, John Hudson established a line of coaches to run from Albany to Schenectady three times a week. John Rogers of Ballston ran a line from that place to connect with Hudson's, thus beginning a regular communication for the convenience of those who visited the springs.

By 1794, there were five great post routes centering in Albany. The first was to New York, the second to Burlington, Vt., the third to Brookfield, Mass., and the fourth to Springfield, Mass., each carrying the mail once a week. The fifth route was via Schenectady, Johnstown, Canajoharie, German Flats, Whitestown, Old Fort Schuyler, Onondaga, Aurora, Scipio, Geneva, Canandaigua and, subsequently, Buffalo. The mail on this route was carried once every two weeks.

The stage coach lines continued to expand so that in the early 1800s, once the Mohawk Bridge and Mohawk Turnpike were built, it was no uncommon sight to witness from eight to twelve coaches on the Scotia dyke, leaving or entering Schenectady at one time. In one instance, "as many as fourteen were counted in a continuous line." Inns and taverns sprang up all along the stage coach routes for the accommodation of hungry, thirsty or tired passengers.

Two notable events occurred in Schenectady just before the turn of the 19th century. In 1795 a

A typical carriage road, which became muddy and rutted during wet weather.

93

charter was granted for the founding of Union College, largely through the persistence of the Rev. Dirck Romeyn, pastor of the First Reformed (Dutch) Church of Schenectady, and its board of elders. On March 26, 1798, Schenectady was officially chartered a city and its first mayor, Joseph C. Yates, took office.

The decade of 1790-1800 may have been a worrisome, uncertain period for the new republic, but if Schenectady was an example of the test of democracy, it was obvious that the people and their government not only survived it but made it eventful. Bigger things lay just ahead for a nation which had only begun to grow.

Scotia's Schonowe Avenue was called the dyke long after it was constructed about 1802. In this northerly view of about 1890, looking toward the entrance to the steel bridge across the Mohawk, the scene looks strikingly similar to that of today — except for the lack of paving. In 1902, the walkway at right became the road bed for the Schenectady Railway Company's trolley tracks.

Section III

FIRE!
FIRE!

Fire! Fire! It has long been a distress signal which has perhaps attracted more immediate response than any other cry.

In this section, we direct attention to fire-fighting in Schenectady, from the time citizens kept their own leather fire buckets in their homes as a legal necessity, through the many years of volunteer fire companies until the paid fire department began in 1900 under Chief Henry R. Yates.

There have been several major fires in Schenectady, beginning with the holocaust in 1690 when the French and Indians put the torch to the sleeping village. The fire of 1819 wiped out much of the lower part of the city, including the wharves along the Binnekill which had provided the major industry of the time. A similar conflagration in 1861 swept through the Stockade area, abetted by high winds, and put the volunteer forces through a severe test. Miraculously, many of the 18th century homes in the lower part of the city have survived Lucifer's tantrums and stand today as mute evidence of man's determination to preserve what he has fashioned from sweat of brow.

Since the turn of the 20th century, fires may not have been quite as devastating, thanks to advanced technology in firematics, but there have been and probably will continue to be blazes of a nature that strike terror into the hearts of those who must face the loss or concern to those who fight the flames.

This is an opportune time to pay tribute to Schenectady's modern firefighters, all part of a system that has preached fire safety and shown such expertise in combatting sudden outbreaks to the degree that the city has for many years regularly been awarded national recognition for its fire prevention record.

In recent years, the popular conception of a fireman is that of a helmeted, black-coated smoke-eater aiming a powerful jet of water into a burning building from atop an aerial ladder. A far cry, indeed, from the rowdy days of the volunteer "fire laddies" who made up in dashing, derring-do what they may have lacked in fire fighting equipment.

The earliest records of organized fire companies in the City of Schenectady go back to the year 1796, when two volunteer outfits banded together to form and direct bucket brigades in the event of a major conflagration.

Company No. 1 had its headquarters in a small building on South Church St. near the northwest corner of State, while Company No. 2 met in a Ferry St. house near the northwest corner of Front Street. This was the beginning, then, of companied firefighters in Dorp City and of a colorful era of volunteer competitiveness which flourished throughout the 19th century.

Volunteer firemen remained organized and continued to battle blazes even after a paid department began operations in Schenectady on the first day of this century. . .that is, until 1960, when the volunteer system was officially disbanded.

The disastrous fire of November, 1819, which wiped out the western portion of the city down to the wharves of the Binnekill, also ignited a reorganization of fire-fighting service here. The Common Council appointed 16 fire watchmen to patrol the city from 6 p.m. to 7 a.m. and named a committee to organize a larger force of volunteers to be "trained under the latest techniques." It also authorized the purchase of a "forcing pump for $560, exclusive of hose and carriage, to be made after the model of the engine in Albany commanded by Captain Brown."

This piece of equipment was little more than a tub on wheels (though called an "engine") which was fitted with a fixed nozzle and dragged to the

Firefighters of the 1880s. Men of the Neptune Hose Co. No. 3, pose proudly in front of the hose house on Fonda Street, now North Jay Street, before a parade. The volunteers were mostly young and boisterous, ready for a fight or a fire at the drop of a helmet.

scene of a fire like a feeble cannon. When the firemen hand-pumped the mechanism, an anemic stream of water shot from the nozzle and was aimed only by moving the cart about. A few wooden ladders were purchased and, or course, the leather buckets were still to be provided by homeowners as the best preventive measure against the spread of fire.

When it met on Jan. 1, 1820, the council resolved that "if any buckets shall have been lost or destroyed at the late fire, such buckets shall be replaced at the expense of the city."

Fire cisterns were constructed later at strategic spots about the city so that water could be pumped out to fill the hand carts. Records show that on Aug. 10, 1849, the Common Council voted to "pay Patrick Gunn the sum of $100 for building cisterns at the head of State St. and one in Smith St. after the plan of the cistern on Barrett St." It also authorized the cistern committee to "have the new cisterns filled if necessary with a view to test them."

The superintendent of streets was told by the council in December, 1849, to "keep the snow from the tops of the city cisterns and keep the joints filled with salt." The fire companies were to be provided poles with which to push the wooden covers aside in the event of fire.

The volunteer companies shortly after took it upon themselves to maintain the cisterns. Protection Hose Co., for example "adjourned meeting to meet Saturday, Dec. 20, 1851, to fill the Washington St. cistern."

In the mid-1800s, volunteer companies had taken on a new kind of glamor and importance in most communities of America — and Schenectady was little different. The companies began to look upon their importance as exclusive, privileged groups as the most essential reason for their being. They engaged in intense rivalries with one another — whether in athletic prowess in boxing or gymnastic teams, decorating themselves and their equipment with prideful disdain or getting their pumper into action first at a fire.

Membership in a volunteer company did not come easy. When application was made, rarely was it accepted within a year — which was the time it took for the volunteers to "look over" the prospect on the basis of his sociability, manliness and/ or interest in fire-fighting. Lucky was the non-member invited to a volunteer company's Saturday night chowder party.

The early fire companies raised funds for their uniforms and equipment in various ways. They began with donations from leading citizens (who became "sponsors" if the gift was sizeable) and then supplemented this with revenues from firemens' social affairs. The firemens' ball was always a

Monitor Nozzle No. 1, mounted on a platform and hauled to fires by horses. This was used in lower State Street fire of Feb. 1, 1905. Three 2½-inch hose lines were coupled to the base with their output leaving the various size tips on the nozzle. Photograph was made about 1901 at the central fire station opposite Crescent Park.

gala event, featuring prizes for best waltzers, drinkers and mustaches.

There was always some additional support from the city treasury by direct appropriations or various tax and fine devices.

Most "big city" records are filled with lurid accounts of rowdy gangs of volunteers so intent on outdoing each other that they resorted to street brawling while the fire raged before them. .or hiring "plug uglies" to guard the fire plugs in the cisterns against rival companies getting their pumps in operation. While much of this raucus behavior appears to have been frowned upon by Schenectady's fire laddies, the spirit of competition was still there.

The only disgrace worse than being passed at a fire was to be "washed." Companies were often positioned in a line between the fire and the water supply — be it a cistern, the river or the canal. Engines nearest the water pumped (through hose) to the water box of the next company which pumped it to the next. When one outfit pumped faster than the volunteers ahead could relay it, the water spilled over the sides of the "washed" engine. "Washed" firemen sometimes draped their rigs in mourning and disgrace until they could erase the ignominy by washing another company or performing some heroic feat.

In the mid-19th century, improved and larger equipment was available. Usually, it was imported from Europe and the metal painted a dull gray. This brought out the artistic talents of rival companies. If, for example, the Swift Hose Company had a bright red hose reel, the Eagle Hose Company decided on a bright orange with shiny brass hubs and a cast brass eagle to add further adornment.

Uniforms, too, came into prominent play as the volunteers sought to be the best dressed and, above all, the snappiest looking outfit in town. Headgear up to about the Civil War era varied from stovepipe to porkpie hat until they gave way to more practical leather fireman's helmet for firefighting. Zouave uniforms with bright, baggy pants and loose blouses were most popular until the 1870's, when most of the fire units across the country switched to tight-fitting pants and a high-collared jacket. The colors usually conformed to the adopted hues of the company.

The fire alarm for years was sounded by tolling bells in the city hall and church belfries. The First Reformed Church was the most reliable in this respect, it sounding the alarms for the great fires of 1819 and 1861 — one of which destroyed the church edifice itself. In many communities, a fire gong was employed. Such a device was used in Carman up until 1933 when the railroad bridge construction was started. The old iron ring, suspended on a wood frame, was then taken down and a fire whistle put into service.

The use of horses to pull fire equipment was not considered in Schenectady long after the Civil War (even though larger cities turned to horse-drawn vehicles about the 1870s) because, in a volunteer company with nobody on full-time duty, there was no one to tend to horses around the clock.

However, on July 7, 1896, the Van Vranken Hose Company No. 2 appointed Henry R. Yates, John E. Brown and Henry I. Van Slyck a committee to buy a horse to pull the hose wagon. They bought a handsome brown animal in New York City on July 26 and called him "Van." On Aug. 1, at the annual inspection parade up State Street, Schenectadians witnessed the first appearance of a horse-driven fire wagon in the city. "Van" served faithfully until his death in 1911.

The volunteers in Schenectady were under a cloud of suspicion during most of 1851-52, especially the rival Swift and Eagle companies who were intense rivals on the "uptown" side of Schenectady. The "Swifties" headquartered on Center Street (North Broadway) while the Eagles nested uneasily just across State Street on Broadway. There were several fires of "incendiary origin" in 1851 that were rather close to one or the other hose houses — in which case either the Swift or Eagle volunteers were on the scene first.

There were two fires the morning of Oct. 9, 1852 — the stables in back of Millard's Hotel near the railroad station and at a meat house connected with the same property. While there was little damage, the public became indignant. The Schenectady Reflector, on Oct. 15, editorialized: "It is to be hoped that there is no connection between these things and the trouble among our firemen. They have too enviable and hard-earned reputation to be lightly esteemed or jeopardized. . ."

Some of the volunteer officers denied that their boys had anything to do with the fires in question. One of them even defended their right to "make sure" the fires were even worth the trouble of being called out.

"One just big enough to make it worthwhile to trundle the truck — and that's all the boys want," he said.

In time, the volunteer outfits reorganized with larger memberships and many of them built new stations.

Protection Hose No. 1 was on State Street near Ferry, Van Vranken Hose No. 2 on South Church Street, Neptune Hose No. 3 on North Jay (then Fonda Street), J.D. Campbell Hose No. 4 on South College Street, E. W. Paige Hose No. 5 on Hamilton Street, and Union Hose No. 6 on Eastern Avenue (then East Liberty Street.)

For many years, the men of Campbell Hose Company would march each New Year's Eve out to the Rotterdam mansion of their sponsor, Col. John D. Campbell, and serenade the family in song. They were then invited inside to partake of a lavish spread of food and wine.

There was a big event in Schenectady in 1897 which lasted from Aug. 17 to 20. It was the 25th annual convention of the New York State Firemen's Association and rated a full-blown parade with rigs, bands and smartly-dressed volunteer companies. Practically the whole town turned out to witness the competition between the units in firematic contests held up in the fairgrounds atop Hamilton Street hill, near Steuben Street.

For all their faults, many championed the volunteers and pointed out that only a minority of them were troublemakers — the rest were honorable citizens interested only in public service, excitement and adventure. Ladies worshipped the feisty groups and youngsters continued to chase after them to fires, yearning for the day when they, too, could become volunteers.

These were Schenectady's volunteer fire chiefs, 1893-94, six years before the paid department took over. From left are Abram Hockford, Second Assistant Chief; William Daley, Chief; and Charles J. Steinert, First Assistant Chief.

An attraction at any firematic display is this ancient steam pumper, a relic of firefighting technique at the turn of this century. This one was shown in Ballston Spa.

Burning steeple of the First Reformed Church of Schenectady, Feb. 1, 1948.

Probably the most celebrated fires in Schenectady's history, aside from the burning of the young settlement by the French and Indians, occurred in 1819, 1843 and 1861. In each case, the conflagration destroyed a wide area of both residential and commercial development.

Bucket brigades were of little or no use in the 1819 fire, which broke out on a windy November night in Isaac Haight's leather currying shop just south of State Street on Water Street. The roaring flames quickly spread to the north, wiping out the wharves and boat building complex along the Binnekill, then fanning out to houses on Church, Union and State Streets in the older section of the city. About 100 commercial buildings and about 60 dwellings were lost in the blaze.

Before the fire, just about all the business activity of the town was at the west end, near the river. When it came time for rebuilding, preparations were already under way for the construction of the Erie Canal and that was a big factor in influencing businessmen to move father uptown where the canal operation was expected to spur mercantile activity. It proved a wise decision, because not long after the railroad also was built through the city at that point.

So it was that by 1843, the area surrounding Wall Street was in the midst of a new commercial center as warehouses and all types of businesses were crowded around the canal and rail routes from the north to the south end of the city. On April 4 that year, a fire started in the New York Central depot and leveled many commercial buildings and homes in that sector. This time, firefighters had some equipment although it was still inadequate and ineffective. The firemen used hand-operated pumps which drew water from numerous large cisterns in the streets. A group of Union College students pitched in by dragging down a small hand-operated fire engine which belonged to the college. After it was all over, perhaps the biggest disappointment — as far as the public was concerned — was that the railroad did not build a large new station to accommodate a growing interest in that mode of transportation. Rather, it constructed a long, low building which the local citizenry soon dubbed "the cow shed" and it was not until 1882 that the city got its first respectable railroad depot.

The fire of 1861 also occurred on a windy day, this time in August. It roared forth from the tar roof of Otis Smith's broom factory at the foot of Cucumber Alley (now West Front Street) and a strong gale blowing across the river from the northwest carried the flames eastward from house to house. Flying embers, tossed high in the air, settled on roofs all along Washington Avenue, Church and Union Streets, and it was only the quick work by individual citizens which kept some homes from being burned. The steeple of the First Reformed Church at Union and Church Streets caught fire from some of the hot embers, but there was such panic in the neighborhood by that time that little effort was made to save the church itself. A new and more impressive stone edifice replaced it by 1863 and it became the pride of the community.

* * *

There have been serious fires in Schenectady since that time, but none so widespread — thanks in no small way to the more sophisticated fire-fighting equipment and a better organized fire department. It is ironic, perhaps, that the most destructive and regrettable fire within recent memory involved the same church that was rebuilt after the 1861 holocaust.

In the late afternoon of Feb. 1, 1948, a fire started within the First Reformed Church that was out of control by the time it was noticed. When the firemen arrived and began hooking up hoses to the fire hydrants, the interior of the great auditorium was already an inferno. A large crowd soon gathered and were kept behind rope barriers as ice-encrusted firemen battled the raging blaze. It was a cold day, and as darkness fell, the temperature began to plummet into the sub-zero range. Miraculously, because the fire was of great proportion, the firemen managed to save surrounding buildings while containing the flames within the church and the adjoining Clark V. Poling House.

The beautiful rose window in front burst outwards as heat and compression built up within the church hall, then the arched trusses caught fire

Boston Store fire, Broadway from Smith Street, Schenectady, December, 1923.

and in a short time the whole roof was ablaze. The fire could be seen for miles around and when the roof finally collapsed, a myriad of sparks flew more than a hundred feet skyward in a pyrotechnics display witnessed by people in Glenville and Niskayuna. Sometime about midnight, the gaunt and blackened framework of the church steeple stood alone over the gutted exterior walls of the 1863 building, as though defiant of the forces which wrought such havoc. It was pulled down the next day as firemen still kept a watch over the smouldering embers, which now and then burst into flame.

The church, the sixth edifice in its history, was rebuilt on the same site the following year. The existing walls were sound, so the exterior is much the same as when it was erected nearly a century before with the exception that the rear wall was removed and a new one built farther back, extending the chancel section. The sanctuary, with its huge vaulted ceiling and beautiful stained glass windows, is of classical proportion held in awe yet today by congregation and visitors alike. The rebuilding of the church was shared by people in the surrounding area, regardless of religious affiliation, as contributions to the building fund poured in soon after the fire. So today, the old Dutch Church stands as a prideful community symbol of a heritage which began before the massacre.

It lacked a steeple, however, until the morning of Nov. 20, 1969, when a Gridley crane hoisted an 82-foot spire atop the belfry tower — a crowning glory to the oldest church of Schenectady.

The fire which raged through the Original Super Market, Broadway opposite Hamilton Street, in the fall of 1948 put city firefighters — both paid and volunteer — to a severe test. Later, after being renovated, it became the Saveway Super Market but has been vacant in recent years.

Two views of the Colonnade Building fire at 240-262 State St. just below the canal bridge. This was the morning of Feb. 1, 1905. Above view is from Wall Street looking west over the canal. Below is front of fire at 9 a.m., four hours after it started. Note Monitor nozzle in action.

A stolen vehicle crashed into an oil tank truck on upper Union Street in 1944 and caused this inferno.

Thick smoke billows skyward from the burning Close Brothers flour and grain storage building on Center Street (now Broadway) as seen from the unfinished State Street railroad overpass on January 26, 1906.

At the height of the First Reformed Church blaze in the late afternoon of Feb. 1, 1948, on the North Church Street side. It was frigid cold. Note the parked car in foreground, some snow still on its roof and with radiator blanketed against the cold. The fire raged from about 4:45 p.m. until after midnight.

Day after the church fire, looking toward front of burned-out edifice from the North Church Street gate.

Later in 1948 as reconstruction was under way and superstructure over the chancel section was hoisted into place.

Businesses on the east side of Broadway, between State and Smith Streets, were consumed by fire in May, 1959. It was the scene of the Boston Co. blaze three decades before. Firefighters are shown battling the stubborn fire which had started in the Carl Co. warehouse just around the corner. The Standard Furniture store at left was ablaze with light but as yet untouched by the fire. There is an empty lot there today. (Gazette photo by Sid Brown.)

Section IV

...THE WALLS CAME TUMBLING DOWN

Down it comes! The stone arches of the entranceways to the old central fire station atop the State Street hill are torn down in October, 1956 to make way for the new county office building. County jail is in background, the courthouse at right. The fire station was completed in 1899. (Gazette photo by Sid Brown.)

The physical character of downtown Schenectady had not changed drastically for many years, since long before the Civil War, so that people who had been away for any length of time came back to surroundings familiar to them since childhood.

In the early part of the 19th century, the city had stood still. Nothing new ever seemed to come its way and very few new buildings were added to alter the scenery. Even with the coming of the Erie Canal and the railroads, Schenectady was called a "sleepy little Dutch town, an old dorp if ever there was one." Some wags even said Schenectady was the only finished city around, that it had "a fence around it and a ceiling above" because it had grown as much as it ever was going to.

Dorp, a nickname which adhered to Schenectady for more than two centuries, is simply an old Dutch word meaning village or settlement. It was originally, of course, a true appelation since it was the Dutch who settled here and pioneered the town's development, but during most of the 19th century it was a term used derisively, it being usually intended as a slur on the city.

With the establishment of Thomas A. Edison's machine works here in 1886, a venture which led to the organization of General Electric within six years, an industrial and population explosion began in Schenectady that perhaps could be matched only by the boom towns of the Gold Rush days. In 1890, for example, the city population was listed as 19,902 by the federal census. By 1910 it was 72,826. The trolley lines were electrified in 1891 and were extended through and beyond the city limits, encouraging widespread housing development and the rapid growth of "suburbs" such as Bellevue, Mont Pleasant and Woodlawn.

Still, despite it all, downtown Schenectady managed to retain much of its 19th century image through the early part of the new century. A few firms, including H.S. Barney Co. on lower State Street and Reeves & Luffman (which became the Wallace Co. in 1909) on upper State Street, expanded their stores, but the city's main stem remained much the same. The post-World War II period has changed all that, however. Former residents have returned to express astonishment over buildings that are gone, new buildings that have taken their place in some cases, entire sections of streets and homes razed with new development in their stead.

With some of these changes have come improvement, even though for old-time Schenectadians there is a momentary sense of loss of a link to the past. For example, the construction of the Schenectady Savings & Loan Bank in 1959 replaced the mid-19th century brick building which had been McCamus store headquarters and next to it, the old Van Horne Hall of Civil War days. On the Liberty Street side of the bank's rear entrance, some mid-Victorian homes were torn down. Few can deny, however, that the bank project has been a plus for downtown Schenectady. Other banking institutions – Schenectady Trust Co., Schenectady Savings Bank and Mohawk National Bank – have also modernized their facilities to help update an old main street.

In 1973, a great change took place in the State Street block between Clinton and Barrett Streets as the Albany Savings Bank was built on premises once occupied by the Lorraine Block, the former Schenectady Illuminating Co. (Niagara-Mohawk) building and the Strand Theater.

Probably the 1950s saw the most widesweeping alterations in the downtown area as urban renewal got into full swing here as in other cities across America. Between 1953-56, the whole section east of City Hall up to Nott Terrace was leveled between Liberty Street and Chapel Street. The brick and frame houses within were pulled down by bulldozers and earthmovers, even the Nott Terrace Elementary School at Morrison Place and Nott Terrace and the south building of Nott Terrace High School. Likewise, dwellings along the south side of Liberty Street from Nott Terrace to Clinton Street were demolished as Liberty Street was widened. The whole project obliterated such former thoroughfares as Blaine Street, Morrison Place, Luther Street and Terrace Place. Modern office buildings were erected along upper Franklin Street, while in that stretch in back of City Hall were built the Two Guys store and parking lot, the Holiday Inn and a few other commercial establishments. Nott Terrace also was widened.

South Ferry Street was widened in 1958 after buildings were razed from State Street to the rear of the Central Fire Station – including the celebrated "house with the blue shutters" that had been run for many years by Renee King. Between 1956-58, Broadway from Hamilton Street south to Pleasant Valley underwent a vast change when ramshackle homes and businesses on the east side were obliterated. Among the new structures built in the area was the Ten Eyck Apartments. Meanwhile, wreckers also tore down buildings along Clinton Street south and on the lower part of Hamilton Street. Clinton Street was extended through to Broadway.

Beginning in 1959, construction of the crosstown connection through Pleasant Valley – eventually to cut over Broadway and Weaver Street to the Thruway spur in the vicinity of General Electric Co. and Edison Avenue out along what was once Rice Road — combined to alleviate traffic problems and change the character of these sections. Again, many buildings were razed.

To make way for the construction of the new public library building in 1968, a wide swath was cut through the north side of Liberty Street between Lafayette Street and the rear of the Schenectady Post Office. The library and later the new police headquarters were erected. Barrett Street no longer exists between Union and Liberty Streets, while Clinton Street was extended from Liberty to Union Street.

The construction of the County Office Building atop the State Street hill opposite Veterans Park necessitated another major wrecking job. Before the piles could be driven and the foundation laid for the new building, the whole area above the courthouse and along Veeder Avenue had to be cleared. Between 1955 and 1958, down came the old Central Fire Station that had been built in 1899 and a number of houses and commercial buildings. Construction of the office building required nearly two years, the county departments moving into it in 1962.

In recent years, demolition of certain buildings has caused considerable controversy. Many people have complained that certain structures of sound condition, and therefore of possible continued service to the community, have been torn down before a real attempt had been made to convert them to new use. Among these were the county annex at 11-13 Union St., razed in 1966 and now a parking lot for the Mohawk Club; the Plaza Theater, razed in 1964 and still an unused vacant lot; Union railroad station, razed in 1972, made part of the parking lot in back of Wall Street between State and Liberty Streets; and, in 1975, the Ellis Building on the northeast corner of State Street and Erie Boulevard, now an empty lot.

Other demolitions, on the other hand, have caused no such public outcry. The Erie (formerly Proctor's and Wedgeway) Theater was taken down in the late 1950s to become a downtown parking lot. In 1955, the old CIO Hall fronting Liberty Street was demolished and that area widened. The new CIO Hall on Erie Boulevard and Fuller Street was built after the old trolley car barn was razed in 1960. Earlier, we mentioned the razing of the McCamus building for the new Schenectady Savings & Loan Bank. Likewise, the loss of the Lorraine Block and the Strand Theater to the downtown scene apparently caused little remorse among the citizenry.

The area just above Veterans Park was beautified considerably when the Polish National Alliance developed a park, known as Pulaski Plaza, on the site occupied by the old state armory that was razed in 1947. It changed again for the better in 1962 when Veeder Avenue was widened and extended through what was known as Armory Place. The traffic bottleneck there, once a sore spot even when there were less vehicles, seldom exists today.

* * *

The continuing change in the Hamilton Hill area, as whole sections of former residential streets are being leveled, leaves nothing but the hope that new housing may someday replace the old — similar, perhaps, to that two decades ago when the Schonowe Apartments and Lincoln Heights improved an entire neighborhood. There is, too, that decayed portion of Broadway between State and Smith Streets which has been much talked about in City Council meetings and by the man-in-the-street. The former Buell & McDonald Building, later part of Standard Furniture, was wracked by fire in 1959 but the blackened and gutted building still stands. The former Mohawk Hotel, which became Hotel Schenectady in later years, is also in a sorry state — long empty and the scene of frequent fires. Along the west side from the hotel building to State Street are other old structures, a few which also have been hit by fire. The snag in restoring this shabby part of downtown may be the uncertainty of city officials and planners whether Broadway at that point should be widened or closed for new development back to Smith Street.

Considering the changes that have evolved in recent years, one wonders what the future holds for Schenectady's "old" section, bounded roughly by the river, Nott Street over to Nott Terrace, down to Pleasant Valley and back down across Edison Avenue to Washington Avenue. The FOCUS downtown redevelopment group has advocated change, but with a blending of "the new with the old" rather than largescale demolition with total reconstruction. Some favor the latter, provided adequate federal aid be restored.

It seems that the architectural makeup of Schenectady's longstanding heritage has reached a crossroads. The metamorphosis that has occurred in the last quarter century will likely be viewed as insignificant to that which is bound to take place before the end of this century.

This is a 1947 view looking eastward as steel girders from the main auditorium of the half century-old state armory were being taken down.

The last show. An interior view of the Plaza Theater in 1964 as seats were being removed before demolition of the building that had stood since 1931. The back portion of the stage loft had already been ripped away. (Gazette photo by Sid Brown.)

Above is a view of the old CIO Hall at Liberty and Walls Streets about 1950. Below, the structure was demolished in August, 1955. In background, the railroad station at left and former Crown Hotel at right would meet the same fate 16 years later.

The contents may seem meagre today when all is taken into account what has transpired in all these years . . . and yet there was an unmistakable legacy of pride and optimism packed within the small copper box which was sealed in the cornerstone of the new Schenectady High School that afternoon of June 18, 1902. And why not? For the first time in its history, Schenectady was about to get its own bona fide secondary school which could cater to a greater cross section of families in a city that was fast developing into an industrial metropolis. Many years before there had been the Lyceum on Yates Street, but it was restricted to young people whose families could afford to pay for private tutelage. In more recent years, the Union Classical Institute held forth at the stylish building at Union and Church Streets (formerly the Mohawk Bank and which today is the Mohawk Club) but, again, for the instruction of those who could pay tuition and might afford the luxury of not having to go to work before age 15.

Under the persuasion of Samuel Burnett Howe, city school superintendent (and for whom Howe School was named), the Schenectady public school system made plans for the new public high school at the turn of this century. The city's Board of Aldermen supported his stand with a bond issue of $60,000 to finance construction of a high school building "up on the hill" on the west side of Nott Terrace near Union Street.

On a September afternoon in 1974, in front of the historical society headquarters at 32 Washington Ave., the entire contents of the cornerstone box were turned over to that organization by the man who directed the demolition of the old high school building that was completed in 1903. Doug Allen, head of D.W. Allen Inc. of Schenectady, not only presented the cornerstone material to the society but deposited the cornerstone itself, all 1,000 pounds of it, on the society's ground for preservation.

On hand to witness the first official perusal of the cornerstone artifacts was Miss Marion T. Posson, who began teaching history at old Schenectady High School (later to become Nott Terrace High School) in 1926 and went on to continue her career at Linton High School when it opened in 1958. She retired in 1965. Miss Posson was especially interested in the event, not only out of sentimentality, but because she had been a cochairman of the cornerstone ceremonies for Linton High School — held June 5, 1957 — and collected the material for that cornerstone box. Coincidentally, she had programs for both the 1902 and 1957 ceremonies.

The material from the 1902 box was crisp, the air-tight box having well preserved the tightly-packed documents for the 72-year interim. Only one photograph, a view of the old Union Classical Institute building, was included. There were copies

The 1903 cornerstone on the ivy-covered exterior of the south building of old Schenectady High, later to become Nott Terrace High School.

of the three local newspapers: The Evening Star and The Daily Union, both dated June 17, 1902, and the Schenectady Gazette, dated June 18, 1902. Three pamphlets included the annual report of Schenectady Public Schools for 1901, the 1900-01 bulletin of U.C.I. and the June, 1902 issue of the U.C.I. publication, "The Palladium." A bound copy of the charter of the City of Schenectady, a program for the cornerstone ceremonies (on the front of which was an architect's drawing of the new high school) and various intrascholastic forms of U.C.I. rounded out the cornerstone box contents. Oh yes, there was also an invitation card to the U.C.I. commencement exercises to be held that night, June 18, 1902, at the Van Curler Opera House, at which 23 pupils were to be graduated.

According to the cornerstone program, the welcoming address was by Mayor Horace S. Van Voast and the principal speech by Dr. Charles Newell Cobb, inspector for the New York State Regents. The 37th Separate Company Band played several selections during the ceremonies and a U.C.I. students' chorus sang two songs, "Corner Stone Ode"

and "America." Superintendent Howe and U.C.I. Principal Arthur Marvin also participated.

In looking back to the Gazette account of the cornerstone ceremony, it appears that those who had arranged the program were pleased that nearly a month of rain ceased the day before and "sunny, seasonable weather favored an auspicious gathering." A good turnout of students and their families, civic officials and the general public attended the program.

The foundation of the new school already had been laid. It was started three months and was being built on the site of an attractive two-story frame residence which had been the home of former Schenectady Mayor Joseph B. Graham since about 1870. Nott Terrace, which was first known as College Terrace, was developed in the late 1850s, and Graham was among the first to build there.

Even with construction of a new high school, the city school board was well aware in 1902 that more school buildings were badly needed. The influx of new families was causing a severe shortage

An early Henry Tripp photograph of the 1880s showing the residence of Joseph B. Graham on Nott Terrace, which was then an uptown dirt road. This became the site of the Schenectady High School.

118

of classroom space and pupils were forced to go on half-day schedules to meet the demand. Brandywine School would be constructed by 1904, and Elmer Avenue School by 1905. Broadway, Edison, Fulton, Lincoln, Horace Mann, McKinley and Washington Irving Schools were all built in 1908.

In 1911, an adjunct of Schenectady High School was completed toward the Liberty Street side. It was called the south building and was connected to the north (or 1902) building by an enclosed bridge. Schenectady High School became Nott Terrace High School in 1930 when Mont Pleasant High School was completed.

After Linton High was opened, the school board decided to use the north building for an elementary school because it contained both an auditorium and a gymnasium (formerly the girls' gym) and in 1962 the south building was torn down for the widening of Liberty Street.

So the 1902 building, the older of the two which made up the high school complex for a half century, was granted a brief reprieve in the interest of education. However, it was decided to close the elementary classrooms after the 1972 semester and it lay idle in the neighborhood which had long since changed from the suburban character which existed in 1902. The building was sold to Ira Blake, Schenectady realtor and developer, but he could find no one interested in acquiring the huge three-story stone edifice. There was talk of possibly renovating it for senior citizen housing, but it was determined that remodeling such a structure (with its thick interior walls and antiquated wiring and heating system) would be impractical and costly.

Doug Allen, who recently bought and renovated the old Craig Hotel across the river from Rexford, was hired as demolition contractor. He and his crew started work in late August and had the old high school building leveled by the first week in September, 1974. Allen was impressed with its construction. There was very little steel, mostly brick-and-mortar bearings and wooden trusses thoughout.

"It was built like a fortress," he said. "Those old walls must have been as sturdy as the day they were built."

The north building, first of the two buildings of old Schenectady High School, as it looked under construction in 1902. Oddly, the cornerstone bore the date 1903, the year of the building's completion.

When one stands today on the corner of Nott Terrace and Eastern Avenue opposite what used to be the Schenectady High School and later Nott Terrace High School, it is easy to feel a twinge of nostalgia — especially if you happen to be an alumnus. It is all so changed now. A quick service restaurant is now located where the north building stood, while Liberty Street cuts into where the south building was.

You think of many things — the noon hour gatherings along the street in front of the school, the pep rallies and fire drills and maybe the anxious moments before the Regents marks were announced.

A long time ago, in 1906, the expansion of the Schenectady Railway Co. streetcar line into Nott Terrace over to Union Street was vigorously opposed by J.W. Smitley, who then lived in the home that is now the rectory of St. John the Evangelist Church. He was against it because, he said, school children would be "ground and mangled under the merciless wheels of the trolleys." He was thinking of the electric cars passing back and forth in front of the Nott Terrace Elementary down by Chapel Street and the new high school farther up the street. That's how much times have changed.

The celebrated bridge between floors of the two buildings which made up the high school. The south building is at left and the north building at right.

ITS LAST DAYS

This was Friday, Aug. 23, 1974, looking northerly from Liberty Street as wreckers began demolishing the auditorium of the north building of the former Nott Terrace High School. By the following month, the entire structure was leveled. Grads of NTHS, and Schenectady High School before, had only fond memories left of their old alma mater. (Gazette photo by Sid Brown.)

The west side of McLane's hotel as it faced the road on the Rexford hill. This and the view on the next page were made by Sid Brown, Gazette chief photographer, a year before it was torn down.

Out Rexford way, the razing of McLane's Hotel in the early fall of 1964 was a necessity with the rerouting and reconstruction of Route 146 and the new Rexford Bridge. The old weatherbeaten landmark was directly in line with the new route on that spot of the Rexford hill where it had stood for countless years, certainly longer than any living human of this area.

Perhaps few buildings of the Schenectady region were as involved with history, yet as obscure as McLane's Hotel. People were just accustomed to seeing the old place as a part of the scenery while crossing the Rexford Bridge to the north, standing against the gentle slope with its curious double-tiered verandas that in later years developed ripple-like sags. Only a few people were left who could remember it in its heyday, when it was a popular hostelry and stop-off point for people using the Erie Canal. It had become simply a derelict, but still handsome enough to be a favorite subject for the easel and paint set — right up until its last day of existence.

The hotel got its start sometime within the 42-year lifetime of Eleazar Rexford, who was born in Rexford Flats Dec. 17, 1787 and died in 1829. Eleazar built a place called the Rexford Flats Hotel and later passed it on to his son, Cyrus W. Rexford. The inn was at first a wooden structure much smaller than the one to be later known as McLane's, but it was on the same site and probably was incorporated into the larger facility.

When the canal was opened in 1825, the hotel's business began to boom. There were two locks at Rexford, making it convenient for canawlers and passengers alike to "stop for a quaff of ale" either at the hotel, at Mickey Travis' Saloon (now the Schenectady Yacht Clubhouse) or at McDermott's Saloon farther down the line. It would take some time for the boats to pass through the locks.

The Rexford Flats Hotel became McLane's Hotel after the place passed out of the Rexford family. A deed in the records of Saratoga County, dated April 3, 1897, registers the transfer of the Rexford Flats Hotel from Cyrus W. Rexford and

One might picture this as something to be seen in a western movie lot or ghost town. McLane's Hotel had an aura of old-time beauty about it, something which has been captured many times on film and canvas.

123

his wife, Hannah, to John McLane, a native of Rexford, for the sum of $4,000.

It was McLane who later enlarged the place to provide accommodations for 100 guests and added the verandas around the building to furnish an exercise area for guests during inclement weather. He also built a ballroom which could hold several hundred dancers and it became the scene of weekly Saturday night dances. Sunday morning breakfast at McLane's was famous for fish caught in the Mohawk River. It is said that fish was not the only item in demand at the hotel on the Sabbath morn, for in those days of strict observance of Sunday blue law, a refreshing spot of beer could be had behind lowered awnings on the veranda.

The closing of the Erie Canal in 1915 was a blow to the hotel's fortunes and its decline probably began that same year. Hotel barns that once housed horses and carriages, often used to meet Utica and Schenectady Railroad trains at Craig across the river, burned in 1924 along with an ice house. After the death of John McLane, the hotel was operated by a son, Harry McLane, and later by a grandson until 1960 when it was closed permanently.

The state purchased the site when it was determined that it would be in the path of the new highway. The hotel was demolished by the C.D. Perry Construction Co. of Troy, builders of the new Rexford Bridge.

A handful of longtime residents of Rexford gathered to watch as the huge teeth of a clamshell digger bit into the roof of the veranda and tore it from the building, then returned to rip away the main structure itself. Finally, only rubble was left. Now those oils and water colors of old McLane's Hotel were more valuable, for nostalgia's sake if for no other reason.

Last of McLane's Hotel, 1964.

Schenectady's railroad depot that was dedicated in late February, 1908, early became a source of pride in a growing community. It won its wholehearted public stamp of approval, as did none of the others in the city's history, as a building which combined both beauty and serviceability.

Its construction, which began in 1905, was in conjunction with the enormous task of raising the railroad tracks throughout the city to form overpasses at the various street intersections. The latter project, which was started in 1903, was completed in time for the grand opening of the new station.

Built on the site of the previous station at the southeast corner of Wall and Liberty Streets, Schenectady's Union Station (which was a popular name for railroad depots) came on the scene when the saga of railroading in America was reaching its zenith. It became a place to welcome distinguished visitors, including presidential candidates, that called for huge public gatherings in the station square. It was also a gathering place for delegates to conventions, industrial personnel and ordinary travelers. Often, within its cavernous interior of vaulted ceilings and gleaming marble walls, people would meet in prearranged agreement whether or not they were taking the trains simply because it was most convenient in the downtown area.

For perhaps a span of 40 years, the station was a busy place, indeed. Horsedrawn carriages and hansom cabs in time gave way to hotel limousines, automobiles and express trucks along its Wall Street perimeter — but people continued to pass through the station in a seemingly unending flow of travel, particularly weekends. The place was regularly packed on holidays. During the two world wars, it was virtually the center of activity.

Then, along about 1950, rail travel began to dwindle throughout America as competition from the air lines, buses and private autos siphoned off passengers who now considered these other modes of transportation either faster, more economical or perhaps more convenient. Railroads tried desperately to balance their operating budgets by cutting back on expenditures previously considered essential to good service. Among these was the maintenance of the huge railroad stations in every major city along the rail routes. In Schenectady, as at most every place else connected with a railroad system, the railroad station in a few short years began to take on a dingy atmosphere, so different from years past. Ceilings were allowed to become discolored through lack of cleaning or painting, the multi-paned windows were clouded with grime, the floors often were not swept with the result that litter gathered from one week to the next, concession stands that once offered shoe shining, re-

freshments and reading material were closed, while up on the platforms passengers could not help but notice a growing accumulation of grime, pigeon droppings and other refuse. Even the big clocks at either end of the waiting room had stopped running for the first time in nearly a half century, the cost of their repair also having been cut. In time, there were less frequent train arrivals and departures. Clearly, the old station had outlived its era of grandeur and there was little surprise among the citizenry here, although with some regret at the circumstances, when Penn Central announced in 1968 it was closing the premises in favor of a small way station out on Colonie's Karner Road.

The City of Schenectady purchased the site on Dec. 11, 1970 for $20,000 and for a time there was some talk of converting the station into a civic center or playhouse. However, efforts to save it

Looking northerly from State Street, July 9, 1971. Part of the overhead railroad crossing had been removed as had part of the tracks along the west side. In far background, Union Station is being dismantled also. At left is the Cushing Building, the lower floors of which were once part of the Edison Hotel.

were balked by two factors — the unavailability of purchase funds and the high estimated cost of renovation. City Council subsequently let bids for demolition of the station and other buildings along Wall Street and awarded the contract to SAS Equipment Co. of North Bergen N.J.

When that firm started work early in January, 1971, the first job was to remove a portion of the railroad overpasses on Liberty and State Streets and two rows of tracks on that west side. By August, the railroad station and Wall Street buildings were down and by Labor Day, the entire area had been blacktopped into a 180-car parking lot.

* * *

On the occasion of the razing of the railroad station a tribute to its memory was written by our good friend and fellow historian, Neil B. Reynolds,

which appeared in the Aug. 6, 1971 Gazette editorial page in his former column, "Raw Materials of History." Here, in part, is what Mr. Reynolds had to say:

"I'm glad I was out of town when the Schenectady Union Station was really demolished. For with it we've lost the nearest thing to a civic center. (The runner-up, of course, was the Hotel Van Curler, in its prime. And a poor third was the old trolley station on the south side of State Street, just below Crescent Park.)

"I'm sure, during my earliest years, the station was the grandest and most imposing structure I'd ever seen. When I think of 'marble halls,' I still see the pale green and white facing of the waiting room. Its echoes were memorable, too; the only two buildings I've ever been in with worse acoustics were the Union College Fieldhouse (before changes were made) and the Albany Armory,

The 63-year-old station is nearly leveled in this northeasterly view towards Erie Boulevard, July 16, 1971. By Labor Day that year, a parking lot had been opened in the area bounded by the boulevard and Liberty Street. (Gazette photos by Sid Brown.)

where I attended the historic New York Central stockholder's meeting at which Robert Young captured control of the line and started it on its downward way.

"Many of the memories of the station are pleasant. From there, I started on my first trip — all alone — to New York. There I remember waiting for an early morning train and meeting the late great singer Leonard Warren, whom I'd heard the night before at a Civic Music concert. We had a good visit and he praised the Schenectady audience as among the most appreciative he'd encountered in years of touring.

"One evening a group of us, all connected with Union College, saw a friend off on the Wolverine on her way to Japan to marry another local friend stationed there for General Electric. At that time the westbound Wolverine stopped only on signal, which was a lantern placed at the edge of the platform. On this occasion, in the rush of well-wishers to the platform, the late organist Dr. Elmer Tidmarsh kicked over the signal lantern and the train almost failed to stop. Years later, I ran into Dr. Tidmarsh just about there, as he was returning from one of his last annual summer trips to Paris; we laughed over the incident.

"There, one welcomed friends home from a long trip, or watched a casket put aboard 'In the Baggage Car ahead.' Some people may remember that, along with the taxis, there was one horse-drawn 'hack' that had its regular place at the northwest corner, where Wall Street widened. The horse got impatient, as even poor old horses will, and pawed the ground with his right foot. For years after, the pavement right there had an oval depression made by that long-dead horse's hoof. And about here used to wait the bulgy Hotel Van Curler bus, which met all the trains and carted visitors down to that hostelry.

"The station served purposes that haven't been replaced. One said, 'I'll meet you at the station.' Or, if downtown, there were always the rest rooms, sometimes smelly but adequate. And there was the vicarious adventure: one could pick up the New York Central's big timetable (Form 1001) which, not too many years ago listed through sleepers to Los Angeles, San Francisco and even for a time, Mexico City. . .

"Those were the days when paying passengers were considered an asset, not nuisances that boosted the deficit. Let's hope that when the station's area is at last a parking lot, there'll be attendants as helpful as the one who use to serve there."

Schenectady station platform. . .once the scene of happy and sad occasions.

Above, the Lorraine Block as it looked shortly after it was opened in 1902 at the northeast corner of State and Clinton Streets. Below, a southerly view from the Barrett Street side on July 23, 1972, as the Lorraine Block neared total demolition.

"Too little, too late" has been a phrase popularly attributed to last minute efforts of preservationists to save certain buildings considered historically valuable or architecturally interesting. In Schenectady, that phrase has been used frequently in recent years as many structures have fallen before the wrecker's ball.

The Ellis Building, located at the northeastern corner of State Street and Erie Boulevard since early canal days, was a prime example of a citizen concern which either came too late or was doomed from the start because of the city administration's firm decision to raze the structure.

Build about the time the Erie Canal was opened in 1825, the three-story brick building was believed to have been first used as a hardware merchandising outlet and warehouse. Robert Ellis, a tailor, later bought the property and it was known thereafter as the Ellis Building. In recent years, the building was in disrepair and all but the ground floor was vacant. Although it was still considered a sound building, there was little question it was fast becoming an eyesore. Finally, the city's Urban Renewal Agency (which actually is City Council) purchased the property with the idea of razing it if it could not be sold.

Sometime in November, 1974, the announcement came that the Ellis Building was to be demolished so that the site would be more attractive for private development. At about this time, through the efforts of a local historic sites survey, the building was being considered for inclusion in the National Register of Historic Places. In January and February, 1975, the URA heard pleas by area organizations and individuals in behalf of preservation of the site — but the die was cast as far as its future was concerned.

By the end of March, the old building was leveled and, at this writing, the vacant lot has been surrounded by a rustic fence and landscaped with a few shrubs and trees.

As an outgrowth of the controversy over the Ellis Building, a committee on preservation of historic sites was formed at the request of Mayor Frank Duci and Councilman Charles Seber for the purpose of determining which buildings or sites within the city should be spared in case of future plans for new highway construction, road widening or redevelopment. Mrs. VanderBogert Shanklin was named chairman of the group, comprised mostly of private citizens, and the survey of historic sites is well under way. The primary concern of the committee, according to its most recent report to City Council, is the preservation of the former county courthouse at 108 Union St., built by 1831. At present, the Greek Revival-styled building is up for sale by the city school district.

If the unsuccessful fight for the Ellis Building did nothing else, it may have been worthwhile, after all, in assuring the preservation of other historic buildings in Schenectady.

Throughout the demolition of the century-and-a-half-old Ellis Building, bystanders watched from across the street as each portion of tin roof or brick wall was chewed loose by the giant crane and claw. However, probably nothing caused quite as much curiosity as a big wooden wheel that was exposed on the attic floor to the right. It looked even bigger after it had fallen among the debris on the Erie Boulevard side.

Like most old buildings and barns in this area, the former canal building was equipped with a block and tackle system used to raise or lower heavy material through upper floor openings. In this case, the upright wheel in the Ellis Building attic indicated the pulley apparatus worked on the Wall Street side in years past. About 12 feet in diameter, the wheel was operated manually from within. The rope, which played out to the block and tackle was hung on the exterior wall and wound around the perimeter of the wheel. Forked

Ellis Building in 1889, then located beside the canal bridge. The section to the rear of the building was added long after the front part was built about 1825. It became a familiar landmark at that corner of Schenectady's main thoroughfare.

129

metal prongs, spaced about 18 inches apart on the outside of the rim, kept the rope intact.

Extremely heavy loads could be lifted and lowered with relative ease by the manual wheel, as much as the horsedrawn drays could handle in those days. Used in its prime period for warehousing shortly after the Erie Canal was completed, the Ellis Building's top floors stocked hardware store provisions such as kegs of nails, metal tools and ironwork. One can imagine some of this material arriving by canal barge and being transferred up to the Ellis Building stockrooms.

Only a few years ago, when the old Freeman paint store building was razed a few doors up Wall Street, a similar but slightly smaller wheel was found in the attic. The block and tackle apparatus still hung outside.

Coincidentally, a letter from Schenectady's Henry Schaffer tells of the all-important attic pulley as used in one of his early Schaffer stores in Old Dorp.

He was recalling the period prior to World War I, when he opened a cash-and-carry Schaffer store on the ground floor of a three-story building on Broadway. It still stands adjacent to and north of the vacant Hotel Schenectady.

"The top two floors were used to warehouse the merchandise for resupplying my stores," he wrote. "I had 10 or 11 stores at that time. What is unique about all this is the block and tackle method of hoisting the merchandise both ways — by hand. I know of no other chain that started in a warehouse with such adverse conditions, and survived. It was another first."

This huge wooden wheel came tumbling down from the garret of the Ellis Building during demolition and puzzled many sidewalk superintendents.

Demolition of the Ellis Building took place during March, 1975, some of the activity being shown in this view from the boulevard side. (Photograph by Ed Schultz, Gazette photographer.)

130

Section V

ON THE
SOMBER SIDE

George R. Blodgett, Schenectady GE patent attorney, is shown in this family photograph about a year before he was fatally shot by a burglar in his Stockade area home on Dec. 3, 1897. He is holding his young son, George, who years later died in an airplane crash. A daughter, Katherine B. Blodgett, was born a few months after the father's death. The murder has remained unsolved to this day.

"The case remains a mystery, as deep as any that has ever enveloped crime, and it bids fair to remain such. A whole week has now passed and still there is not a person under arrest and probably not under justifying suspicion. Will the murder go unavenged?"

This was an excerpt from a feature story which appeared in the Utica Globe on Dec. 11, 1897, eight days after George R. Blodgett, a prominent General Electric Co. patent attorney, was fatally shot in his home at 11 Front St., Schenectady, an incident which precipitated a widespread manhunt throughout the northeast for a gun-toting burglar.

The story of the Blodgett murder is not generally known in Schenectady today, but there are still a few residents of the city's historic stockade district who occasionally refer to the tragedy — even though they may be somewhat hazy about the details of the case.

The solitude of the Stockade area was shattered by four gunshots the morning of Dec. 3, 1897 at about 2:40 a.m. Actually, they were fired from the Blodgett's bedroom window by a hysterical wife moments after her husband had been mortally wounded by an intruder. As she told police later, it was the only way she could think of to attract neighbors and get quick assistance. And it worked. The police were quickly notified and medical aid was called upon in a vain attempt to save Mr. Blodgett's life.

Diagonally opposite the former Blodgett residence, in a quaint little dwelling at 18 North Church St., today lives a woman whose life was directly affected by that long-ago tragedy — even though she was born a few months after it happened. She is Dr. Katherine Blodgett, world famous for her work in the old GE Research Laboratory, and now retired.

Dr. Blodgett's knowledge of the slaying of her father comes mostly from accounts she later read in news columns. Her mother, she recalls, rarely discussed the matter with friends, much less her children, after she sold her Schenectady home and moved her family to New York City.

However, Dr. Blodgett maintains she has a "sketchy recollection" of developments which conflict with the contention that her father's death remained an unsolved crime. She vaguely recalls a story that the killer's sister convinced him to give himself up to authorities and that, while in jail awaiting prosecution, he hanged himself.

There seems to be no record of that macabre twist to an already grisly tale. Schenectady police know nothing of it and a search of the department's daily blotter for a little more than a five-year period following the murder has turned up only the fact that the case remained unsolved.

As reconstructed by police at the time, this is what happened on that fateful night:

Mrs. Blodgett, sleeping beside her husband in an upstairs bedroom, was awakened by a strange sound and screamed when she saw a dim lantern light moving toward her. (The head of the bed was near the hallway door which led to another bedroom in which their young son, also named George, was sleeping.) Mr. Blodgett jumped out of bed only to face a burglar who held a gun in his left hand and oil lamp in his right.

The intruder ordered Mr. Blodgett to put up his hands, while retreating toward the hallway. Either Mr. Blodgett tripped or lurched toward the burglar, but in any event the householder was in a bent position when he was fired upon, a .38 caliber bullet entering the body to the right of the spine.

Immediately, the burglar dashed down the stairway and escaped through the front door, pursued part of the way by Mr. Blodgett. The latter, not knowing he had been shot, attempted to seize the intruder and had gone down the stairway almost to the foot before he realized his weakness. Wearily, he returned to his room where he died at 2:30 p.m. on Saturday, Dec. 4 — some 35 hours after he was shot.

Police Chief William Campbell (Schenectady's chief of police from 1872 to 1904) quickly took charge of operations shortly after police arrived. The men searched the grounds and found two of Mr. Blodgett's overcoats just outside the house. There was evidence that the house had been ransacked by the burglar and reported missing were a silver handled hairbrush, a child's spoon and fork, a silver sugar bowl, a dozen silver spoons, a pair of scissors and two pair of overshoes.

Dr. Van der Veer, an Albany surgeon, was immediately summoned and he arrived in Schenectady 55 minutes after the shooting, coming over on a special engine, the Mohawk, provided by the New York Central Railroad superintendent. Dr. Van der Veer remained at the bedside of the stricken Mr. Blodgett until death terminated his services.

Chief Campbell put 10 men on the case and alerted area residents to "be on the lookout for a left-handed man who might have a gun and must be considered dangerous." GE officials authorized the Pinkerton Agency to send out 15,000 handbills for the arrest and conviction of the burglar (or burglars) and offered a $5,000 reward for anyone giving information leading to that eventuality. E.W. Rice, Jr. of GE also sent a telegram that morning to Pinkerton National Detective Agency in New York to "send good men to play tramp. . .will pay usual price and expenses and a $5,000 reward. . . come tonight."

District Attorney W.W. Wemple also put out an order: "Get the men and spare no expense in this matter."

As it turned out, Pinkerton's assigned Detective John S. Coyle to the case and he worked surreptitiously in and around Schenectady for more than a week. He uncovered not the slightest clue as to who might have perpetrated the Front Street killing.

There were several persons brought in for questioning within a few days after the incident, including two men found wandering in the Glenville hills and another man who had been picked up in Cohoes for loitering. . .but they were released after their innocence of the Schenectady crime had been established. A short time later, Schenectady police interrogated two men ("hard-looking citizens" arrested in Troy on vagrancy charges) as prime suspects; but they, too, were set free after several days of questioning.

On Dec. 16, Solomon Bradshaw, a Princetown farmer, called police to tell them he recalled something that might have a bearing on the Blodgett murder. He had thought little of it at the time but later "began putting pieces together." He told authorities that on the morning of Dec. 3, a well-dressed man stopped at the Bradshaw farm and asked for something to eat. The man was about 26, weighed about 130 pounds and had what appeared to be a "crippled hand." Bradshaw told police he thought it was the right hand that was injured, because the man could not use it in inquiring for the direction of the Duanesburg railroad, pointing over the hills.

The visitor, Bradshaw said, was "not the usual beaten track type of tramp and was well-dressed." This was the best lead the police had come across but it led nowhere. Railroads, depots and yards were checked for miles around and bulletins were sent to communities serviced by any kind of railroad in the state to keep a lookout for "a man with a crippled hand." Nothing came of it.

Police had issued a bulletin minutes after the shooting which called for the arrest of a man to be charged with burglary, assault with a deadly weapon and attempted murder. After Mr. Blodgett's death, the charge became murder.

Mr. Blodgett, 35 years old at the time of his death, came to Schenectady with his wife in 1893 as an expert on patents. He came from an established New England family and attended one of the finest prep schools in the country, Phillips Academy in Andover, Mass. He was buried in Bucksport, Maine.

The former Blodgett home at 11 Front St. near North Church Street, scene of the murder of George R. Blodgett in 1897. Photo was made in 1938.

The assassination of President Lincoln in Ford's Theater the night of April 13, 1865, of course created a tremendous sensation in Schenectady.

The news was received here late that night and Schenectady had its first extra. William D. Davis was at that time one of the proprietors of the Evening Star, having just returned from the front. He himself set up in type what he knew about the assassination, making in all about three-quarters of a column, and printed it on slips of paper.

They were eagerly sought along the downtown streets and in the vicinity of the railroad depot just north of State Street along the ground level tracks. The sentiment was generally that a dastardly crime had been committed and most people were shocked at the news. It is related, however, that someone that night made a remark that "they are beginning to kill pigs down in Washington" and that he had to be rescued from an infuriated mob by cooler heads. Schenectady had its share of Copperheads.

The day after the assassination, the people of Schenectady began to plan a fitting expression of their grief over the death of Lincoln. Committees were appointed and on the following Wednesday, April 19, the obsequies were held. There was hardly a house in the city which did not have some sort of mourning emblem on it. All business places were closed for the day. The church bells tolled all day long and the firing of minute guns was kept up from sunrise to sunset. Services were held in all the churches and they were attended by large congregations.

In the morning, there was a parade which included members of the 83rd Regiment, Mayor Andrew McMullen and the Common Council, St. George's Lodge and St. Andrew's Society. In reality, it was a funeral procession with an elaborately draped hearse pulled along the line of march by four black horses, symbolic of the death of Lincoln.

After the procession, about 1,500 people went to the First Reformed Church for services conducted by several local pastors, including the Rev. Dennis Wortman of the Dutch Church.

A mass meeting also was held in the County Courthouse at 108 Union St. the night of April 17 as an expression of the community's regret over the death of the president. County Judge Judson S. Landon was chairman of the proceedings. John W. Veeder, who was postmaster at the time and in later years went to the State Legislature, was in charge of arrangements for the observance which was to be held the following Wednesday. Judge Landon called for the drafting of suitable resolutions and named the following committee to pursue it: Prof. Benjamin Stanton, Union College; Alexander J. Thomson, a Schenectady attorney; and Howard Barringer of the well-known Barringer family of Schenectady.

While the committee was preparing the resolutions, addresses were made by the Rev. Horace G. Day, pastor of the First Baptist Church, and the Rev. Arthur Jutkins. The meeting was largely attended and there was absolutely no sign of political differences. There were no dissenting views to the expressions of sympathy and sorrow at the nation's loss.

* * *

The train bearing the remains of Abraham Lincoln did not stop at Schenectady. It passed through the city on the early afternoon of April 27, 1865. An immense crowd gathered along the tracks from Engine Hill off Broadway down to the station at State Street. At the station, the funeral train slowed almost to a stop but did not come to a complete standstill. The crowd uncovered and many wept as the train steamed slowly over the river bridge on its circuitous route to Illinois.

Above, passenger train crossing the grade level tracks on State Street about 1895, looking southeasterly toward Broadway. Patrolman Mynderse was killed in area where men are standing at left. Below, typical track crossing scene on Schenectady's main street before the tracks were raised by 1907.

Fatalities at the several grade level railroad crossings in Schenectady were not unusual, but the heroic death of Ptl. James A. Mynderse at the State Street crossing three quarters of a century ago got wide-spread attention which helped precipitate the replacement of those danger spots with overhead bridges.

It was nearly dark that early evening of Saturday, March 31, 1900, when a group of pedestrians stopped for a westbound Delaware & Hudson freight train which had warned of its approach with several whistle blasts. At the same time, a switcher engine was traveling east toward the crossing on an adjacent track. Then, it happened.

A woman began to cross the board walk across the tracks from the canal side. Suddenly she was aware of the approaching freight and turned to go back when she saw the other engine coming from the opposite direction. She stopped as if transfixed in the glare of the oncoming headlamp.

Witnesses later reported details of Mynderse's quick action, a matter of a few seconds, which saved the woman's life at the cost of his own.

The policeman was standing at the crossing between Track 3 and the Edison Hotel (as police customarily did at busy times of the day to assist the flagman) when he saw the woman's predicament. He shouted a warning as he leaped at her and pushed her forward to safety. As the freight train passed, Mynderse stepped back toward Track 3, apparently forgetting about the other engine, and he was struck and killed. His mutilated body later was removed to the Timeson & Fronk funeral parlors on Church Street.

Among the effects found in the patrolman's coat pockets was a silver watch, its case broken and its hands stopped at 6:22.

It was several days before the identity of the rescued woman was known. Several witnesses were heard but the "lady of mystery" did not come forward until after the funeral. She gave her name as Mrs. A. Behrisch of 65 Schuyler St., Albany, and told authorities that she was still so "frightened and shaking" after the incident that she did not leave her house. She had no idea of how she was saved until she read it later in the paper, Mrs. Behrisch said. After crossing the tracks, she had walked hurriedly up State Street and finally boarded an interurban trolley for home.

The Gazette sponsored a campaign for the dead patrolman's family the morning after the accident. About $500 was raised within a week and presented to the widow, who lived at 14 Close St. with their three children.

Mynderse was born in Princetown in June, 1857, and spent most of his early life working on his

Patrolman J.A. Mynderse. . .died a hero's death.

Mrs. A. Behrisch. . .whose life he saved.

father's farm. In 1893 he was appointed a special patrolman for the Schenectady Police Department and the following year, after passing a Civil Service exam, received permanent appointment. He was said by Police Chief William L. Campbell to be "fearless in the performance of his duties. . .he never thought of danger."

A solemn funeral procession took place shortly after 2 p.m. the Wednesday after the accident. Members of the police department walked in front and alongside the horse-drawn hearse as it made its way slowly across Veeder Avenue from the Mynderse home, turning off Albany Street into Summit Avenue for the service to be held at the First English Lutheran Church where the police officer had been a member.

The sanctuary was filled to capacity and crowds thronged outside the church as the Rev. W.E. Crouser officiated at the funeral. When it was over, the cortege then went down to Hathaway's livery on Broadway where the funeral party took carry-alls to the cemetery.

The patrolman's broken body was laid to rest in a silver gray casket in the family plot at Viewland Cemetery, next to the Cobblestone Reformed Church in Rotterdam. Members of the Schaughnaugh-ta-da Tribe of the Order of the Red Men conducted the burial rites.

The day after the funeral, about 8:30 p.m., D&H flagman Jack Cain was credited with saving the life of another woman who was crossing the State Street tracks and became "petrified" at the sight of an approaching train. Cain rushed forward and pulled the woman aside just as the engine passed by. Neither was injured.

There had been considerable agitation for overhead tracks in Schenectady since about 1890, but the railroads balked because of the expense involved and the inconvenience of disrupting schedules while the tracks were being raised. Following the death of Ptl. Mynderse, however, extreme pressure was brought to bear through newspaper editorial comment and an indignant Common Council. The citizenry, too, made their feelings known to both the railroad and the council.

Finally, in the spring of 1903, the project was started with the hiring of D.D. Streeter & Co. of Chicago as general contractor. Overhead crossings were to be built in 13 locations throughout Schenectady, temporary wood trestles to be constructed while steel and concrete foundations were put into place.

It was calculated to be a five-year project. Work on the State Street crossing was started March 1, 1905 and completed the latter part of 1907, when the entire project was finished.

The Mynderse funeral procession on its way up Summit Avenue for service at First English Lutheran Church the afternoon of April 4, 1900. Newly built state armory is in background.

138

Schenectady was shocked and angered on July 31, 1901, when a 22-year-old woman was killed by a fast-moving mail train at the State Street crossing. Her death made the eighth fatality at that hazardous spot since 1897 and it came a little more than a year after Patrolman Mynderse was crushed beneath the wheels of a locomotive.

The tragic death of pretty Miss Clytie C. Curtis once again stirred a public and official outcry against the New York Central Railroad, which after the Mynderse incident had promised to rigorously obey safety rules within city limits (most prominent of which was to reduce speed to 10 m.p.h. and sound whistles and bells at frequent intervals) and to prepare plans for the track-raising project. The feeling was that railroad officials had broken promises on all scores, meanwhile ignoring the danger which the grade level crossings presented daily to the people of Schenectady.

Again, as in the Mynderse case, a hero was involved — but this time the victim was the person he was trying to save. Miss Curtis, who was employed in the drafting room at General Electric as a tracer, was returning to the plant after a midday meal uptown. She was riding her bicycle and as she came to the State Street crossing, the second section of the fast mail, known as Number 3, was approaching the city from the east at a high rate of speed.

The engine was not yet in sight so the young lady disregarded the signals of the flagman, apparently thinking she had time to cross before it arrived. As the train came around the curve she seemed to realize the frightful danger she was in and so made a desperate effort to cross the tracks. Flagman Henry Maloney, only his third day on the job at the State Street crossing although employed by New York Central for several years, saw that it would be impossible for Miss Curtis to clear the tracks in time. He shouted and ran towards her, frantically waving his arms, but she seemed determined to go on.

Just as the cycle was about to go on the tracks in front of the engine, Maloney caught the woman about the waist in the hope of dragging her back from a horrible death. The handlebars of the cycle struck him in the chest and knocked him backwards, while Miss Curtis fell directly in front of the engine. Her body was carried for a moment on the pilot of the engine then thrown with awful violence against the gate across the Troy tracks.

The street was quickly thronged with people, who for an instant were paralyzed with horror at the sight they had witnessed. Policeman Tom O'Connor and Fire Chief Henry Yates were the first to be at Miss Curtis' side after the accident and at first glance realized there was no hope for her. She was unconscious but barely alive, her body shockingly crushed.

A horsedrawn ambulance soon arrived and took the victim to Ellis Hospital (then on Jay Street) where she remained in a coma until death mercifully came at 4 p.m. Hospital authorities said she was beyond human aid for the left side of her face and the back of her head were crushed and her left arm fractured.

Meanwhile, Maloney had been taken to his Albany Street home at his request. He was in a state of shock, not from the injuries he had suffered, but over the condition of the person he had tried vainly to save. Over and over again, he asked those who looked after him, "How is the young lady. . .is she alive?"

Maloney finally was prevailed upon to go to the hospital himself because he had sustained a cut on the top of his head and several bruises about his body. At Ellis Hospital, where he was treated about 5 p.m., he learned the awful truth — Miss Curtis had succumbed to fatal injuries.

Miss Curtis was born in Guatemala, where her father worked as a steamboat captain. The family moved from there to New Orleans where they resided for 10 years and from there they went to Bath, Maine. Later they moved to Lynn, Mass., and then came to Schenectady in 1898. At the time of

Henry Maloney, the heroic flagman who tried vainly to save a life at the State Street railroad crossing.

her death, Miss Curtis lived at 817 Locust Ave. with her mother, Mrs. Adriana Curtis, and her brother, James F. Curtis, who was a GE draftsman. She also had a sister, Miss Addie B. Curtis, of Lynn. Her father had since died.

Editorial comment in local newspapers once more decried the loss of life at the fatal crossing and rebuked railroad and city officials for allowing such conditions to exist. One such editorial stated:

"Who is to blame? That is the question which occurs to all. Not the flagmen of the Central, D & H or the street railway, for they were as usual on the alert and strictly attentive to their duty. Not Miss Curtis, for when she realized her danger it was too late for her to act. Only those who have escaped death in such a form can realize the utter confusion and paralysis of the mind under such conditions.

"There are but two other possible doors at which the blame may be laid — the New York Central Railroad Company, which persisently and with contempt violates the law regulating the speed of trains within the city limits, especially upon grade crossings; and the city, which weakly permits such violations to continue.

"From a date about one month after the cruel killing of brave Officer James Mynderse down to the present time, there had not been a day in which one or more passenger or mail trains have not greatly exceeded the speed limit, some of them crossing State and Union Streets at a speed of 40 miles an hour. . .Not only is the law in regard to speed violated, but that in regard to the passage of several trains over the same crossing at one time is violated every day. . ."

It was clear that 20th century Schenectady could no longer put up with a situation that was tolerable in the previous century. The boom in population naturally promoted a vast increase in street traffic, so that the heretofore inconvenience of having trains pass through the center of town at grade level had now become a distinct menace. As we reflect on it, the raising of the railroad tracks which began two years after Miss Curtis' death was an all important event in the saga of modern Schenectady.

Portrait of Miss Clytie C. Curtis as it appeared with a newspaper account of her tragic death.

Inscribed on one of the weathered granite headstones in Viewland Cemetery, next to the Cobblestone Reformed Church, are the words: "In memory of N. Augusta Carpenter. Killed by the falling of the Central Baptist Church at Syracuse, N.Y., June 23, 1874. Age 24 years and 10 months."

The 'Syracuse disaster' happened beyond the memories of the oldest inhabitants of North Rotterdam today, except by faint recollection of what their elders used to tell of it. Residents of this area 85 years ago were shocked at news of the tragedy and the untimely death of young "Gussie" Carpenter.

Her father, John M. Carpenter, died in 1856, and shortly after that the widow Carpenter decided to move her family from their small home near the first canal lock in Rotterdam (what is now the vicinity of Lock 8). Mrs. Carpenter gratefully accepted the offer of her brother, Alijah Vedder, to come to Utica to live with him and his wife, Cornelia.

They left behind many relatives in Rotterdam and in the intervening years came back regularly to visit them. So, when two days after the accident, Augusta's broken body arrived at the Schenectady station on the 3:40 eastbound train for burial in Rotterdam that same day, there were many who wept genuinely for her.

But for the story of the church disaster:

It was a warm Tuesday evening, and more than 200 persons crowded into the second-floor social hall of Central Baptist Church for a strawberry festival and a musical program by the young people of the Sunday school.

There were proud parents and relatives, children dressed in lacy finery and many out-of-town guests. Among these were Augusta and her Aunt Cornelia. They had arrived in Syracuse the day before to visit Augusta's cousin, Amanda Reynolds.

Folding chairs had been set up around three sides of the room, facing a platform at the far end which served as a stage for concerts.

Until the performance began, about 7:30, people simply milled about and ate strawberry shortcake, ice cream and cookies.

Augusta, in her pale pink bonnet and white taffeta gown, sat quietly with her aunt in one corner of the hall. She was relieved when the pastor stepped on the platform and made his brief welcoming speech to start the program; the overcrowded room had become stuffy and she thought it would help if there was not so much confusion.

More chairs were brought in to fill up much of the center part of the hall, even as Charlie Collins,

14, opened the musicale with a violin solo. His sister, Minnie, then came up on the platform to play the piano and when it was announced that she would be 13 the next day, her embarrassment caused her to strike more than one wrong key in the first few bars.

The performance must have been half over when a man near the back of the hall jumped to his feet and, pointing overhead with a quivering hand, loudly exclaimed: "My God! Look. . .the ceiling!"

There hardly was time for anyone to look up at the badly-cracked plaster ceiling, which by now sagged ominously at the center. An instant later, a deafening roar brought down an avalanche of plaster, beams and trusses. Nearly all who had been in the hall were carried with the collapsed ceiling into the first floor below, the heavy timbers of the roof breaking the second floor.

For a split second there was silence — darkness had spread its cloak over the scene, gas lines having been severed, but there was enough light to see a pall of dust rising from broken plaster and wood.

When the reverberations of the crash died away, screams of the injured and dying filtered from out of the wreckage. Soon rescuers began to arrive, police, firemen and neighbors. In the light of the kerosene lamps, the lifting haze revealed a scene of incredible destruction and horror.

An old man, face smeared with blood and grime, was crying hysterically because he had lost his Bible. A half-naked woman whose flesh was torn from one side, pleaded for help, then fell back dead. Some who managed to crawl from under the jackstraw rubble wandered about in a daze, calling for relatives in hoarse, unreal voices.

A large crowd quickly gathered at the scene, almost before the full force of rescue workers had arrived. The explosion-like sound of the crashing roof had been heard throughout the area. Some of the onlookers were hysterical; a police cordon had to be thrown about the roofless church so that rescuers would not be impeded in their search. As the bodies of the dead and injured were brought out to be carried to nearby homes or barns, shrieks of anguish were heard from those who recognized their loved ones.

Minnie Collins, her white dress stained red, was taken out barely alive and carried to a house next to the church. She died an hour later, still 12 years old. Her brother, Charlie, was found dead in the debris early the next day.

Some persons who had been seated next to windows when the ceiling fell saved themselves by grabbing hold of the sills. One of these was John Horton, who assisted in the rescue operations and helped carry out the lifeless body of his daughter, Lula, 13, from the wreckage.

All told, 11 persons were killed outright, and two died later in neighboring homes that had been turned into temporary hospitals. There were 146 injured.

Many were trapped beneath timbers and flooring and had to be sawed free by rescue workers. The bodies of Augusta, her pink bonnet still tied to her head, and her Aunt Cornelia were not found until the next morning, when a large beam was sawed in sections and lifted out.

The Rev. Dr. Dowling of New York City was erroneously reported killed in the disaster with his son George. However, when he turned up very much alive at his home the next day he told his wife "it was the hand of God that spared our lives." He was on his way to the depot with George after visiting his college son; they stopped at the church but found it so crowded they left in about 10 minutes — just before the accident.

Why did it happen? The blame was laid on the shoulders of the church committee members who heeded the advice of architect H. N. White. The architect, vacationing in Europe at the time of the tragedy, had told the committee that the first floor

Sunday school rooms could be made more adaptable if the supporting iron pillars under the second floor were removed. They were, and that left only a series of iron rods to support the upper floor. The rods went through the lower, but not the upper chord of a wooden truss under the church roof. The wooden truss also was found to have been weakened by dry rot, which accounted for the rods finally breaking through under the weight of the large crowd of people.

The church was rebuilt and served its congregation until 1910, when Central and First Baptist churches combined to form First Baptist Church of Syracuse. The old building was torn down and replaced by the beautiful six-story Gothic structure which now graces the corner of East Jefferson and Montgomery Streets.

On Christmas Eve the following year a similar tragedy occurred at Hellika, Switzerland. During a holiday program in a schoolhouse there, the flooring suddenly gave way and plunged its occupants into the cellar below. Eighty persons were killed, 50 injured. An investigation revealed that several iron posts supporting the main floor had been removed when basement rooms had been converted into a gymnasium.

Augusta Carpenter's headstone in Viewland Cemetery, Rotterdam. (Photograph by Ed Schultz.)

Public hangings always drew large crowds, whether out of morbid curiosity or a plain desire to see justice done. It is recorded that a hanging which took place in Schenectady on Feb. 25, 1825, broke all attendance records.

As the day dawned bright and chilly, all roads leading into Schenectady were filled with a steady stream of people arriving by wagon and horseback. They made their way to the City Hall block at Union and College Streets where the hanging was to take place.

The scaffold had been erected in the courtyard of the stately white building, and around it milled an increasing throng of spectators, who came well before the appointed hour of noon. The city's population was about 7,000 but officials estimated "anywhere between 10 and 20 thousand" came to see John F. Van Patten pay for his crime.

The 23-year-old school teacher had been tried and convicted the month before for the slaying of a Rotterdam housewife, Mrs. Maria Schermerhorn. It had taken the jury only 15 minutes to deliberate and hand up its verdict, after which presiding Judge Duer solomnly pronounced the death sentence.

The case had received widespread publicity because of its complexities. There were many who secretly sympathized with the young schoolmaster's plight despite his confession before and after trial that he had murdered the woman.

For one thing, it had been established that he suffered frequent spells of deep despair, almost to a point of "feeble-mindedness," and that this condition was hereditary in his family. Henry Yates, Jr. and Abraham Van Vechten, defense counsels, had tried to argue insanity on behalf of the prisoner but the court held "whosoever sheddeth man's blood, by man shall his blood be shed."

Moreover, it was hinted strongly that the murdered woman had driven the distraught Van Patten to blind vengeance. This is information taken from the condemned man's "Life and Confessions," written in the death cell less than two weeks before the hanging:

Born in New York City, May 22, 1801, he moved to Albany with his parents in 1806. When his mother died three years later and his father had been declared insane, young Van Patten moved to Glenville to live with his grandparents. In 1814, he went to live with his uncle across the river in Rotterdam.

He began teaching in a one-room schoolhouse there in the spring of 1824, took an active part in young people's religious meetings at the Henry Vrooman Putman residence and made many friends among the families of that area — the Putmans, Schoonmakers, Bonds, Smiths, Bradts.

THE TRIAL,
AND
Life and Confessions,
OF
JOHN F. VAN PATTEN,
WHO WAS INDICTED, TRIED, AND CONVICTED OF THE
MURDER

OF
MRS. MARIA SCHERMERHORN,
(ON THE 4th OF OCTOBER LAST,)
AND SENTENCED TO BE EXECUTED ON THE
25TH FEBRUARY, 1825.

SCHENECTADY

FROM THE PRESS OF THE MOHAWK SENTINEL.

1825

One evening, at a meeting of the young people's society, he met a young lady named Josenah Fonda to whom he became attached. They began to keep steady company and in time promised "nothing but death should part us."

Then Mrs. Maria Schermerhorn made her fatal move — that of interfering in the love affair. She convinced the blushing Josenah that her lover was a sickly, weak-minded young man and some day would be like his father, committed to an asylum.

Mrs. Schermerhorn also warned the girl that the schoolmaster was lazy, that he purposely took time off from school because he disliked work. Apparently the young lady believed her, because she suddenly developed a coolness toward her erstwhile beloved.

So great was the depth of Van Patten's despondency that he decided to do something desperate. Mrs. Schermerhorn already had admitted to him that she had spoken to Josenah and that "if I have said anything wrong, I am sorry for it; but I am not afraid to say what I am obliged to."

On Sunday morning, Oct. 3, 1824, Van Patten's brooding reached a conviction while he listened to the Rev. S. Van Vechten, pastor of the North Rotterdam Church. The text was "Whatsoever thy hand findeth to do, do with all thy might."

The next day, he dismissed school at noon and borrowed a gun at the Putman home under the pretext of going squirrel shooting. As he neared the Schermerhorn home, he wadded the blunderbuss with a double shot of powder, rammed it down hard, cocked the weapon and went on.

The confused young man's account of the shooting follows:

"When I came near the house my courage failed me, but I went on til I came to the house and (Mrs. Schermerhorn) invited me in. She seemed frightened and began to talk to me: I now was sorry I came and wished myself away. I thought I could not go through with the deed, but if I went away I should be confined for life.

"I was much confused and rose up two or three times and went to the door with a design either to do the deed or go away. She seemed distressed . . . and while about her work, she seemed to begin everything and finish nothing. Then I thought I could go through with it. I took up my gun with the left hand about the middle of the barrel, drew the breech up the right side of me, pointed the muzzle a little upward, fired and stept out of the house."

Van Patten entered the woods and walked until he reached the area of the South Rotterdam (Fisher Methodist) Church. There a posse of farmers, headed by Mr. Schermerhorn and Mr. Springer, intercepted him and took him into custody.

Speaking of the deed, Van Patten later wrote in his cellblock confessions: "This was an awful scene; from the time I first rose from my chair, till I was out of doors, was not more than three or four seconds. It seemed as though the heavens passed away, and hell gaped wide to receive my soul; I first walked, but the horrid cries from both mother-in-law and children soon made me run.

"In about a hundred yards, I entered the woods and loaded the gun, not meaning to go away, but determined not to be taken until I came to the

city; I meant to come to the prison myself, set the gun down at the door and deliver myself up; but when I came to the south Rotterdam church I stopped; there were a number in pursuit of me.

"Mr. Springer called to me and threatened to shoot me if I did not deliver myself up. I consented, not through fear of his threats, but on condition they would not tie me. I was so affected that for some time I could not speak to them.

"Met Mr. Schermerhorn by the way, and shook hands, but could not speak to him. He exhorted me and I was much affected. I was then taken to the police office, where, after a short examination, I was committed to prison."

Van Patten's trial commenced on the Wednesday morning of Jan. 12, 1825 in the courtroom of the building before which he was to be hanged six weeks later. Judge Duer presided, assisted by Judges Boyd, Ryley and Potter. The prosecution was handled by Alonzo C. Paige, district attorney, and Nicholas F. Beck, assistant, while Abraham Van Vechten and Henry Yates represented the prisoner.

In the ensuing testimony, the defense called many witnesses who had known the prisoner both in Glenville and Rotterdam in an attempt to bolster its case based on a plea of insanity. However, none would say they considered Van Patten deranged but rather weak-minded. The prosecution entered Van Patten's signed confession into evidence and called Mrs. Schermerhorn's mother-in-law and 10-year-old daughter, Sarah, to the stand as witnesses to the murder, in addition to others who testified they had heard Van Patten say four days before the crime he had but one enemy in the world and "she will not live long."

After the jury returned its verdict of guilty, Judge Duer pronounced the death sentence. In his lengthy address before the prisoner standing before him, the jurist at one point observed:

". . . But with the exception of some expressions of sorrow, which were wrung from you upon your arrest, it does not appear from the time of your perpetrating the deed to the present moment, you have exhibited the feeblest mark of contrition — the slightest symptom of remorse, or the least sign even of feeling! Miserable man! Can nothing soften your obdurate heart? Does it remain callous to every impression that may open it to penitence?"

The clock in the belfry of the Dutch Reformed Church was tolling noon when Jailer Van Zandt led prisoner Van Patten from the jailhouse at Ferry and Union Streets. A wagon had been provided for transportation to the gallows, but John Van Patten said he would prefer to walk the single block. It was to be his last walk, so there was no objection.

The crowd was silent as the small party trod up the flagstone walk and into the courtyard where the shadow of the noose lay across the top steps of the scaffold. And there was not a sound, save for the barking of a dog somewhere in the distance, as the prisoner ascended the steps. He did not turn his head or appear to take any notice of the multitude about him.

When he first stepped on the drop, it gave way and he fell to the ground. It was soon replaced and he again walked up the steps to the gallows. The Rev. A.H. Brayton, who had visited the prisoner often during his stay in the jailhouse, delivered a long sermon as was the custom for public hanging. Several other speakers followed.

Finally, the condemned man was asked if he wished to speak. He did. Van Patten first thanked various individuals for their kindnesses to him during the past few months, then warned "all people, old and young, but especially the young, not to resist the spirit of God, nor procrastinate repentance, but yield to conviction and not rest till their peace is made with God."

The last words put to him, by Mr. Brayton, were "Does Jesus appear precious?" Van Patten replied, "I am happy." Then the drop fell.

The West College building, erected by 1804 for an expanding Union College from design plans furnished by colonial architect Philip Hooker, is shown in this view of the 1880s. The courtyard in front of the building was the scene of Van Patten's hanging in 1825, it being Schenectady's city hall from 1814 when the college moved up to its present campus until 1857 when the city's school system took it over. In the foreground is Union Street, while at left is College Street. The Erie Canal was to the right. The Union School was built on the site in 1892 and was razed in 1960; today it is a parking lot for the Van Dyck Restaurant.

Mr. and Mrs. S. Dana Greene. . .their deaths stirred a city.

Harry Proper

Greene funeral procession turning into Wall Street.

Back in the days when the Mohawk River was more widely used for commerce and recreation by business firms and private individuals, it was frequently the scene of fatal and near fatal mishaps no matter what the season.

Probably the most celebrated of them all occurred on the late Monday afternoon of Jan. 8, 1900, when a well-known Schenectady couple plunged to their death through thin ice while skate sailing on the river. The double tragedy saddened the entire city and was talked about long after that week of mourning.

It had been a frigid winter but with little snowfall, with the result that skating was excellent — particularly on the wide expanse of the Mohawk. On that fateful afternoon, about 5 p.m., S. Dana Greene, 37, and his wife, Cornelia Chandler Greene, 33, left their home at 7 Union St. and walked down to the river to enjoy a spin on the ice. They changed to their skates in the small shed provided by the Mohawk Golf Club near the iron bridge at Washington Avenue.

The couple spent some time skating in that area when finally Mrs. Greene proposed that her husband put up the skating sail because a brisk wind was blowing. There were several boys on the ice at the time and one of them, Alex J. Thompson, Jr., warned them of the danger of open water caused by the removal of ice by river ice cutters. Greene thanked him for his thoughtfulness and added that he was aware of the danger.

Daylight was waning when the Greenes sped off toward the railroad bridge, their skating sail catching the wind and sweeping them along with increasing speed. Suddenly there was a terrified shriek of a woman, to be repeated again and again.

N.D. Proper, the ice man, and his son, Harry, were in their office on the river bank not far from the railroad bridge. As soon as the cries were located by them as coming from the opposite side of the river, near the Glenville shore where the open water was, Harry caught up two long pike poles and they both ran to render assistance.

When they arrived at the scene, they found the body of a woman floating nearly erect in the middle of a broken section of thin ice which had frozen over the open water, held so by the fur boa which she wore, one end of which was frozen to the thin scale of ice. Only the one body was seen. By this time, J.A. McCue had also responded, bringing with him a plank. They were not successful in reaching the unconscious woman, however, so Harry Proper and McCue hurried back to the city shore and procured a boat which was pushed across the ice to the scene of the accident. The body was at last removed from the water and taken

back to Proper's office within 15 minutes of the time the cries were first heard.

The Propers did not know whom it was they had taken out of the water. They telephoned the police station and to several physicians while unsuccessful efforts were made to revive the victim. Meanwhile a crowd began to gather and the first that anyone up until that time knew it was Mrs. Greene was when Spencer B. Knowlton, an employe at General Electric and an affiliate of Mr. Greene, recognized her. Drs. Charles McMullen, Charles G. Briggs and George E. McDonald arrived in that order but there was nothing for them to do save concur in the opinion that her death was due not to drowning but to shock and exposure to extreme cold. The body was removed to the Greene home.

Strangely, up until this time, no one suspected that the husband had also perished in the river since the boys who had seen the couple take to the ice were not around after the mishap. But there was no one at the Greene house and when Mr. Greene's mother, brother and sister were told of the accident, they felt certain he had been with his wife. Coroner Joyce immediately began a search with two boats and grapnels. At 8:30 p.m., about a half hour later, Mr. Greene's body was raised from the water.

Later, in reconstructing the tragedy after talking to witnesses, authorities attributed its cause to the supposition that the couple was carried with such speed by the increasing wind that they reached the ice cutting region, which was partially hidden by the sail, before they had a chance to turn aside or stop. The ice cutters were held blameless as they had guarded the opening the ice in accordance with requirements of the law.

The sad news spread quickly through the neighborhood and soon the whole city knew about it through a newspaper extra. It was the more sensational because the Greenes were among the community's leading citizens.

They came to Schenectady in 1893 when Mr. Greene was named manager of the lighting department and general sales manager of General Electric. Before that, he had been employed by the Sprague Electric Car and Motor Co., which was the pioneer in the electric railway industry, and then served as assistant to the general manager of the United Edison Electric Co. until it became a part of General Electric in 1892.

Mr. Greene's family background was notable in service to the country. His ancestors were closely connected with Gen. Nathaniel Greene of Revolutionary War fame. His grandfather, who died in 1899 at the age of 97, was a man of great distinction, both as a soldier and an engineer. He volunteered in the Civil War at the age of 60 and served with honor throughout that conflict. Mr. Greene's father was none other than Lt. Dana Greene who, at the age of 21, commanded the U.S.S. Monitor in her famous battle with the confederate ironclad, C.S.S. Virginia (popularly known as the Merrimac,) after the Monitor's commander, J.L. Worden, was critically wounded at the outset of the Chesapeake Bay battle.

Mr. Greene's war record was nearly as impressive. He was graduated from Annapolis in 1883 at the head of his class and served in the navy for four years as a junior officer. During the Spanish-American War, he again served in the U.S. Navy, this time as a lieutenant and represented the navy on Theodore Roosevelt's staff.

At the time of the Schenectady tragedy, Roosevelt was just beginning his second term as New York governor and that fall would be elected U.S. vice president. In September the following year he would succeed to the presidency upon the assassination of William McKinley. When he was told of the Greenes' deaths, Roosevelt immediately made arrangements to attend the double funeral, coming over from Albany by train.

Mrs. Greene was the daughter of Rear Admiral Ralph Chandler of the U.S. Navy. She was born in Poughkeepsie in 1866. Everyone, in the neighborhood and in church circles, knew her as a gracious and intellectual person, well liked as a devoted wife and civic worker.

The funeral was held on the Thursday following the accident. Before the rites at St. George's Episcopal Church, a brief family service was held in the home. Long before the beginning of the 1 p.m. church service, throngs gathered on Union and Ferry Streets in the vicinity of the home and the church. It was estimated that about 10,000 persons were on hand.

Old St. George's Church was filled by the time the funeral procession filed through its entrance. Prominent General Electric officials were seated up front, along with Governor Roosevelt and his staff. Also present was the detachment of the Naval Battalion and Company E of the Second Regiment, commanded by Capt. J.M. Andrews. The burial service was read by Right Rev. William Croswell Doane, bishop of Albany, and Rev. Dr. John P.B. Pendleton, rector of St. George's.

After the church service, the funeral cortege was escorted over Ferry Street and up State Street to the railroad station. The remains, accompanied by the funeral party, occupied special cars attached to the 2:35 p.m. train and conveyed to Bristol, R.I., where burial took place Saturday morning.

* * *

Two years later, local residents were again reminded of the Greene tragedy by another accident down at the frozen river involving the ice cutting industry. This was the afternoon of Feb. 4, 1902, when a driver, a team of horses and a sleigh loaded with river ice broke through a thaw-weakened surface of the Binnekill at the rear of Washington Avenue in Schenectady and went under for a split second — but the man and the animals were saved.

N.D. Proper & Sons had a contract to supply tons of ice to Swift & Co.'s warehouse on Center Street (now Broadway, between Liberty and Union Streets). The men were cutting in the vicinity of the iron bridge which connected the Washington Avenues of Schenectady and Scotia.

Charles Fry, one of the sleigh drivers, was hauling a freshly harvested load of ice back towards shore when the accident occurred. There was a sickening crunch as the patch of thin ice gave way and just as suddenly the whole rig went under, leaving a gaping hole now frothed with river water.

There were a lot of men on the job that day and help was quickly at hand. But just as luckily, both Fry and the horses bobbed to the surface (it was afterward surmised that the struggling horses broke free their traces and also forced Fry directly up to the opening in the ice.)

The half-frozen driver was pulled out by rope, wrapped in horse blankets and rushed by a company sled to Ellis Hospital. Hauling the frightened animals out of the river proved quite a task, but after a good deal of grappling and pulling (with the aid of other horses) the team was rescued. Mr. Proper, even before the work of saving the horses was started, sent out a call for a veterinarian — but two responded and were on hand to administer to the shivering animals. One of the horses was badly cut but managed to survive the ordeal.

The accident caused considerable extra work for the firm besides the loss of ice that could have been cut long after the 2 p.m. mishap — but all concerned were grateful that only a sled had been lost. The next day, a new channel of ice was opened about 200 feet from shore and a more careful check was made of the thickness of ice where it was to be hauled to land.

Mr. Proper said his men were cutting 18 inches of solid ice from the river at the time and expected to "cut several hundreds of tons more yet this winter."

Section VI

RANDOM STORIES
OF THE PAST

Between 1867 and 1870, Schenectady was a precinct in the Capitol Police Force, created by the State Legislature to uphold the law in Schenectady, Albany and Troy. These are the men of Schenectady's force, of which only Assistant Chief William Jones (seated right) is identified. The police station was then on Wall Street, near State.

One of the mysteries which bugged Schenectadians some 50 years ago was . . . whatever happened to the McKinley bust?

The granite likeness of President William McKinley, mounted atop a stone pedestal, had graced the restful confines of the city's Crescent Park (now Veterans Park) since it was dedicated in 1902. But it disappeared one night in the early 1920s and no clue could be turned up as to its whereabouts or the perpetrators of the theft. Some citizens were inclined to say it was "another college prank" by some playful Union students, but the presidential bust never did turn up in any of the dorms or fraternities and the college to a man disowned any connection whatever to the incident.

The statuary was presented to the city as a gift of the Italian-Americans of the community and as a suitable memorial to President McKinley, assassinated at the Buffalo Exposition the year before.

Memorial Day 1902 was chosen as the date for its dedication and the ceremony highlighted the memorial services in Crescent Park that year. Those of Italian extraction were proudly represented in the gallery of honor as Mayor Horace Van Voast gave the acceptance speech on behalf of the city. The Italian Band played several numbers and representatives of the Garibaldi Society and the Italian Mutual Aid Society participated in the service.

The bust was placed at the time near the foot of the park where Lafayette Street crosses State at that juncture. A few years later it was moved to a new spot just above the Civil War monument. There it remained until its sudden departure.

* * *

Spring had just bloomed hereabouts in 1908 when the residents of upper State Street in the Hulett Street area were alarmed over some mysterious white chalk marks on their fence gates or doorways.

There was a variety of symbols appearing almost overnight — crosses, circles, double crosses and three dots arranged in the shape of a triangle. Many of the housewives became frightened. They thought perhaps their family had been marked for some strange hex they knew nothing about. So the police were called in.

Chief James W. Rynex put two of his best men on the case to go up to the neighborhood, examine the markings and ask questions of residents and anyone else walking through the area. However, before they even began their assignment the officers had a good hunch what it was all about — and as far as is known, their hunch was correct.

It had long been a tradition for panhandlers, or hoboes, to put chalk marks on houses for the information of their brothers-of-the-road. It was sort of a hobo's "directory." A certain symbol meant the residents of a certain house were a soft touch, another that they were accommodating but demanded work for a handout, still another that they were highly uncivil to itinerants, etc.

In the end, the police let it be known that they were on the lookout for hoboes in the area while advising householders to erase the chalk marks and report any further annoyances. It worked, at least for the balance of that year.

* * *

Back in the 1870s, when the Schenectady police department was located on Wall Street and the force was not nearly as large as today, there was an officer by the name of Sgt. Pat Rooney whose astute practicality in police matters was matched by his Irish wit. Many stories about his humorous escapades have been handed down.

There was the occasion when an alderman from the Second Ward complained to Rooney that he "never yet saw a policeman down my way." The sergeant soberly took note of the complaint and about 11 that night, the alderman was awakened from a sound sleep by the jangling of his front door bell. The drowsy politician peered out of his window and asked what was wanted.

"Nothing is wanted, Alderman" said Rooney. "I only wanted you to know that if you looked out of the window you would see a policeman in front of your house." The alderman returned to bed, grumbling over the interruption of his sleep.

At midnight his bell rang again and once more he went to the window only to find Rooney on his front stoop begging the alderman to look him over and assure himself that he was looking at a policeman. This time, there was an outburst of profanity but it had little effect on the sergeant, who walked slowly down the street. And every hour thereafter that night, Rooney stopped at the alderman's home, each time calling the latter's attention to his badge, his night stick and uniform.

Needless to say, from that time on, there never again was a complaint by the alderman about the lack of police vigilance in the neighborhood.

* * *

A furor was caused in Schenectady in the summer of 1901 when Police Chief William Campbell issued an order, after consultation with the mayor, which banned hurdy gurdies and similar "street instruments" from the city's streets.

The reason given by Chief Campbell in his July 15 order was that complaints were received from some local citizens that the roving street grinders disturbed the sleep of late shift workers or bothered the ill. Also, the chief said, the street or "cart" pianos had been obstructing traffic on Wall, Jay and Centre Streets as people gathered to listen to the music.

The Gazette editorialized against the ban, stating that the music privided much-needed entertainment for people of moderate means and argued that if they were objectionable to some neighborhoods, they should simply be asked to move on. Then letters to the editor began to pour in with all (but one from Chief Campbell) in defense of the street musicians and strongly opposed to the ban. One letter writer said, "The street pianos offer at present the best music ever played on the streets."

Mayor John H. White then took matters into his own hands, recognizing the popularity of the hurdy gurdy trade. He issued a public statement to the effect that "the wishes of the people should be respected" and prevailed upon Chief Campbell to rescind the order.

The organ grinders came back to the Schenectady scene, cautioned to stay away from congested, narrow streets and to move along if requested by anyone unappreciative of the music. They remained, in lessening numbers, until the 1930s, and then disappeared the way of the all-night diner, the German band, the scissors grinder and the rag man.

* * *

It may be difficult to comprehend in the midst of today's complicated financial structure, but there was a time when it was not uncommon for people to be paid semi-monthly or even monthly. Then after all the bills were paid — including the groceries which at the turn of the century averaged $5 a week for middle income families — the wage earner could hope that there might be a little left over for "rainy day" money.

Take the case of the Schenectady police back in April, 1908. Practically every policeman signed his name to a petition presented to the Common Council asking that members of the force be paid every two weeks instead of once a month. The petition cited the hardships of paying accumulated bills should any savings be used up by the end of the month. The Gazette supported the petition in an editorial:

"It is a perfectly reasonable request and the number of signatures indicates that the police are all of the same mind in their view of the matter. The employes of the two great industrial concerns here, as well as similar corporations in other cities, are paid every week. It gives them the opportunity to buy provisions and other necessities at the reductions which cash payment affords in some instances.

"Furthermore, it permits them to pay their bills for other things as they come in and they are not confronted at the end of the month with a mass of bills that take most of their month's pay check. To pay the police every fortnight would not only help them, but it would be better for merchants and others with whom the public has to deal. The aldermen should do what they can to see that the request of the policemen is carried out."

The city's aldermen did just that and the following month, in May of 1908, Schenectady's finest went on a semi-monthly pay basis.

Schenectady's finest. . .in the 1870s.

152

During the post-Civil War period, the United States underwent a fundamental transformation from a culture that was essentially agricultural to that of an industrial order. Likewise, in Schenectady, the change which took place in the space of a few decades was amazing.

Schenectady in the 1870s consisted of a cluster of homes and small businesses on a plateau below the old Albany Hill. Union Street became the Troy Road just beyond Park Avenue; there were farms, nurseries and a brick yard off Union Street in the vicinity of the present boulevards. Stone quarries were all about, one near the site of St. Clare's Hospital and others to the west. Way out in the country, a lane (now Brandywine Avenue) connected State and Union streets. Near the present intersection of Brandywine Avenue and Union Street stood the Van Voast mill. Where the former Maqua Co. plant stands was located the Brandywine Knitting Co. In an earlier period, the mill and distillery of James C. Duane, son of the founder of Duanesburg, had occupied this site. And even farther back, in 1683, Adam Vrooman established his grist mill on the same spot alongside the creek then called the Sand Kill.

On old Center Street (now Broadway), south of the foot of Franklin Street, stood the Barhydt and Greenhalgh spring works which had grown from a smithy's shop and whose high square chimney had loomed a landmark since 1857.

On Fonda Street (now North Jay), was the John Cantine Co., a foundry which produced ornamental fencing and the distinctive iron works which topped the stall partitioning in the stables of the area. The iron fences in front of the homes on Union Street just below Seward Place were made at Cantine's.

On the site of the former Ryan's Garage on Broadway, nearly opposite Smith Street, the Coraline works began as one of the early manufacturers of celluloid products. When business demanded expansion, the works moved to Front Street where a brick building was erected. During the 1880s, the building blew up. The same plot was occupied by the American Locomotive Co.'s war-time tank shop. Before Alco and Coraline, the site was occupied by the Alpha Knitting Mill.

Another knitting mill, the McLachlan and Conde Co., had its beginning in Gleason Alley and later moved, to continue the making of hosiery on South Ferry Street.

During this period, Schenectady still had many broom-making shops. Among the better known were C. Whitmyer & Co., Washington Avenue; Frederick Dunning, Ferry Street at the river, and Flinn's on Front Street. Just as broom-making was one of the oldest industries in Schenectady, so the Kilmer Wire Works was one of the newest of the period. Oddly enough, the wire works moved away in the 1880's because of labor troubles. The Kilmer plant had been located in a brick building along the canal (now Erie Boulevard) opposite South Church Street.

Probably the best known paint works were those of Engleman and Bellinger on the flats below Edison Avenue. Marble works included those of J.W. McMullen in the Wyckoff building at State Street and Washington Avenue and Thomas W. Wallace on Nott Terrace.

On North College Street, George Weller had a soft drink and bottling works. The favorite drink in those days was sarsaparilla. There were three well known brick yards. Barker's was located in old Tannery Lane (Blaine Street), Case and Yates Co. was situated on Union Street above Park Avenue, and Sweet and Johnson Co. was on upper Blaine Street.

Carriage (and sleigh) builders included Shaible & Butler on Broadway just in from State Street, Peter Magee on Albany Street and Van Vranken's on Washington Avenue about where the community college now stands.

John Weiderhold's Mill on Broadway, opposite Hamilton Street, was busy making hoopskirts and ladies' muslin underwear. Harness making shops were owned by the Lyon brothers and Andrew Benedict, both on State Street.

These few shops, and many more, illustrate the diversity of Schenectady's early industry. Such shops were important factors in the city's economic system then, just as their giant counterparts have become in the present century.

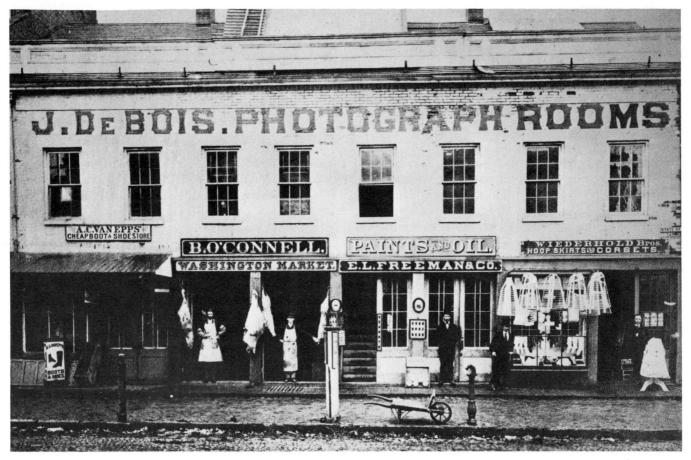

The Wiederhold brothers (John on the left and George on the right) pose at the entrance to their hoop skirt and corset shop on the lower right of this old building which once stood on the southeast corner of State and Ferry Streets. The date: 1874.

Looking down Hamilton Street in 1890 toward old South Centre Street (now Broadway) with John Wiederhold's brick factory in far right background.

Among Schenectady's leading businessmen of the latter part of the 19th century, when the city became industrialized and outgrew the lethargy of a typical canal town, was a friendly, big-framed German by the name of John Wiederhold.

Like others who sought to escape political tyranny against those who held socialistic beliefs, Wiederhold left his native Germany for good in 1865 and embarked for the U.S. — a land which had just endured a tragic civil war but held out promise of a new and prosperous life for those willing to work for it. After having been for some time in Amsbury, Mass., he came to Schenectady in 1869. In partnership with his brother, George W. Wiederhold, he purchased a retail fancy goods store at the southeast corner of State and Ferry streets.

In 1874, the Wiederholds commenced manufacturing hoop skirts. There are photographs in existence today which show the store front lined with steel-corseted mannikins along the curbside.

In 1882, now in partnership with Charles S. Washburn, John Wiederhold built a large brick factory opposite Hamilton Street on what was then called South Center Street (now Broadway) and began the manufacture of muslin underwear. The business was very successful and the firm gained a reputation for reliability throughout the country.

In 1883, Wiederhold married Mary Dunbar. They had two children — a son, Edward J., and a daughter, Marguerite. He was a charter member of New Hope Lodge No. 730, F. and A.M., and a member of the Schenectady Elks Lodge. While he took a great interest in philanthropy and civic affairs, including the city's politics, he never held public office nor did he seek it. He was a liberal supporter of the First Presbyterian Church.

There came a twist of irony in the closing years of his life. Although he had been a longtime respected Schenectady businessman whose firm had done extensive work with the U.S. War Department in military clothing contracts after 1900, the outbreak of World War I resulted in what was called a "routine check" of Wiederhold's patriotic leanings. This, of course, happened to many another stalwart U.S. citizen who had come to this country from Germany — including the renowned GE mathematician, Dr. Charles P. Steinmetz.

Investigations over a six-month period in 1917 were made by the government before a report back to the federal government established Wiederhold as no threat to national security. No one but John Wiederhold, who lived for nearly a half century in Schenectady and contributed greatly to its welfare, could know the personal grief of such an inquiry.

He died in February, 1918, at his home at 612 Union St. (which is located next to the former German Methodist Episcopal church, later used by the Senior Citizens Center) after being ill a week with pneumonia. He was 74 years old.

The old Wiederhold manufacturing center was closed not long after and was used for various purposes after that, mostly as a warehouse. It last became a Saveway Market but that, too, has closed. The empty brick building, which a few years ago was the site of a Halloween "Haunted House" for area youngsters, still stands on the Broadway corner next to the market square.

John Wiederhold, shortly before his death.

Three doors in from Francis Avenue, next to the PNA Hall at 803 Crane St., there is a structure known as the Graybar Building which has a plaque attached with the following inscription:

"On this site, thereafter known as 'Engine Hill,' starting from a small brick building used as the western terminal station, the Mohawk and Hudson Railroad Co. operated the first steam propelled railroad transportation service in America. The De Witt Clinton engine with three passenger cars was used on the initial trip between the cities of Schenectady and Albany, August 9, 1831."

The bronze tablet was erected in August, 1938, by city officials and the Schenectady County Historical Society to designate the site of the first railroad station in the state and perhaps the first in the nation, and as a tribute to the memory of George W. Featherstonhaugh, whose determination led to the creation of the Mohawk and Hudson Railroad.

The exact date of erection is not known, but it was soon after the first ground was broken on July 29, 1830, by Gen. Stephen Van Rensselaer. And it was to the unfinished structure that the famous DeWitt Clinton drew its first load of 14 passengers in Concord coaches to inaugurate the age of steam locomotion.

The station was not an impressive building but was of a simple rectangular design 42 feet long and 24 feet 10 inches wide. It was one story and of brick exterior. On the inside, there was a hall through the center with rooms on each side.

The station had a short life as a railroad depot. The coaches of the Mohawk and Hudson at first were let down an inclined plane on Crane Street and drawn by horses to the bank of the canal where Peckham and Wolfe's lumber yards once stood (then Dock Street but now Erie Boulevard). However, this operation was abandoned by the railroad in 1841 when the line was moved about a mile south of the old road. It brought the road into the city over Broadway and Edison Avenue.

Soon after 1841, the railroad depot was sold to a man named Lang or Long who converted it into a private residence. He added a front porch and a summer kitchen to the rear . . . and this was as it stayed through the years until it was torn down. Of course, after it had stood vacant for several years prior to 1921, the old station looked dilapidated with several windows broken and its porch sagging.

But even so, when it was announced in the spring of 1921 that plans were afoot to do away with the landmark there was some agitation to preserve it. Even Mayor George R. Lunn stepped into the brief controversy, suggesting that perhaps public subscription might be encouraged to have the building removed to some nearby place where it might stand as a shrine to early railroading.

He thought Pleasant Valley Park would be a good spot. However, the idea never got past the planning stage when impatient developers of the Crane Street site decided nothing would ever be done and went ahead and razed the old station.

Ten years later, in 1931, there was some lamenting that the original depot had not been saved. It was the centennial celebration of the DeWitt Clinton's historic trip and now, too late, many people were saying that it was too bad that more foresight hadn't been shown by preserving the western terminal of the Mohawk and Hudson Railroad.

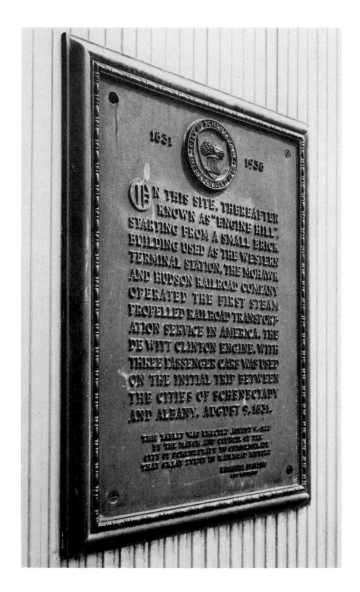

Plaque on the building at 803 Crane St., marking the site of our first railroad depot.

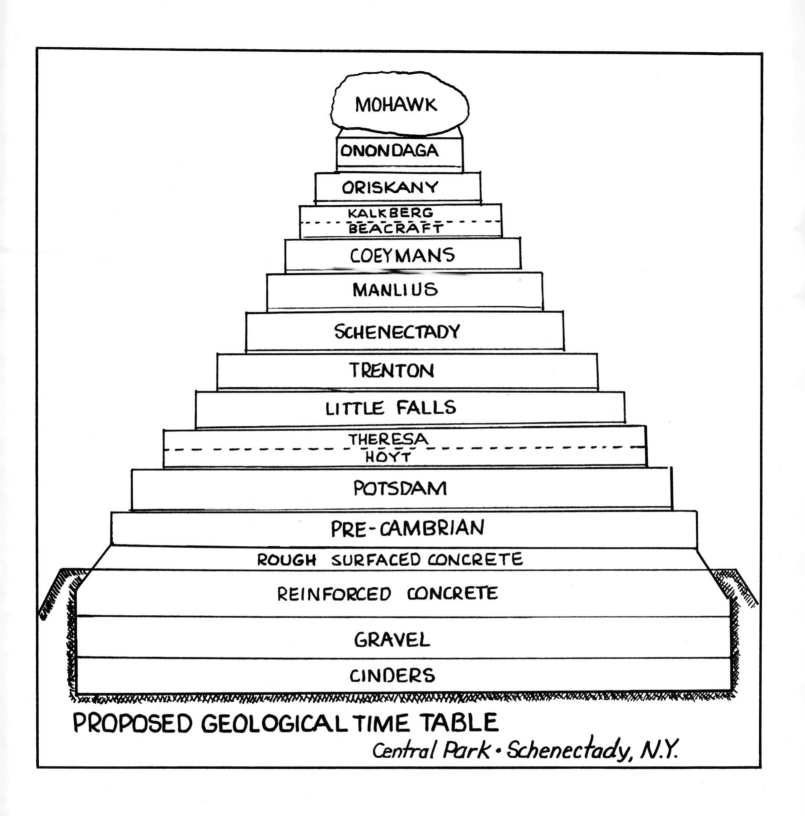

This was the working diagram for the Geological Time Table or "park pyramid" when it was proposed in 1934.

Some time ago we were on a radio talk show when a caller asked about the "Central Park pyramid." The question floored us, as it did the host, because neither of us had ever heard of, much less seen, the subject in question — and we were both natives of Schenectady.

Several subsequent callers shed some light on the mysterious object but it was not until we received a personal call some days later that we were able to dig into the background of the pyramid. The revealing source was Albert M. Getz of Schenectady, who with H. W. Dill, Jr., was in charge of its construction. Here's the lowdown on the park pyramid as reconstructed from a Gazette story dated Jan. 5, 1934.

It was the time of the Depression Thirties, when the federal government was desperately finding ways to provide local employment through agencies set up by the Roosevelt administration.

One of the projects devised by the Civil Works Administration (CWA) was the construction of a "Calendar of Eons" to be set in a newly purchased portion of Central Park. It was a spot near Oregon Avenue but off Fehr Avenue that was selected for the stone pyramid and which was to be built with funds provided by the CWA (incidentally, the CWA lasted only a year and was replaced in late 1934 by the Works Progress Administration, more generally known as the WPA).

The project was to represent a story of the past covering a period which reached back through millions of centuries and concerned geological happenings in the vicinity of Schenectady. E.W. Allen evolved the "geological time table" with assistance from the late Dr. E. S. C. Smith, professor of geology at Union College.

It was to be built in the form of a pyramid, 14 separate layers of rock to depict 12 great eras of geologic time covering a period estimated to be between one and two billions of years. Allen stated at the time that the general design would be similar to a "time table" he saw on the campus of the Penn State College adjacent to the school of mines.

It required several months of the spring of 1934 to obtain the rocks recommended by Professor Smith, but it was done and the pyramid was completed by late summer that year.

The rock pyramid was built 10 feet square, resting on a 13-foot concrete base. The rock layers were about seven inches thick, separated from each other by a space of one inch concrete.

As worked out by Professor Smith (who died in November, 1971) the series incorporated in the pyramid included certain rocks of the Precambrian, namely, gneiss, schist and the quartzite part of the Grenville series; the Potsdam and Theresa sandstones, Hoyt limestone and Little Falls dolomite of the Cambrian period; the Trenton and Schenectady beds of the Ordivician; the Manlius of the Silurian; the Coeymans, Beacroft and Kalkberg limestones, the Oriskany sandstone and Onondaga limestone of the Devonian and topped by the Mohawk conglomerate of the post glacial Pleistocene period. Thus completed, the "time table" visualized in a novel way representative rocks of the Archeozole, Paleozoic and Cenozoic eras.

The pyramid was intended to be the focal point of a nature trail in the new park area and had the backing of the Mohawk Hiking Club. However, the project never reached the expectations of its planners and in a few years the area around the pyramid became overgrown with weeds and brush. There is, however, a small dirt road leading into the trail. It became known as "lover's lane." It is on upper Fehr Avenue, just north of Golf Avenue.

Occasionally a park pedestrian or a cyclist will venture into the section and will be mystified by the sight of the strange pile of rock, some of it vandalized over the years. But now, when someone asks us about the park pyramid, at least we will have a little more information.

A last look at the Rice Road boulder was taken by H.L. Reed (left), then GE manager of community relations and communications, and the late Chester J. Woodin in December, 1964, before construction of the $20 million Thruway spur along that route. The plaque was removed and turned over to the Schenectady County Historical Society for its archives. Mr. Woodin was part of the group that in June, 1936, arranged for the dedication of Rice Road in tribute to Edwin W. Rice Jr., renowned GE engineer.

A one-week celebration was held in Schenectady in mid-June of 1936 to commemorate the 50th anniversary that Thomas A. Edison took possession of the two unfinished buildings of the ill-fated McQueen Locomotive Works to establish the Edison Machine Works. In 1892 it became the General Electric Co.

One of the features of the week's celebration was the dedication of what had been known as the Old Dyke Road along the Mohawk River as Rice Road, named in honor of Edwin W. Rice, Jr. who died the year before. This was two years before the new WGY studios would be opened at the apex of Rice and River Road at Washington Avenue.

The Dyke Road was developed about 1925 when the old Erie Canal bed was transformed into Erie Boulevard, billed as one of the widest and best-lighted boulevards in the country at the time. Of course, the plant that Edison and his associates started in 1886 had by this time grown into a tremendous establishment, stretching far beyond the confines of the plot he had at first purchased so that it extended along the river flats into Rotterdam.

The idea of naming the thoroughfare after Rice came from J.R. Lovejoy, director of the company and a close associate of Rice during his lifetime. So it was Lovejoy who, about 4:30 p.m. on June 12, 1936, unveiled a bronze tablet affixed to a huge boulder at the entrance to Rice Road alongside Washington Avenue. The event, broadcast over WGY, was attended by Owen D. Young, Gerard Swope and other high-ranking executives.

The tablet, which today is a permanent exhibit at the Schenectady County Historical Society, read: "Rice Road — Dedicated to Edwin Wilbur Rice, Jr. A great pioneer of the electrical industry who had the vision, competence and patience of the investigator — the daring and strength of the practical engineer. Dedicated by the City of Schenectady in commemoration of 50 years of electrical achievement, June 12, 1936."

The huge boulder, the weight of which was estimated from 14 to 20 tons, came from a wooded area opposite 1220 Waverly Place on what had been the old Van Voast farm. Many years before, the story ran, Indian squaws ground corn against the rock's rough top. The truth of this may or may not have been doubted, but at least the knowledge that so large a boulder lay within Schenectady was almost forgotten. The story of the Waverly Place boulder reached J.S. Apperson, chairman of the memorial committee, who thought he would have to go north for such a specimen. He arranged for it to be transported to the Rice Road corner for the ceremony.

The big rock and the bronze plaque had been a familiar sight to local residents, but in 1965 it was removed when work on the Thruway spur began. But a word about E.W. Rice, the man for whom the road was dedicated.

He played an important part in the history of electrical progress in Schenectady. In association with Charles A. Coffin and Prof. Elihu Thomson (of Thomson-Houston fame at Lynn), he contributed much toward the building of GE. He was largely instrumental in bringing Charles P. Steinmetz to the company's engineering staff, he encouraged the investigation by the company of the Curtis Steam turbine and gave it a fair trial through a period of uncertainty until it became the foundation of a vast electrical power system. He was chiefly responsible for the establishment of the GE Research Laboratory.

In 1913 he succeeded Coffin as president of General Electric, a post which he held until 1922 when he became honorary chairman of the board of directors. He held that position until his death in 1935.

There were several big dinners during the commemoration of GE's 50th year of electrical progress in Schenectady, most of them held in the Hotel Van Curler. Among the speakers were Charles Edison, son of General Electric's founder, Dr. George R. Lunn and Gov. Herbert H. Lehman.

In honor of the celebration, a huge birthday cake about 50 feet in circumference was erected in the park across from the hotel (now Schenectady Community College). There were 50 candles on it, all illuminated with electric lights.

This view of the former Lyceum was made in 1910, a year before it was razed. At the time, the old school building was serving out its last days as a blacksmith shop run by M. LaMontaine.

There were lots of memories stored within the old Lyceum building when that curious piece of architecture was torn down in the summer of 1911 to make way for a new storage house for the Fitzgerald Brewing Co.

The Lyceum, an eight-sided wood and stucco building, was located at 5 Yates St. and was erected in 1835 by G.F. Yates to serve as a private school for boys. It was operated as such for almost 20 years until about 1854 when public schools were established in Schenectady and lessened the need for private schooling. Professor Cook, the last instructor at the Lyceum, was appointed superintendent of the Union School on the old West College grounds at Union and College Streets.

Among the students attending the Lyceum was Chester A. Arthur (later to become a U.S. President) whose father was pastor of First Baptist Church and lived at the time in the parsonage at the corner of Liberty and Yates Streets. Arthur later went to Union College.

David Crittenden, who was author of Crittenden's Arithmetic, the standard text book of that day, was the first instructor at the Lyceum and held that position for several years. Inside the schoolhouse, seats were arranged around the sides of the octagonal room in a sort of balcony and were separated by partitions so that the pupils — about 50 in number — were not subject to interruptions or distractions but were in sight of the instructor.

The old school, when it ceased to be used for that purpose, for a time served as the meeting place for Sigma Phi of Union College and then became one of the first fraternity houses in the country. This was shortly before the Civil War.

Still later, it was converted into a private dwelling, then as a storage building and finally lay in vacant disrepair for several years before succumbing to the wrecking bar.

The Lyceum in its heyday. It was a curious piece of architecture, an octagonal building erected on Yates Street in 1835 as a private school for boys.

An 1893 view of the Great Flat looking toward the river from above the New York Central tracks. General Electric Co., which grew out of Edison's machine works, was rapidly expanding its facilities and eventually would occupy the whole area shown in background. The street which led to the company gate from alongside the Twoomey House in right foreground was once named Kruesi Avenue.

When Thomas A. Edison decided to set up his electrical machine works in Schenectady in 1886, he entrusted much of its organization and opening operation to one of his chief aides, a native Swiss by the name of John Kruesi.

Not only was Kruesi an able executive, as general manager of the Edison Machine Works when it opened in Schenectady in December, 1886 and later chief mechanical engineer when the firm became the General Electric Co., but he was also a mechanical genius whose talents were fully recognized and used by Edison. The names of "Honest John" Kruesi (so called by his men because of his fairness to them and utter devotion to his work) and William "Pop" Turner were well known for years in Schenectady because they were the ones who got the plant rolling after 1886 and were in charge of hiring personnel.

It was by no means mere chance that Kruesi had been selected by the great inventor for his new role in the upstate city. Shortly after coming to America in December, 1870, Kruesi worked for a time with Singer Sewing Machine Co. as a machinist but changed jobs after hearing of a young experimenter named Edison in Newark and the things he was working on — like the telephone, stock ticker, telegraph printing press and electric pen. Kruesi, who signed on with Edison in 1871, was more adept at the mechanical execution of ideas conjured up by the inventor.

One day in 1877, Edison handed Kruesi a sketch with a notation, "Kreusi, make this." (It is interesting, from a human interest standpoint, to note that Edison misspelled the surname of his trusted employe). The story goes that Kruesi naturally was curious as to what the contraption was intended to accomplish and was rather dubious about the whole thing but went right to work on the model, even after Edison told him, "I'm going to make it talk."

In a few days, Kruesi had the model finished and brought it to Edison. One turned the crank and the other recited the whimsical doggeral, "Mary had a little lamb. . ." Then the reproducing needle was applied at the beginning of the little grove of dots on a strip of tinfoil and the crank being turned once more gave forth the recorded sounds. Kruesi is quoted as exclaiming, "Mein Gott in Himmel!"

At any rate, that occasion gave Edison one of his greatest sensations of fame and marked the beginning of the recording industry.

Kruesi was born May 15, 1843 in Heiden, Canton Appenzell, Switzerland, and was soon taught numerous trades. However, he was satisfied with none of them and when old enough apprenticed himself to a locksmith and then went to

John Kruesi

Zurich as a journeyman machinist. He excelled in the trade and by the time he immigrated to the U.S. from England, he was more than ready to make his mark in American industry.

Soon after joining Edison's firm, Kruesi married Emily Zwinger, whose parents also were Swiss. Meantime the little shop in Newark had been outgrown and they all moved to Menlo Park where the phonograph, electric incandescent light, electric car and other revolutionizing inventions were born.

From 1876 to 1881, Kruesi was the invaluable mechanical foreman of the Edison laboratory. In 1881, he developed the celebrated underground electric tube system and became general manager and treasurer of the Electric Tube Co. In 1885, this company merged with the Edison Machine Works of which he became general manager. This was the same firm which moved to Schenectady from the Goerck Street site in New York City in 1886.

While in Schenectady, Kruesi and his family lived at 16 Union St. which is now the site of part of the Mohawk Club parking lot on that corner. There were nine children, one of whom died in infancy, but none are alive today. Elizabeth Joyce, daughter of August (Gus) Kruesi and granddaughter of John Kruesi, lives at 1436 Lowell Road with her husband, J. Warren Joyce, former city historian. A great-granddaughter, Cynthia Kruesi Duval, and her husband, Thomas D. Duval, also live in Schenectady. She is the daughter of William Kruesi and granddaughter of Frank Kruesi.

It is said that John Kruesi never got over the loss of his wife Emily, who died in early 1897 after a lingering illness. He grieved for her. After returning from a trying business trip to New Orleans, he died within a few days on Feb. 22, 1899. Both were buried in a family plot near the Brandywine Avenue entrance in Vale Cemetery.

The street which led to what became known as the subway gate of General Electric was named Kruesi Avenue in honor of the pioneer GE machinist and executive, but in more recent years it has become known simply as Lower Broadway.

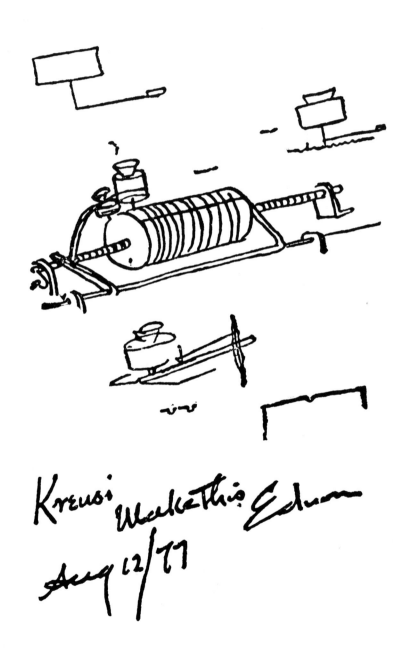

The famous sketch, drawn by Thomas A. Edison, of the first phonograph with the notation, "Kreusi, make this." (He misspelled the name.) The date was Aug. 12, 1877, and soon the world would have its first talking machine.

Two of the most familiar figures on the streets of Schenectady a century ago were Jim Cuff, the Indian "yarb" peddler, and Joe Bones, the rag picker.

They were much alike in many ways — each lived alone in a small shack, never showed any sign of violence and was too proud to beg although grateful for any kindnesses. And each, though he may have wished otherwise, spent his last hours of life in the city almshouse on Emmett Street near the old fairgrounds.

Jim Cuff probably ranks as the all-time Number One character of the Schenectady area as the gaunt halfbreed (he was nearly seven feet tall) lived here almost all of the last century before he succumbed to pneumonia in March, 1893.

But surely, then, old Joe Bones would have to be a close second, settling in Schenectady in the 1840s and making it his hunting ground until he died in May, 1882.

Much has since been written about Cuff, who daily roamed the surrounding townships in search of herbs and edible weeds and peddled them in the city, but the memory of Joe Bones all but died out after the turn of the 20th century.

Not until his death did it become publicly known that his real name was Joseph Arnold, that he was about 84 years old and was an immigrant from the grand duchy of Baden in Germany. He was simply known as Joe Bones and it is not likely that anyone would have called him anything but that even if his true name had been known earlier.

As with Cuff, Joe Bones never seemed to grow old. Many adults with families of their own were amazed in later years that the two men still had dark hair and were quick of step.

Unlike his Indian counterpart, Bones was of short stature and smiled a lot at passersby — whether they taunted him, as some youngsters did, or nodded a greeting.

He was thin and wiry, he had teeth as clean and sharp and strong as a rabbit's, and he could crack hazelnuts. He could skin over a high board fence with the agility of a cat and he was no slouch at running — the boys found that out when they would yell, "Old Joe Bones, here's some stones!" and then pelt him.

If the stones were small and did not hurt him, old Joe would merely shake his fist and jabber at the offenders. Then he would turn away with a smile. But if hurt by a large or sharp stone, he would give chase.

Joe was a naturally kindly man and liked children. Even when his face had been cut by a stone and he had caught the boy who threw it, he

Joe Bones, from an old tintype, with the "tools of his trade" — a burlap bag and a pointed stick.

would merely give him a "shaking up" and warn him not to do it again.

His vocation was that of a rag picker and for many years his odd figure was a familiar sight on weekdays in some part of the city. His daily tours took him into the backyards of the residential sections in his search for old paper, rags, bones and metal. He carried a bag on his back and a short hickory stick with a steel spike in one end, with which he would fish bones from barrels or dig them from the frozen ground in the winter time.

His sole companion for many years on these incursions was a small dog which was as wiry and active as its master. Joe's dog followed close to his heels and helped search out bones that neighborhood dogs had buried or market owners may have deposited in trash cans.

Joe plied his trade with an industry that was indefatigable. He had a rough exterior and his clothes were most disreputable, the patching and repairing being done by the old man himself. He was a recluse, living in his filthy shack in the wilderness that was then McClellan Street just off State Street (Cuff, by the way, lived nearby in a similar one-room shack on South Brandywine Avenue just off State).

And he never begged. He was known to housewives and they frequently gave him food or hot coffee. When their children would be troublesome and failed to obey, mothers threatened to "give you to Joe Bones who will carry you away in his bag."

It was Joe's unending search for bones that gave him his sobriquet. The junkmen, who in turn sold the bones to fertilizer manufacturers, paid him a half-cent a pound for bones and one cent a pound for metal. One of the dealers who had a scrap yard on White Street (now Clinton) between Liberty and Franklin Streets, discovered some iron in the bones sold him and he spoke to Joe about it.

"I tried to tell Joe to keep the bones and iron separate, for the iron was worth more than the bones, but he couldn't get it through his head," the dealer once said. "He knew iron weighed heavier than bones and the more iron he had in his bone bag the more money he got for the bones."

Subsequently, Joe got wise to himself. He saw the scrap dealer paying a boy for some metal. After that Joe separated metal from the bones before selling them.

The industry of the old man and his taciturn habits led to the general belief that he was a miser and had acquired a great wealth mysteriously hidden in or about his shack — and it was at first thought this may have been his undoing. In mid-May of 1882, he was found by a neighbor, Henry Brown, lying unconscious and nearly nude outside his shack.

It was believed he had been attacked and robbed, although there was no evidence of bodily injury. The interior of Joe's simple abode was disarranged and a few clapboards had been torn off the outside — but since he never had a reputation as a neat housekeeper, no one could know for sure whether anyone had been searching for possible riches.

Joe was taken to the almshouse. He never regained consciousness and died on May 16 while attendants, under the direction of Superintendent William G. Van Patten, were putting clean underwear upon him.

Dr. M.G. Plank, who was summoned after the old man's death, testified that no marks had been found on the body that would lead to the belief that he had suffered any violence at the hands of others. His opinion was that death resulted from old age and exposure.

Only a dollar or so was found in the shack and this was in pennies and small silver. Later a small amount was found to his credit in a local bank.

As to Joe's worldly possessions, a priest of St. Joseph's Catholic Church said that in 1878, at a time when the rag picker had had some trouble about his dog, he came to the rectory and left the sum of $70 for safe keeping. Four weeks later he showed up and took the money back.

"I gave it all back and he never left money with me since," said the priest. "On May 5, 1877, he donated $100 to the church, which was turned over to the trustees. I published the fact to the congregation on the next Sunday. That was all he ever donated to the church. The last conversation he had with me, he told me he had no money."

Schenectady's first almshouse, or "poorhouse" as most city dwellers called it, at Emmett and Craig Streets where Jim Cuff and, later, Joe Bones spent their last hours.

Over 100 years ago, Route 159 or Mariaville Road was once called the Fort Hunter Road. It was a plank road, popular for turnpikes developed in the early 1800s, and was officially called the Fort Hunter Plank Road until about the time of the Civil War when that portion of it from Hamburg Street to the Five Corners in Rotterdam became Curry Road, and the remainder Mariaville Road.

The Fort Hunter Plank Road became a reality less than two years after application by a private turnpike company was made in Albany in 1849 in accordance with the Plank Roads Act of 1847. It began at the junction of what is now Hamburg Street and ended at Fort Hunter, the approximate route of today's Route 159. (Today's Fort Hunter Road, which meets Curry Road at the point where a toll house once stood, was named after the former turnpike.)

The plank road was an important highway in its day, penetrating the Mohawk Valley on the south side of the river. Like all plank roads, it had innumerable toll houses at which horseback riders or drivers of horsedrawn vehicles paid a few pennies for using that stretch of the highway. There were also many taverns along the route.

When it reached the point now called the Five Corners in Rotterdam, the Fort Hunter Road cut across the Duanesburg Plank Road. On the north side of the Duanesburg Road at this junction stood for many years the well known Van Wormer's Tavern. There was a blacksmith shop and a half dozen other buildings also clustered about the

corners. Nearly two miles west of the junction was a toll gate located at a point where the Fort Hunter Road met the road leading to the Princetown settlement. There were two dwellings there, one owned by J.T. Wasson and the other by William Gordon.

Passing the old Princetown (or Cobblestone Church Road) Road, crossing and recrossing the Poentic Kill, Fort Hunter Road made a wide swing through the Poentic Valley up to Rynex Corners. At this junction were McClyman's Tavern, two saw mills and several dwellings.

A quarter mile farther west, beyond the old tavern, was Lake Maria (later known as Featherstonhaugh Lake). A third toll house was located a mile and a quarter past Rynex Corners, then Fort Hunter Road ran north for another mile to Mariaville with its mill house and small industrial and agricultural community. The settlement was at the confluence of the Chuctanunda Creek and the mill pond. A church, tavern, store, grist mill and saw mill provided the needs of those in the surrounding area.

The Fort Hunter Road went on to Pattersonville and the Fort Hunter community. The latter, named after Governor Hunter who was crown authority of the British province of New York at the time, was built as a bastion against the French in the early 1700s. Hendrick Vroman of Schenectady was architect and builder of the fort and a church when Fort Hunter was developed.

Typical toll house on early 19th century turnpikes, this one atop the Broadway hill known as Pierson Toll.

The Salvation Army Citadel is shown shortly after its construction at 218 Lafayette St. in 1908, from a glass negative by Will Underhill. Moses Viney's home was to the left. This building was demolished early in 1974 when the new citadel was erected, part of it over Moses' former dwelling site.

170

Wide news coverage locally was given the death of Moses Viney when the former coachman and attendant of longtime Union president Eliphalet Nott succumbed to a three-month illness at the outset of 1909.

Viney, who had been attended by Dr. W. L. Pearson throughout his sickness, died at 11 p.m. on Sunday, Jan. 10, in his tiny home at 220 Lafayette St. where he had lived for 35 years. He had lived to a ripe old age, just two months shy of 92.

The story of Moses Viney was well known to virtually every Schenectadian at the time, how he was born a slave in Talbot County, Maryland, and while a young man successfully escaped bondage to freedom in the north. Actually, he and two sturdy companions decided to make the break on Easter morning, 1840, and in a few weeks were in the Schenectady area on their way to Canada. However, Viney liked the looks of this place and remained on the Glenville farm of a Dr. Fonda where he worked for a time as a laborer at $5 a month with board.

Not long after, Viney followed the advice of newfound friends and went on to Canada rather than risk the chance of being taken as a refugee slave. In a few years he had saved up enough money to buy his freedom from his erstwhile master in Maryland, a Mr. Murphy, and returned to the Schenectady area.

Dr. Nott heard of the young man, took an interest in his welfare and hired him as his coachman and valet. In the two decades that Viney served the college president, a strong bond of friendship grew between them. He loved Dr. Nott and the latter's affection for the ex-slave was as deep. After the aged Dr. Nott died in 1866, Viney stayed on as coachman for Mrs. Nott and upon her death several years later purchased the horse and rig and went into the cab business for himself. His services were particularly in demand by the college faculty and visiting alumni, so familiar a figure had he become around the campus.

In 1903, the 86-year-old coachman decided it was time to retire. He spent more time at his home but still was seen on his daily stroll around the Crescent Park section. Often he would sit on the tiny porch of his small abode near the Smith Street corner and in cold weather he could be seen looking out the front window from his easy chair. He was a friendly sort. It seemed everyone knew him, and he always had a smile and pleasant greeting for passersby.

He was especially fond of his neighbors, the Schenectady corps of Salvation Army, and often said he loved to listen to their hymn-singing and band music. When the Salvation Army decided to build its new citadel at 218 Lafayette St. in 1908,

Moses Viney, an ex-slave who spent his more than 60 years as a free man in Schenectady.

Viney gladly donated a fringe of land to enable the corps to meet its building requirements. He meant it as a gift but the grateful corps gave him $200.

Likely as not, the old man listened to the spiritual music that Sunday night he lay on his death bed.

Ironically, the new citadel was dedicated a week after Viney's demise. Commander Evangeline Booth, who was on a preaching tour in this country at the time, was supposed to take part in the ceremonies but her illness from a recent operation prevented her from attending. She remained in her Edison Hotel room that Saturday. However, the next day she preached an afternoon and evening service at the Van Curler Opera House. Mrs. C. Jehu, wife of the local corps captain, was a personal friend of the commander, having served in London under Mrs. William Booth, wife of the Salvation Army founder and mother of Evangeline.

The years marched by and on Dec. 1, 1973, the Schenectady corps dedicated another new building, this one at the corner of Lafayette and Smith Streets, part of the site which includes the former residence of Moses Viney. The 1909 citadel was razed in February, 1974.

The Schenectady Corps of the Salvation Army moved into this residence at the turn of this century as a permanent home, next to Moses Viney house at the left. Capt. Edward Jehu, corps officer at the time, is standing at right at the headquarters entrance. Both this and the accompanying photograph were tiny prints found in the cornerstone of the 1908 building when it was demolished in 1974.

Salvation Army Capt. and Mrs. Edward Jehu, Schenectady corps officers while Moses Viney lived next door as a friendly neighbor. He loved the corps' music and hymn-singing. This photograph was dated Sept. 13, 1908.

Collectors of old photographs or postcards relating to Schenectady are familiar with what seemed a favorite scene for the photographers of the past century — a southerly view of the Erie Canal looking down Dock Street from State Street.

The vantage point usually was such that the picture included the Brown Furniture Co. store located on what is now the site of the Masonic Temple (with Bond's Clothing on the ground floor.) Not many today recall the prominence once held by the Brown firm among furniture buyers of the day — almost up to the day it folded in 1917 after being in business in Schenectady for 88 years.

Albert Brown came here in 1829 from his native Stockbridge, Mass., and opened a retail store on lower State Street, just below the present Breslaw building. He specialized in making chairs (each of which was stamped "Guaranteed by Albert Brown") but also manufactured other pieces of furniture. In a short time, he was retailing furniture, especially chairs, throughout the surrounding area while wholesaling the remainder in Albany, Utica and other cities.

Local deliveries were made by shop apprentices on a push cart with two wheels and a platform about three by five feet.

A son, Theodore, joined the firm as a partner in the 1850's and it became known as A. Brown & Son. When Theodore died in 1864, another son, Clinton, became a partner once he had been discharged from service in the Union Army.

Shortly after this, Brown's had moved into a two-story wood frame building at the corner of Dock and State Street, a building which once was the City Hotel. Albert Brown, ailing at the time his second son joined the firm, died by 1880 and Clinton became sole owner.

The old wood building was wrecked in 1910 by the bursting of a water main on Dock Street (which extended along the east bank of the Erie Canal from State to Washington Avenue, earlier called Rotterdam Street.)

Immediate plans were made to erect a modern building in its place. Meanwhile, the furniture stock was moved to the old Center Street Opera House then located in the vicinity of what is now Broadway between Smith and Hamilton Streets.

The impressive new Brown's furniture buildings was completed in 1912 and the firm moved into it that fall. One of the former clerks of the firm, J. M. Laverty of Corinth, once recalled that one of the first orders of furniture which he personally sold at the new store was for two mahogany beds to the wife of Gov. William Sulzer (who served only one year before being removed from office in October, 1913.)

"As a furniture store, Brown's was said to be the most up-to-date of any store between New York City and Cleveland. Sterling Welsh was our rival," Mr. Laverty told us. "But I regret to say that we did not enjoy our new store too long."

Brown's went out of business in 1917 and sold the property to the Masonic Order, which converted it into the Masonic Temple that stands today at the southeast corner of the State Street and Erie Boulevard.

A rather interesting sidelight to the story of the Brown family in Schenectady is that they lived in a large residence at 237 Liberty St. which was razed in the mid-1950s. Here was born Miss Helen C. Brown, daughter of Theodore, and here it was she formed the Brown School before the turn of the century.

The patronage of prominent General Electric Co. officials, who wished to send their children to a private school, prompted her to move her school up to Rugby Road in the GE realty section of the city. It is there yet today.

A 1905 view of Dock Street (right) along the canal and State Street (left) with Brown Furniture Co. store in foreground, now the site of the Masonic Temple.

A rare view of the Maxon grain elevator, easterly view looking across the canal toward Pine Street and the locomotive works. Barge at right, partially under the Jefferson Street canal bridge, is unloading grain through the boxed chutes that were equipped with chain-driven riser scoops.

As Erie Canal commerce grew and prospered even before the 19th century was half over, it became evident that local merchants must also expand with the trade if they wished to share in the larger profits.

George G. Maxon, who was the seventh president of the Mohawk National Bank, later recognized the fact that a bigger facility was needed to store grain which was coming into this area in ever-increasing quantities from the midwest. In 1865, he and John Thompson built a seven-story grain elevator next to the canal at Jefferson Street and it enjoyed a quarter century of lively business.

The main building of the grain elevator complex was 60 by 100 feet and was 95 feet high. Many an "aerial" photograph was made from atop the structure of the Union College campus to the east and the American Locomotive Works to the north. The grain holder's capacity was one and a half million bushels and from 15 to 30 men were employed there, depending on the season.

After 1881, Maxon bought out his partner and ran the business with his sons, Ethan and Frank, as the Maxon Elevator Co. The elder Maxon died in 1886, two years after a stock company was formed as the Schenectady Elevator Co. and the firm was leased to Ralph Thatcher of Albany, who operated the business. Shortly thereafter, the Delaware & Hudson Railroad demolished the Maxon buildings and erected a freight house on the premises. More recently, the railroad building has been converted to a lumber and hardware business by Grossman's supply center.

George G. Maxon, who married Ann M. Wood, was a descendant of the Maxon family who came to this country from Wales in the early part of the 17th century. Several generations of Maxons long before the Civil War operated a profitable produce and commission business in Schenectady. Maxon Road was named after the family.

Besides the storage and sale of grain, George Maxon also had a flour and seed store on Wall Street in what was known as the Maxon Block, extending from Liberty Street south towards State Street. It burned in 1906 and was replaced by the Crown Hotel, later to become known as the Shear Block, razed in 1970 when the parking lot there was being developed.

The Maxon family residence was a yellow brick building at 404 Union St., which became the Physicians' and then Mercy Hospital before World War I. Today it is occupied by Spencer's Business Institute. The family also had a summer estate at 2519 Van Vranken Ave., then seemingly quite a distance from the city.

Ansel Cobb Maxon, a grandson of George Maxon, died in the Van Vranken Avenue home in 1970 at the age of 85. He had lived there with his sisters, Miss Ann M. Maxon and Mrs. Cordelia M. Kendall. The family furnishings were sold at auction and many items of historic value were bequeathed to local historical groups.

The Maxon home on Union Street about 1878. Center Street, now Broadway, is at right. In 1911, the building became Physicians' Hospital and from 1913 until 1917, it was Mercy Hospital. Today, still at 404 Union St., it is the Spencer Business Institute. Originally, it was the Archibald Campbell mansion.

These two views are from the same vantage point, Smith and Lafayette Streets, but about a century apart. Above is the original house built for Robert Furman in 1857 and below is the rectory of St. Joseph's Church, showing the addition towards the front.

When Robert Furman married Catherine Ann Van Guysling on Dec. 2, 1857, he took his young bride to their new home near the top of the spring-filled clay banks on Smith Street, overlooking sparse uptown section of Schenectady. While not the most sumptuous residence in town, it was surely looked upon as the mark of a wealthy man.

Furman, then 31, was a prosperous merchant of the city, having recently assumed the drygoods business of Myndert Van Guysling (Catherine's father) on the corner of State and Ferry just a few doors from the competitive H. S. Barney & Co. But at this point, when he and his new wife began housekeeping at the 51 Smith St. residence, he had only begun to garner the wealth and distinction that made him one of Schenectady's leading citizens within another decade.

He had come far since the day he arrived in Schenectady — a shy, 17-year-old farm boy from Oneida County — to become a clerk in the clothing store of his older brother, Rensselaer Furman. This was next to Van Guysling's store, so that when in a few years Robert bought his brother's small but flourishing business, the old Dutchman made a shrewd move by inviting the capable young man to join his firm. This, too, was a turning point in the fortunes of Robert Furman.

He was not satisfied with being just a merchant, no matter how successful. His interests were allied with civic development and politics. Although he came to Schenectady with the equivalent of high school training, having attended a classical academy at Mohawk, Herkimer County, Furman later succeeded by private study in gaining admittance to the bar and thereby branched out into new fields of endeavor.

This was about the time the Furmans moved into the fine two-story brick home at Smith and Lafayette (now the rectory of St. Joseph's Church). Probably his participation in the development of Crescent Park can be recorded as his first venture — into what was to become a regular series of public-spirited enterprises.

The first plan of the contemplated park as "a delightful breathtaking spot at the head of the city" was outlined in the Weekly Reflector in 1857. It suggested the ugly clay gully be fortified with trees and grass, later to be enhanced by benches, walks and perhaps a bandstand. The success of the project, however, hinged on the problem of widening the plot as a suitable park site. At that time it was a thin slice of land wedged between the road on the left which led up the hill to the Albany Turnpike and a road on the right going up to Albany Street.

Furman and Platt Potter, Supreme Court justice, got the ball rolling when they both donated fringes of their property on the south portion of the proposed park so the road could be angled to the right. It is not a matter of record, but it is said property owners on the opposite side also gave part of their frontage to assure a wider park.

Just how it finally got to be named Crescent Park has not been confirmed. The story is that Furman suggested the name because the contour of the new park resembled a half moon. It is a fact that after the park was laid out the following year, the thoroughfares on either side were intended to be called North and South Crescent — but somehow this never came to be, so that today they both remain simply State Street.

Furman's participation in civic endeavors came in quick succession. He was a member of a cemetery association, headed by Edward Rosa, which purchased a large tract of wooded glen just east of Nott Terrace known as the Vale. Its brook was turned into a succession of miniature lakes and the whole ground laid out for a park and cemetery. Vale Cemetery was dedicated in 1857.

He was one of the founders of the Schenectady YMCA in 1858, later donating $1,000 to its building fund.

Just after the outbreak of the Civil War, in the summer of 1861, a fire started in Otis Smith's broom factory near the corner of Front Street and Washington Avenue swallowed up many dwellings in that area. One of the casualties was the old Dutch Reformed Church, of which the Furmans were members.

Not long after, the congregation met to consider plans for a new church and Robert Furman was appointed to the committee that would see to getting the job done. When it was suggested a wooden church be constructed within conservative means, Furman roared, "Let's build a big church!" and backed up his words by initiating a drive to obtain financial pledges from its members.

The beautiful stone edifice, designed by architect Edward Potter, was soon erected and the Rev. Edward S. Seelye preached his first sermon in it the following year. Although the church was again a victim of a disastrous fire Feb. 1, 1948, its original structure remains.

Furman earned the rank of colonel when, during the draft riots of 1863, he was requested by Gov. Horatio Seymour — a personal friend as a result of his accomplishments as a lawyer in the state and U.S. courts — to raise a regiment of soldiers from the Schenectady area. This he did and the 83rd Regiment got its preliminary training on the fairgrounds located in what is now the Steuben Street district.

Although the outfit never did see action in the war, it continued in service as the 83rd Regiment for home defense until Jan. 17, 1874, when it was disbanded.

The only political office Furman ever held was that of member of the Assembly, when Reuben E. Fenton was governor. The colonel, a Democrat, was elected by the narrow margin of 50 votes over his Republican opponent, Austin A. Yates. One of his accomplishments during his single term of office was to obtain a state appropriation of $30,000 to construct an armory in Schenectady.

Many influential and farsighted Schenectady citizens are credited with convincing Thomas A. Edison and his associates that they should choose this location for the Edison Machine Works. It is not surprising to know that the energetic Furman was foremost among them. He was one of those who raised the $7,500 difference in purchase price (the Stanford Estate, owner of the old McQueen Locomotive Works property, demanded $45,000 but Edison would not go beyond $37,500) in a dramatic, last-ditch effort to bring the new industry here in 1886.

Impressed by the street railway system in larger metropolitan centers, Furman for many years thought Schenectady should move with the times and establish a horse railway here that would facilitate public travel. It so happened that during a visit to New York City, he broached the subject to A. R. Chisholm, railroad promoter. Chisholm came to Schenectady and laid the groundwork for the organization of the Schenectady Street Railway Co. in 1886. The horsecar line — which extended from Washington Avenue up to Brandywine Avenue — was formally opened in dedication ceremonies held at the foot of Crescent Park the following year. This was the beginning of the Schenectady Railway Co. with its miles of city and interurban electrified trolley lines.

Colonel Furman, who did not live to see the 20th century, certainly played an important role in the phenomenal transformation which resulted in the development of the small, quiet and seemingly self-satisfied city of Schenectady into a leading industrial center.

* * *

The brick dwelling at Smith and Lafayette Streets, now the rectory of St. Joseph's Church, is quite different today from the home built by Colonel Furman nearly 120 years ago. Both its structural design and its surroundings have changed drastically with time.

There were only two houses farther up Smith Street to Veeder Avenue, where a few dwellings were being built against the summit. Furman, a prosperous businessman, considered the suburban

Robert Furman

surroundings ideal for raising a family in a genteel atmosphere.

The streets then were of cobblestone with flagstone set at the crosswalks. Cisterns covered by planking nailed tightly together were at strategic corners to hold water that could be pumped out in case of fire in the neighborhood.

When the Furmans were raising their lively household of seven children, the house was not as large as today. It was of two-story brick, painted gray, with a straight roof line. A broad wooded frontage wall had been built up to keep the soil from washing downhill. There were two entrances from Lafayette, including a "cow gate" and two more on Smith Street. The one farthest up that street led into the rear of the property where a huge barn was located. There were other outbuildings in back. One was a shed in which Abe Vedder, carpenter, worked to keep up home improvements. There was a combination woodshed and ice house (where blocks of river ice were stored in sawdust). A brick stable and carriage house, still on the grounds today, housed four riding horses, a pony and a goat — plus two carriages and a pony cart.

Of the children born to the Furmans between 1860 and 1877, the last was the only girl. She was Miss Katharine A. Furman, who died in 1956 at

78. The others, in order of birth, were James, Robert Jr., Van Guysling, Franklin, Earle and Harry. Earle, last surviving child, died in 1963 at age 91. At the time of his death, he lived at 8 Union St.

As a prosperous businessman and budding lawyer, Colonel Furman owned real estate all over the city's suburbs. One of these sections was the flats below lower Hamilton Street, now encompassing the Broadway-Van Guysling Avenue area, which he bought about 1870 for a few thousand dollars because it was mostly swampy land. He restored it to usable land by building dykes along the upper hillsides, then tapping them after a rainstorm to wash down the clay and sand. The Furman's pasture land for two milking cows was located on Van Guysling near Edison Avenue.

During 1961 interview, Earle Furman recalled that when he was about seven years old, he would go from his classroom at the White Street School (which was located at what is now the rear of City Hall, Clinton and Liberty Streets) to the pasture and bring home the two cows by way of Hamilton and Smith streets.

* * *

Soon after midnight on Friday, Jan. 5, 1894, Colonel Furman knew he was dying. The 68-year-old civic leader had been ill only about two weeks, beginning with a sudden loss of appetite and severe stomach pains. Now he called his family to his bedside.

There were only five children left, James and Franklin having died young. Robert Jr., 31, was a New York City physician and Van Guysling was 30. The others were Earle, 21; Harry, 18, and Katharine, 16.

The last thing he told the boys was, "Take care of your mother and Kitty." He died at 2:20 a.m.

The former Civil War officer was given a military funeral the following Monday afternoon. After a brief family service at the home, a funeral cortege was formed at the foot of Crescent Park with the Citizens Corps Band and the 36th and 37th Separate Companies of the state militia at the head. As the procession moved slowly down State Street on its way to the First Reformed Church, the route was lined with people who had left work to witness the last honors paid a man who had been a great benefactor to the city.

The marching militiamen, Crescent Park, the beautiful stone edifice of First Reformed Church — even the Vale Cemetery which on this day was his final resting place — all were part of Colonel Furman's civic endeavors. But now, as the Rev. A.C. Sewall observed in his eulogy: "He has done with roofs and men. Open Time, and let him pass."

It was Earle Furman who completely remodeled the family home soon after his father's death. Since then it has changed little to this day or when it was sold to St. Joseph's Church and opened as a rectory in the fall of 1928.

Recently, the county administration arranged to acquire a portion of the spacious yard of the rectory as additional parking space for employes of the nearby county buildings. A vast change, indeed, from the days when Earle Furman brought the cows in from pasture.

Above, Liberty Street looking east toward Jay Street as it looked when Chester A. Arthur lived here. The house at left, corner of Yates Street, was the parsonage of First Baptist Church where the Arthur family resided. Spire of old Second Reformed Church is in center background. That edifice was razed in 1908 to make way for the post office and federal building. Below, the same scene as it looks today.

Chapter 49

YOUNG CHESTER ARTHUR

Chester Alan Arthur lived in Schenectady four years. Three of them were spent at Union College, thereby enabling that institution to claim him as one of its most illustrious alumni.

He first came here in August, 1844, when his father, a Baptist preacher, left a West Troy pastorate to accept a call to First Baptist Church of Schenectady. Rev. William Arthur, a Scotch-Irishman of stout character with a "scorn of conventionality and of the fashion which passes away," brought with him his Vermont-born wife and seven children to live in a two-story brick house on the east corner of Liberty and Yates Streets.

The Arthurs had been moving in and out of a number of communities since 1835 when they left Chester's birthplace in Fairfield, Vt. And although the Rev. Mr. Arthur would still serve churches in Lansingburgh, Albany and Newtonville before his death in 1875, Schenectady was to be the last place that Chester would live with his parents before striking out on his own.

He was a strapping 13-year-old lad when he came to Schenectady, which only recently could boast of both Erie Canal traffic and railroad transportation. The first year here he continued his education at the prominent Lyceum School, one of the better-known pre-college institutions in upstate New York, then located on Yates Street around the corner from Union.

The Arthurs did not own the Liberty Street house. Apparently it was leased as a parsonage of First Baptist Church as the Rev. Mr. Arthur's successor, Rev. Horace G. Day, is listed in the 1862 city directory as "boards at 79 Liberty, corner Yates." That same dwelling, which still stands, now is 425 Liberty St.

For many years, up to the mid-1930s, the site was occupied by the Jersey Ice Cream Co. which manufactured what it called "Schenectady's premier ice cream." Although the firm painted its name in huge letters across the top front of the building, the corner brick structure still had the appearance of a former residence. It does not look that way today. Liberty Electric Co. later purchased the property, modernizing the front with large plate windows and an entranceway in the center of the whole. The old brick exterior also has been cement stuccoed and painted.

The parsonage was unpretentious, yet it was an attractive home for the times. There was more room between the front porch step and the sidewalk in those days and, like so many other homes, it was filled with a small green lawn bordered by flowers. There also grew bushy sprawling plants with a brilliant scarlet fruit called "love apples." They were considered poisonous then, and it was not until farther into the 19th century that the idea proved false and tomatoes began to be cultivated as edible fruit.

The Methodist Episcopal Church was almost across the street from the Arthur home. That building today is St. John the Baptist School, now vacant.

* * *

No doubt when the Rev. Mr. Arthur first visited his church on coming to Schenectady, he was more than a little concerned over its location. It was on South Center Street, opposite Franklin, and was built shortly after First Baptist Church was organized in 1822 with 36 charter members. The congregation, too, was dissatisfied with the location now that the railroad had come. Only recently, the Utica & Schenectady Railroad had been completed and its tracks passed beneath the rear window of the brick edifice. Even the Rev. Mr. Arthur's strong, evangelistic delivery could not compete with the hiss of steam engines and the incessant clanging of bells in the midst of a sermon.

When the church finally did erect its 407 Union St. building in 1856 (now Friendship Baptist Church), the Rev. Mr. Day already had completed the first decade of his 50-year tenure as pastor of First Baptist. The Rev. Mr. Arthur and his family — except Chester — moved on to Lansingburgh in 1846.

Chester Arthur began his studies at Union College in September, 1845. He enrolled in the Class of 1848, having been permitted to start in the sophomore year through college examination. A statement in the college treasurer's book, now in Union's Schaffer Library, reads: "Chester Arthur, Baptist, Age 16."

Unusual to be entering college at so tender an age? Probably not, since those attending private schools in those days went on to college if their grades permitted. But, according to retired Prof. Frederick L. Bronner, former head of Union's history department, the entry in the treasurer's book raises interesting questions:

"Now if Arthur's birthday was in October as he said, and if in September 1845 he was 16 as his record says, then he was born in 1828. If he was born in October 1830 as he said, he was only 14 in September 1845. Was he really born in 1828 or did the registrar make a mistake? Or did Arthur lie about his age with the registrar's approval since the college rule still held that admission was forbidden to those under 16 — or did he know the rule and add a couple of years to gain admission? Did he lie or tell the truth? Did the registrar make a mistake intentionally or not? It is perplexing."

Actually, it had been charged in Chester Arthur's lifetime that he falsified his date of birth and his birthplace to accept the nomination as vice president at the Republican convention in Chicago in 1880.

It was only a few months after he became the 21st President of the United States by virtue of the assassination of President Garfield in 1881 that an "unfriendly writer" charged the new executive was not an American-born citizen but really was born in Canada. The author of "How a British Subject Became President of the U.S." claimed Arthur was the oldest son, not the second oldest, and therefore was born in Canada in 1828. He said Chester Arthur appropriated the birthday, and Vermont birthplace, of a second son who died in infancy and even made a secret trip to Canada to make sure there were no conflicting records to disprove his story.

The damaging brochure was discredited as without foundation, and the whole issue has since been dismissed by historians.

While at Union College, Chester Arthur preferred to live on campus so he moved his belongings from the Liberty Street parsonage up to his North College dormitory soon after enrollment. A section of a window sill from Room 25 of North College today hangs on a wall of the public relations office in Wells House. It bears the neatly carved letters: "C.A. Arthur."

The young man, growing yet taller and independent, followed the pattern of a model student. He got good grades and was elected to Phi Beta Kappa — but about one-third of his class of 79 students was, too. During the long winter vacations, he conducted schools in neighboring communities to earn a portion of his tuition. In those days tuition at Union cost him $28 during his three years; room and board ran about $125 a year.

The future President left Schenectady in 1848 after he was graduated from Union. He "read law" at Ballston Spa for a while and then took teaching assignments for several years which eventually led him to accept the job as principal of Cohoes Academy in 1852.

There is a curious coincidence relative to those few years he spent as a teacher. When he became schoolmaster of a country school in North Pownal, Vt., he succeeded the man whom he also would some day succeed as chief executive — James A. Garfield.

President Arthur, denied the opportunity to seek an election on his own account in 1884 when the Republican party nominated James G. Blaine, retired to private life to New York City where he died Nov. 18, 1886, from Bright's Disease. He was buried in Albany Rural Cemetery, Menands, where in the 1950s a huge Guardian Angel monument was installed to replace an original but smaller stone at the gravesite.

The gravesite monument to Chester A. Arthur in Albany Rural Cemetery, Menands.

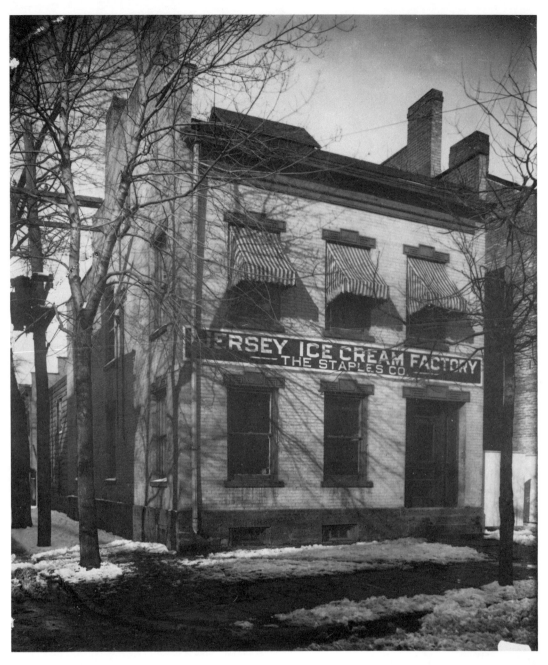

The old parsonage was used as a commercial establishment by the Jersey Ice Cream firm a half century ago. Above, Arthur's boyhood home as it looked in 1925. At right, Chester A. Arthur in 1880.

183

Above, work gang of the Jones Car Works in the 1880s. Below, workers of the Westinghouse Agricultural Works testing equipment on a Duanesburg farm in the 1890s. The sites of both firms, down on the great flat, were taken over by General Electric Co.

The Jones Car Works had a rather brief but industrious existence in Schenectady, lasting for some 10 years before it folded and ultimately was absorbed by the growing General Electric Co.

Walter A. Jones was president of the firm which produced mainly drawing room cars for the railroads. Its first such car, appropriately, was named "Schenectady" when it rolled off the line in 1882. Jones was the second person to build a home on Union Avenue when it was opened about 1880. He purchased five acres of land which included the pine grove and part of the "brook that bounds through old Union's grounds." It later became part of the GE realty plot.

Jones had erected his plant, consisting of a long one-story brick building, on the westerly side of what was then called Mill Lane (now GE's main avenue) in 1882 at about the same time Walter McQueen was building the two structures on the easterly side for what was supposed to be the McQueen Locomotive Works. The latter firm went into receivership, however, before it began operation and the two buildings were sold to Thomas A. Edison for his machine works that opened in December of 1886.

The Jones Car Works went out of existence in the early 1890s and was used for a time by the Gilbert Car Manufacturing Co. as an auxiliary plant to the factory at Green Island. The Gilbert firm, one of the principal early manufacturers of railroad cars in the U.S., also constructed hundreds of street cars for New York, Chicago and St. Louis.

In 1897, GE acquired the factory building and used it as a carpenter shop until it was torn down in 1908.

* * *

Near the head of the lane, along the south bank of the Erie Canal just beyond Rotterdam Street (now Washington Avenue), stood another former early Schenectady industry that also later was absorbed into the fast-growing acreage of General Electric.

This was the Westinghouse Agricultural Works which was built in Schenectady in 1856 after George Westinghouse Sr. decided his small shop in Central Bridge was not adequate to manufacture the new thresher he had devised. Westinghouse, a native of Pownal, Vt., had earlier established a machine shop in the Town of Florida in Montgomery County.

G. Westinghouse & Co. did well at its Schenectady site until the latter part of the 19th century, when competition from bigger firms in the farm machinery field caused business here to slump. By the time General Electric took over the old Westinghouse factory site after 1900, the latter firm had been run by Jay and John, sons of the founder. Westinghouse retired from active business shortly before his death in 1884, he having seen the fulfillment of the ideas he had conceived a half century earlier. In its heyday, the farm machinery plant employed between 250 and 300 men.

Incidentally, while the family lived in Schenectady, another son, George Westinghouse Jr., attended Union College. He went on to magnificent industrial heights with the Westinghouse Corp., the impetus of which was caused by the young man's invention of the railroad air brake. The latter was manufactured at Pittsburgh when it was first put on the market.

When General Electric took over the old Westinghouse factory site, all buildings were razed with the exception of a square, two-story brick structure topped by a cupola that stood nearest the canal bridge across Washington Avenue. This had been the Westinghouse office building and GE kept it as a local sales office and numbered it Building 34.

However, early in August, 1932, the local sales force under George Campbell moved into the first floor of Building 36 nearby as preparations were made to demolish the last of the Westinghouse plant. By Aug. 27, the ivy-covered building was gone.

Plans were made almost immediately for construction of a new WGY studio since the growing radio station was long since overcrowded in its Building 36 quarters. The stylish radio building, erected almost on the spot of the old Westinghouse offices, was dedicated in 1938. The surroundings had changed drastically since the days of the farm machinery operation. The canal was gone, replaced by the expansive boulevard, and now Rice Road veered westward past the sprawling General Electric plant into Rotterdam.

Times continue to change. The radio studio that opened to public plaudit in 1938 was torn down not long after it was replaced by the new WGY-WRGB-WGFM facility on Balltown Road in 1957.

Two old views of the Westinghouse plant, now the junction of Rice Road and Edison Avenue. The trolley cars crossed the canal bridge at this point. In center of both pictures is the Westinghouse office building (with cupola) that finally was torn down by GE in 1932 to make way for the new WGY studios.

One of the many unusual exhibits at the Schenectady County Historical Society, 32 Washington Ave., is a small portable sewing machine which played a dual role in the saga of American ingenuity.

This same crude device is one of the early models manufactured by Elias Howe soon after the Connecticut inventor patented the sewing machine in 1845 — and was used by Phineas T. Barnum to repair his circus tents. The hand-cranked machine weighs about 30 pounds, is black lacquered with inlaid mother-of-pearl. It fits into a heavy wooden box, marred and battered through years of rough use on the road.

Barnum, the master showman who later was to prove his philosophy that the public loves to be fooled as well as entertained, organized his tent shows out of Bridgeport, Conn., a few years before Howe set up a small manufacturing plant there. The two were good friends, and soon after obtaining his first U.S. patent on the sewing machine, Howe presented one to Barnum to take along on the sawdust trail. Barnum had often complained that much time was lost in sewing up canvas that had been rent by wind, wear and ticketbeaters.

After Barnum consolidated his traveling groups into one big circus in 1870, to be billed as "The Greatest Show on Earth," he gave the sewing machine to Madison Vedder, a Schenectadian who worked with Barnum's shows for many years. It is said that Vedder operated a sideshow concession and later married the "fat lady." When the Vedders quit the circus and came to Schenectady to live at 30 South Ferry St., the old sewing machine again changed hands. About 1897, Vedder gave it to a neighbor, Isaac D. Wessels, who lived at 14 South Ferry and managed the Singer Sewing Machine shop at 110 State St., just above the H.S. Barney Co. store.

The machine remained in the Wessels family until Dec. 23, 1919, when Stewart Wessels, a son of Isaac Wessels, presented it to the historical society.

The small machine is a pioneer in its own right. It set the stage for commercial adaptation of Howe's great invention that eventually would revolutionize the American garment industry. And when a corps of seamstresses with treadle sewing machines became a vital part of the "Big Top" after Barnum joined his chief rival, J.A. Bailey, in 1880, it must be remembered that a small portable Howe sewing machine was the forerunner of the service to the traveling circus. Only it is not now so much to repair canvas as to mend and produce dazzling costumes for the performers.

Above, carriage maker George Shaible in front of his establishment on South Center, now the east side of Broadway near State Street corner. Below, an old view looking northwesterly across Niskayuna Road (now Eastern Avenue) toward the John C. Ellis mansion (now the rectory of St. John the Evangelist). Ellis bought the child's sleigh for his young son.

In one corner of the toy room of the Schenectady County Historical Society is a tiny pull-type cutter which invariably catches the eye of visitors to the society's museum.

It is more than just an antique toy. A bit of Schenectady's history is connected with it.

It goes back to a winter's day shortly after the Civil war, when a heavy-set man with mutton chop whiskers called at the impressive brick Ellis mansion at the corner of Union street and Nott terrace.

George Shaible, considered the city's leading manufacturer of carriages and sleighs, had made the trip from his downtown establishment to deliver an order from John C. Ellis, president of the young Schenectady Locomotive Works and probably the wealthiest citizen of the area at that time.

It was an unusual order, calling for a child's sleigh no longer than three feet that was carefully constructed of hardwood and metal as a replica of the speedy horse-drawn cutters of the day. Shaible, proud of his craftsmanship and anxious to please his customers, had built the miniature model with the same care with which he turned out its larger counterparts.

Ellis was highly satisfied with the trim little cutter, painted with bright yellow enamel and trimmed with fancy red curliques along its runner and chassis. The business executive had ordered it for the infant son, John Ellis, who was born in 1865 to him and his young wife, Jane Schermerhorn Ellis.

A four-foot wooden shaft and handle were attached to the front so that the cutter and its small occupant could be pulled along on family walks. A straw-filled, upholstered seat cushion and tufted back rest provided built-in comfort. There was even a monogrammed "E" carefully lettered in red on the footboard.

The fancy decorative work was done by an artist known as a "carriage striper." That is now a lost art, just as so many other facets of handcraft disappeared with the advent of automation.

So elated was Shaible over Ellis' enthusiastic appraisal of the miniature sleigh that the artisan made another one in his South Center street shop — this time for his own young son, William G. Shaible, who was born in 1866.

Throughout the ensuing years, which saw the growth of Schenectady extend far beyond the Ellis home and eventually convert that residence into the rectory of St. John the Evangelist Church, the tiny Ellis sleigh was handed down to relatives.

It was last in the private possession of Miss Maude Stauring of 129 Elmer avenue, who donated it to the historical society in 1960.

She used it as a child as did others in her family before her after it was first built for John Elmer Ellis. She was a descendant of both the Ellises and the Shaibles. Mrs. Ellis was her great aunt and William G. Shaible her great uncle.

What of the Ellises and the Shaibles of the past century?

When John C. Ellis died Oct. 4, 1884, his two brothers, Charles and Edward Ellis took over the business helm at the locomotive works. His widow later married Joseph W. Smitley and they continued to live in the white-painted brick home at the top of College hill, then referred to as the Smitley Mansion.

John Elmer Ellis, the boy for whom the small cutter was made, lived most of his 36 years at the Smitley Mansion, but died in New York city on Jan. 21, 1901.

After the elder Shaible died Feb. 8, 1894, the carriage business at the downtown shop (which was located on the site of the razed Standard Furniture building) came to an end.

His son, William G. Shaible, later became an official of the former Citizen's Trust Co. here and was an officer of the Chase National Bank in New York city at the time of his death July 3, 1932.

All are buried in the family plots in Vale cemetery.

Wilfred Dalton, former historical society curator, and the tiny sleigh.

From an old engraving of the famous "Lightning," first locomotive made in the Schenectady Locomotive Engine Manufactory in 1848.

Receipt of June 17, 1848, signed by Edward A. Norris acknowledging payment of $293.68 by Simon C. Groot "being a full settlement between the Locomotive works and Septimus Norris."

About the turn of the 20th century, Schenectady had earned the title "The city that lights and hauls the world." On the southern extremity of the Erie Canal which was cut through Schenectady in 1825 was the General Electric Co., already a leader in the age of electricity, while down at the northerly city limits was the American Locomotive Co., a reputable manufacturer of steam locomotives for more than a half century.

Today, the Alco plant is gone and the canal has long since been replaced by a boulevard but General Electric has continued production, now at both ends of the city. Its global output of electrical machinery — including massive turbines and generators powered by steam, diesel and jet propulsion — has served to revise Schenectady's title to "The city that powers the world."

The story of the Alco takes in a big chunk of Old Dorp's long and illustrious history, however, and its importance to the city's growth and economy in the past century qualifies it for more than mere mention of its passing. Indeed, the founding of the steam engine manufactory in 1848 at once moved Schenectady out of the classification of "a sleepy little Dutch town" into an industrial phase it has enjoyed ever since.

Schenectady already had a stake in the exciting era of railroading, thanks in no small part to the vision and energy of George W. Featherstonhaugh of Duanesburg. He spent nearly a decade in promoting his dream of a steam railroad that would connect the Hudson River at Albany with the navigable Mohawk at Schenectady. That dream came true on Aug. 13, 1831, when the historic DeWitt Clinton drew the first train from Albany to Engine Hill (at the top of Crane Street hill) in Schenectady for the grand opening of the Mohawk and Hudson Railroad. In 1832 the Saratoga and Schenectady Railroad was completed, later to become part of the Delaware and Hudson system. By 1836 the Utica and Schenectady Railroad was opened and eight years later, the Troy and Schenectady line was in operation.

So it became quite apparent, at least to a number of prominent Schenectady businessmen, that the Mohawk Valley was ripe as the center of railroad construction in New York State. In 1847, John Ellis and Judge Platt Potter called together a group of progressive citizens for the purpose of organizing a locomotive works. Daniel D. Campbell, Simon C. Groot and J.C. Wright shared the enthusiasm of Ellis and Potter to the extent of underwriting a subscription of $50,000 to set up the enterprise.

Edward, Septimus and William Norris of Philadelphia, who had already established a good reputation in locomotive manufacturing, were invited to organize and manage the operation which began as the Schenectady Locomotive Engine Manufactory. They agreed, contributing what amounted to $10,576 in tools and machinery, and the articles of agreement were entered into on Jan. 20, 1848.

The plant was started on a triangular plot of some 12 acres south of the drydock (swing bridge) of the Erie Canal and east of Fonda Street (now known as North Jay Street) which was acquired from Union College for $1,000. In less than a year, the firm delivered its first locomotive which was sold to the Utica and Schenectady Railroad. It was the famous 15-ton "Lightning," an unusually fast and powerful locomotive which, unfortunately, was ahead of its time and existing light roadbeds.

The Norris brothers became discouraged with the lack of orders within a year of operation and company affairs were growing from bad to worse down at the young plant. The Philadelphians decided to pull out of the venture and the plant was idle for a year. But it was not the end of the locomotive industry in Schenectady.

On May 26, 1851, a new company known as the Schenectady Locomotive Works was formed and business conditions improved such that by 1854 the goal of building a locomotive in eight days was achieved, then bettered. New orders were now coming in rapidly from railroads in other parts of the country.

John Ellis, that canny and talented Scotsman who did so much to establish the works here, had been doing a good job as business agent and titular director of the company. He had already been a principal stockholder but in 1857, when a general business panic gripped the nation's economy, Ellis chose the opportunity to buy up a major share of stocks and take control of the company.

He again demonstrated his shrewdness at the outbreak of the Civil War when he began construction of a large number of locomotives without any orders on the books. It resulted in a windfall for Schenectady's economy and vaulted the locomotive works into industrial prominence. Within a few months the federal government purchased all locomotives on hand and the plant operated at peak capacity for the remainder of the war.

Ellis died in 1864 before the war's end, but he had lived long enough to see the firm he had helped establish take rank among the leading industries of America. As will be told in the story of the Ellis family to follow this piece, the fortunes of the locomotive works would continue to be directed by an Ellis until a giant merger in 1901 formed the American Locomotive Co.

* * *

It was about the time of the Civil War that those in this area began referring to the Schenectady Locomotive Works as "The Big Shop," a nickname which was affectionately attributed to it until the Edison works came into greater prominence by the 1890s. The government census of 1880 gave Schenectady a population of 13,655 — of whom about 1,000 were employed by the locomotive plant to keep pace with the annual production of 175 locomotives, a far cry from the meagre turnout of only a few years previous.

Management problems developed in 1882 when Walter McQueen, a skillful master mechanic and brilliant designer of steam engines, resigned as vice president to form a rival locomotive company. Joined by State Senator Charles Stanford and several other Schenectadians, McQueen bought eight acres of land along the south river flats and began construction of two factory buildings. However, Senator Stanford died suddenly and the project was left without its principal financial backer. In 1886, Thomas Edison bought the two unfinished buildings for his Edison Machine Works, the inception of what today is the General Electric Co. Meanwhile, McQueen and the Eillises reached a mutual understanding and he returned to his old job at the locomotive works.

In 1905, four years after a merger caused the firm to change its name to the American Locomotive Co., Alco entered the field of automotive man-ufactory and produced high-priced Alco cars, limousines and trucks. However, the assembly line techniques and lower priced vehicles mass produced by men such as Henry Ford were too much for the Schenectady plant to overcome, and in 1913 it quit the auto industry to concentrate on steam engines.

The company had always been an important contributor during wartime. It built hundreds of steam locomotives for the allies during World War I. During World War II it went into the manufacture of tanks and was the first in America to produce an M-3 (General Grant) tank satisfactory to the U.S. Army. All told, Alco produced about 6,000 tanks as well as 1,086 steam and 157 diesel electric locomotives for the War Department during the last world conflict.

The steam locomotive era came to an official end in 1948 when the American Locomotive Co. had built 75,000 units. A pioneer in the diesel electric locomotive field, Alco produced in 1924 the nation's first diesel electric unit — a 300-horsepower switcher locomotive, and in 1929 the first diesel electric passenger unit.

The company prospered down through the years, suffering through several economic depressions but still providing extensive employment for many citizens.

Immediately after 1901, when the "Big Shop" merged with seven other companies, the Schenec-

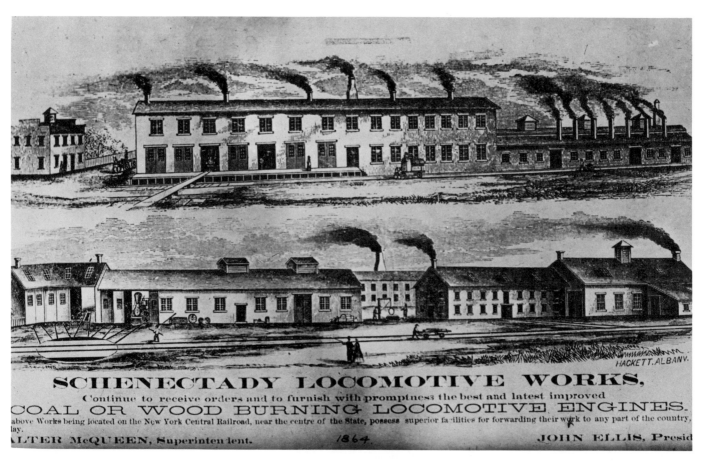

From an 1864 Schenectady city directory.

tady plant was expanded into what is known as the "West Side" — beyond the Erie Canal to the Mohawk River. This section was part of the early Schenectady settlement. The land was willed by Hans Janse Enkluys to a church organization about 1864, for the benefit of the poor, and was known as the "Poor Pasture."

The plant gradually expanded its facilities to 47 large and 110 smaller buildings on an area of 112 acres — about 10 times the acreage of the original plant constructed in 1848.

In 1955, after the acquisition of additional plants in various parts of the country, it was decided to change the well known name, American Locomotive Co., to Alco Products Inc. The new name, it was felt, would accommodate products other than locomotives now being manufactured by the firm.

The Latrobe, Pa., and Chicago Heights, Ill., plants, manufacturing industrial forgings and springs, were now a part of Alco, as was the plant at Auburn, N.Y., manufacturing diesel engines for stationary and marine application as well as for locomotives.

In addition, a new power generating unit known as the Alco Power Package, was soon to be added to the roster of the products built by the company.

With the acceleration of foreign railroad development after World War II, the company expanded its international operation and built close to 3,000 locomotives still in service on every continent in the world.

Alco Products became a subsidiary of the Worthington Corporation in 1965. After the merger of Studebaker with Worthington in 1967, it became a unit of Studebaker-Worthington Inc.

But the end of the saga of locomotive manufacturing in Schenectady, which had in truth ended several years before, was officially declared in 1968 when Alco's doors were shut by Studebaker-Worthington, never again to reopen as a locomotive plant. Several buildings were razed and a few were leased to private industrial interests. But the bulk of the old locomotive works has been taken over by General Electric, which went to considerable expense in renovating the former Alco buildings as an adjunct to the main plant across town.

The Ramada Inn, which opened in Schenectady in 1974, is located on the site of the original locomotive works and where one of the assembly buildings once stood. As an in-house attraction for its guests, the inn has set up a room as a "Railroad Hall of Fame." Directly across from the inn, corner of Nott Street and Maxon Road, is a shopping center where the Alco round house and paint shed at one time put the finishing touches on the engines which rolled out of the assembly shop.

Alco automobile, about 1906. In front seat are William L. Reid (left) and James McNaughton, both Alco officials.

193

Yard of the Schenectady Locomotive Works at about the time of the Civil War.

Gardens in the rear of the home of John C. Ellis, son of the works founder. The mansion, which can be seen in background, is today the rectory of St. John the Evangelist.

For more than a half century — up until June 24, 1901, when the Schenectady Locomotive Works was merged with seven other locomotive plants in different cities of the U.S. to become the American Locomotive Co. — the "Big Shop" was guided by the Ellises, the father John Ellis, and his four sons, John C., Charles G., Edward and William D. Ellis.

They are gone now, but much remains yet in Schenectady to make us remindful of their presence in another century. The beautiful brownstone homes where Edward and Charles Ellis and their families once lived are still a part of the lower Union Street scene. The Edward Ellis home at 215 Union St. is today used by the First Presbyterian Church as a Sunday School while the former Charles Ellis home at 217 Union St., later occupied by James W. Yelverton, became Amity Hall in 1948. Ellis Hospital is named after Charles Ellis, its chief benefactor. And the present rectory of St. John the Evangelist Church was once the home of John C. Ellis.

John Ellis saved the locomotive works from extinction in 1851 after the Norris brothers of Philadelphia pulled out of the failing two-year operation of the Schenectady Locomotive Engine Manufactory. The Schenectady Locomotive Works was founded under his presidency and prospered thereafter to become this city's leading industry. Death came to John Ellis in 1864, but he left the works in the hands of his four sons and their presidencies followed in order of their seniority.

John C. Ellis succeeded his father as head of the company, serving until 1878, six years before his death. Next came Charles G. Ellis, who was president until his death in 1891. Edward was president until he died in 1897. William, the fourth son of the founder, was in charge of the locomotive works until it became the American Locomotive Co. in 1901.

The amalgamation resulted in Albert J. Pitkin, well known for his work at the Baldwin Locomotive Works and also at the Rhode Island Locomotive Works, moving up in position from superintendent of the Schenectady works to its new vice president. He was to be influential in having the company produce heavier and heavier locomotives as an advocate of large boilers and increased grate areas. In 1904, with the death of Samuel R. Callaway, the first president of American Locomotive Co., Pitkin was named president and served until his death Nov. 16, 1905.

When he became company president in 1864, John C. Ellis and his wife lived at 86 College St. but at the war's end he decided to build the stately white mansion atop Union Street hill across from the college gate. In those days, his residence was on the outskirts of town and only vacant fields stretched eastward in the region of what today is Eastern Avenue.

A picturesque formal garden adjacent to the east side of the mansion was carefully tended by a groundskeeper and the carriage house at the rear (still there today, at the corner of Eastern Avenue and Nott Terrace) had living quarters on the second floor for the liveryman and his family.

After the death of John C. Ellis, his widow married Joseph W. Smitley and they lived in the former Ellis residence which then came to be known as the Smitley Mansion. It was Smitley and his brother, John H. Smitley of Pittsburgh, who provided the $15,000 to build and furnish the Ellis Hospital nursing home, called the Whitmore Home in memory of their mother, Keziah Whitmore, who died in 1893 at her Pittsburgh home. (The Whitmore Home was razed in 1973.)

The home of John Ellis, the works founder, was at Liberty Street and South College Street at the point of the canal crossing. After his death, his widow continued to live in the house — long since known as the Ellis Mansion — as well as two of her sons, Charles and Edward.

In time, however, Edward moved into a house at what was then 216 State St., next to the residence of Dr. Harman Swits. The Edward Ellis house later became the home of Jonathan Levi, Schenectady wholesale grocer, and that building still stands, now 428 State St. The Swits home was torn down when Charles W. Carl built his new department store on that site by 1916.

* * *

In 1883, this news item appeared in the Evening Star: "Edward Ellis and his brother, Charles G. Ellis, are negotiating for the purchase of a large plot of land on the north side of Union Street, extending from the residence of John O. Horsfall at 51 (old number) to the home of John B. Clute at 63 Union St. (old number)). The property was formerly a part of the estate of, Harmanus Peek, deceased. If successful in acquiring the property, the purchasers each intend to erect a handsome brownstone residence on the site."

By 1885, the two brownstones were up, each with a large carriage house in the rear, and pictures of the side-by-side mansions were featured in brochures of the day as "examples of fine residences in Schenectady."

Shortly after Dr. Charles P. Steinmetz, later to become renowned as GE's "electrical wizard," came to Schenectady he leased the former Ellis Mansion next to the canal and lived there until he built his Wendell Avenue home in 1903. The old Ellis house was demolished in the 1950s and today is the site of the Jack-in-the-Box drive-in eatery.

At the death of Charles G. Ellis in 1891, it was found that his will bequeathed the sum of $25,000 to be used in establishing Ellis Hospital in memory of his father, John Ellis, the founder of Alco. So it was that on March 27, 1893, the hospital moved into an attractive three-story brick building on Jay Street next to the old City Hall. When it moved up to its present location on Nott Street in 1906, the institution retained the name Ellis Hospital.

William Dewar Ellis, unmarried, spent much of his time in the New York City area until he became the last of the Ellises to assume the company presidency in 1897. Then he lived in a suite of rooms at the Edison Hotel. He was a member of some of the most exclusive clubs in New York State, among them the Union League Club, Society of Sons of the Revolution Republican Club, New York Athletic Club, Suburban Riding and Driving Club, Automobile Club and Transportation Club, all of New York City; the Saratoga Club and Golf Club of Saratoga, and the Mohawk Golf Club and Mohawk Club of Schenectady.

While a young man he received a liberal education, not only in American colleges, but also in France and Switzerland.

Edward Ellis as a boy in military school clothing. Old print was found among material in cornerstone box of 1892 works assembly shop on Nott Street when it was razed in 1959.

The residences of Edward Ellis (left) and Charles G. Ellis (right) still standing at 215 and 217 Union St.

196

Charles G. Ellis

Edward Ellis

Alfred J. Pitkin

The Harmanus Peek houses, demolished in 1884 for the building of the two Ellis homes on lower Union Street.

Rows of tank hulls off Seward Place during full tank production for World War II. Alco made good use of the former college pasture.

The last tank to roll off Alco line in 1954.

Quite a startling announcement appeared in local newspapers following a decision by the Union College Board of Trustees on Jan. 9, 1901 to sell a large portion of the sloping western extremity of the campus which for years had been known as the College Pasture.

Shortly after Union College moved from its West College building in 1814 to the new campus up on "the hill," taking residence in the few structures already built according to the design by Jacques Ramee, students and city residents alike dubbed the area just west of the renowned "seat of stone" as the "pasture." Which it was, indeed, as cattle once grazed along portions of the out-of-town plot and grain was harvested from other sections of it in the late summer.

There are stories galore about the old pasture, including the earliest known golf matches played along its extremity in the late 19th century by prominent Schenectadians who in time organized the Mohawk Golf Club. It was near the end of that last century, however, when Schenectady had so grown in population and industry, that the pasture was becoming encircled by urban life and was no longer to be considered excess real estate.

The college trustees, probably recognizing this fact (besides the extra revenue to the institution), announced that the pasture land fronting on Park Place from Nott Street to South Avenue would be divided into 44 lots, about 160 feet deep and varying in frontage. The property, with prices set from $600 to $1,500, was to be sold by realtor George W. Van Vranken, with offices at 334 State St.

Many offers came from developers, soon after the announcement was made, to buy the property as a whole but the college board decided to cut it up into building lots and dispose of them in this way.

"This affords home builders an opportunity to secure a lot at a reasonable price, and not at high speculative prices," a board spokesman said at the time. It was also stipulated that lots were to be sold with modern restrictions — such as the establishment of a building line and strict residential zoning.

A large advertisementsof the land sale appeared that week in Schenectady newspapers, noting the fact that "The location is a very desirable one, and with the beautiful shade trees, electric cars and convenient location, a better site would be difficult to find."

The response was tremendous. Van Vranken told a reporter that his office was crowded all the next day by persons seeking facts on the properties to be sold. The realtor called it "Schenectady's Oklahoma."

"This reservation has been fenced in, dividing the growth of the city since 1814 and now it is suddenly ordered open for development," Van Vranken said. "The College Pasture, in song and story endeared to the friends of 'Old Union,' is soon to become an integral part of the city's growth. Sacredly guarded from settlement since 1814, it is now to be taken by the 20th century from the cow and given the colonist."

Some of the city's leading citizens, including Charles H. Benedict, John N. Parker, Alfred Stoodley and George A. Cassidy, bought early. Mrs. Catherine Webb, formerly of Pawtucket, R.I., purchased a huge corner lot at the corner of Park Place and South Avenue. In no time, by that summer of 1901, homes were going up.

Because of the huge success of the sale, the college decided to sell more of the pasture later that year. A new thoroughfare was developed, called Seward Place in honor of William H. Seward, Union College graduate of 1820 and secretary of state in President Lincoln's cabinet. The newest lots ranged along the west side of Seward Place and almost overnight became one of the city's most attractive streets. By 1903, the city's first permanent public library was built at the corner of Union Street and Seward Place.

* * *

In later years, the college pasture — now less than half its original size — continued to be a grazing ground. Even up through the college administration of President Dixon Ryan Fox, in the 1930s and early 1940s sheep roamed the pasture between Library Field and Seward Place. However, with the advent of World War II, things again changed on that plot. The college agreed to cooperate in the war effort by leasing the north portion of the pasture for parking facilities as the Alco plant hummed with tank production.

After the war, Union College decided to use the pasture for its expansion program. West College dormitory was the first to go up in the early 1950s and other buildings soon followed. Today, the old college pasture is but a memory to older alumni and residents.

At left, the drug store which Henry A. Kerste built at 402 Union St. in 1892 and where he soon became one of the city's most popular druggists. Ercole Conti, who took over the business in 1940, retained the Kerste name and it is at the store front yet today. Above, in this 1878 view, young Henry Kerste is shown standing at left in front of Gustavus Steinfuhrer's drug store at 209 State St. (then No. 85) just west of North Ferry Street. With him are the store owner, center, and his father, Reverend Steinfuhrer of Astoria, L.I. Kerste was a clerk at the time, later attending the Albany College of Pharmacy and becoming a pharmacist in good standing.

Just mention the name Henry A. Kerste at any gathering of senior citizens of Schenectady yet today, and most eyes will light up in recognition of a man well known as "the Union Street druggist."

Indeed, Kerste made his mark as an enterprising and efficient drugstore operator before the turn of this century and many families relied on him for prescribed medicine any time of the day or night. And while he was careful not to overstep his bounds as a pharmacist, he had been known to be handy in emergencies in treating burns, scrapes and bruises within his establishment.

Kerste was born in Schenectady in 1865, four months after the Lincoln funeral train passed through town. He was the eldest of three boys and when he was only six, his father — a wholesale butcher who had come to America from Germany as a boy — drowned in the Erie Canal. His mother remarried. Young Henry attended the Union Street School at College and Union Streets (now the Van Dyck parking lot) and went on to the Albany College of Pharmacy from which he was graduated in 1886.

He got some early training at Gustavus Steinfuhrer's drug store at 209 State St. but in 1889, Kerste bought out the E. L. Davis pharmacy at Union and Yates Streets, beginning with $100 capital and earning $7 for his first day's receipts.

In 1892, Kerste built the handsome structure at 402 Union St. with a pharmacy on the ground floor and living quarters upstairs. The business, which still carries Kerste's name, is now run by Ercole Conti, one of his "boys"whom he trained as an apprentice and who succeeded him upon his retirement in 1940 after more than half a century as a "pill roller."

Shortly after his retirement, the old-time druggist recalled during an interview, "In the old days we had to make everything ourselves. We made our own pills, suppositories, infusions and ointments. We worked mainly with herbs."

It was a time when the mortar and pestle were the druggist's symbols, and mystical glass globes filled with colored water stood in each store window, a kerosene or gas light behind each at night as a sign that he was available in emergencies. Incidentally, Conti still has those symbols and many other artifacts from the old days when Kerste was one of Schenectady's best known pharmacists.

There was a period just after the introduction and popularization of the ice cream soda and phosphate drinks when Kerste succumbed to public demand for a soda fountain. But after a few years, it became evident to Kerste that "either I had to spend my time preparing sodas or I had to devote it to prescriptions. . .the soda fountain had to go." As a matter of fact, although he did close down the ornate wood and marble soda fountain in later years, it remained inside the Kerste store after Conti purchased the property and business. More than a decade ago, after an unsuccessful attempt to get it stored in a local museum, Conti finally sold the soda bar to a New England village museum.

During his youth, Kerste was noted as an area "dare-devil" of sorts. He was an ardent bicyclist in the 1880s in the days of the "high wheeler" when cycling was almost as dangerous as driving "hot rod" jalopies is now. He was also a bobsled enthusiast when bobbing was a favorite winter sport in Schenectady. He captained the Snow Queen team that competed on Union Street hill, sliding almost as far as the Erie Canal (now Erie Boulevard). Later, in 1902, Kerste was one of six persons to own an automobile in Schenectady. His car was a Pierce Motorette. The next year, the Pierce Arrow was on the market.

* * *

We hear much today of armed robberies of business establishments. Kerste once recalled that he had his share of incidents which involved persons who broke in to obtain drugs and/or money. The most serious attempted break-in occurred in November, 1938. His clerks had gone for the night and he was sitting at his desk in the rear of the store about 10 p.m. when he heard a scratching noise at the rear door. Thinking his dog wanted to enter, Kerste opened the door and a masked man thrust a revolver into his face and tried to come in with a companion, also masked.

Kerste struck at the gun but failed to knock it to the floor. The man hit Kerste in the face with the weapon, fracturing the druggist's jaw and knocking out his front teeth. The injuries kept Kerste in bed for a long time, but he had foiled the robbery attempt.

After he returned to work, Kerste must have mulled over the possibility of retirement. He soon stopped filling prescriptions, leaving that to Conti and the late Harry Dodge. But the store was familiar ground and it was with difficulty, even after he officially retired, that he could face up to not putting in a full day either behind the counter or chatting with his old customers outside the store.

Kerste married Susanna Glass of Schenectady in Temple Congregational Church on North College Street. They lived over the drug store until she died in 1949. He died on Aug. 30, 1955 — 26 days after his 90th birthday.

Above, the Burr Bridge as viewed along the Scotia dyke road. Schenectady is in right background. Below, one of the two lanes within the bridge.

For 66 years of the previous century, the bridge which connected the Washington Avenues of Schenectady and Scotia was well used and widely appreciated. It should have been, for it was the first bridge to cross the Mohawk River in the Schenectady area.

After it was constructed in the dawning of the 19th century, the span had many names — the Burr Bridge, the covered bridge, toll bridge and Mohawk River Bridge — but there is little question that no matter what name was attributed to it, the old structure served the traveling public well.

Until the bridge was constructed, a ferry was the only means of transportation across the Mohawk, operating locally at Hoffman's between Rotterdam Junction and Glenville, at the foot of Ferry Street in Schenectady to the opposite shore, and in the vicinity of present-day Freeman's Bridge. While it was better than nothing, the ferry was slow and inefficient for all the commerce of the busy merchants, farmers and their families.

In 1800 the Mohawk Turnpike and Bridge Co. was formed to erect a bridge and toll road from Schenectady to Utica, about 80 miles, to be called the Mohawk Turnpike. The bridge became a project separate from the turnpike, of which it was the eastern terminus in 1805. Even before the bridge was finished, the turnpike company had constructed the dyke road along the Scotia shoreline that today is called Schonowe Avenue. The present Amsterdam Road or Route 5 was the course of the Mohawk Turnpike as it headed westward from Glenville, replacing a path that accommodated only hikers or horseback riders.

The Mohawk River bridge, an engineering marvel of our new nation, was designed by Theodore Burr, cousin of Aaron Burr, and was said to be the crowning glory of the well-known architect. It was a suspension bridge 900 feet long, with cables made of massive pine planks bolted together.

Its completion on Dec. 6, 1808, was an occasion of grand celebration in honor of the event. Gov. Daniel D. Tompkins, the state comptroller and other men prominent in state and local politics attended the opening ceremony and, for the only day in the bridge's history, crossed each way without paying toll.

Some years after 1809, four other piers were added to the original three, ruining the appearance quite unnecessarily, because fears of the durability of the three piers were groundless. Then, in a few years after its construction, a protective covering of clapboards was added, giving the bridge a ragged look quite different from what the architect had intended.

Lighting by day was through an opening three feet square on each pier and the cracks between the siding. A visitor to Schenectady in 1872 wrote: "Through these openings along with the sunlight come also the swallows and other birds that have a taste for the picturesque. Dear especially to the bats is the network of beams overhead with its sombre twilight."

At night a total of four oil lamps, each of three candlepower of brightness, seared the shadows of the covered bridge. The two lanes of the bridge, separated by a three-foot high chord down the center, had two little lamps each. The floor was uneven and 18 inches lower between the piers than on them.

For 50 years, David Hearsay was the bridge keeper while Christopher Beekman, better known as "Uncle Stoeffel," was toll taker for the cavernous structure.

In 1873, the Town of Glenville purchased the bridge from William Van Vranken, as treasurer of the Mohawk Bridge Co., for $12,600. Some distance east of the old bridge, Volney Freeman had erected a bridge over the Mohawk in 1855 and this the town also purchased in 1879.

The covered bridge was declared unsafe and the town closed it and sold it at auction in parcels for about $500. Most of the timber went to a firm which made matches.

While in the process of demolition in the summer of 1874, after the covering was ripped off, the bridge returned in its last hours to the beauty of its youth. The superb arches and the graceful curves of the original structure were revealed.

Once it was gone, the old covered bridge was replaced by a simple steel structure built upon the same broad stone piers. Glenville collected the toll from all users of the bridge except Glenville taxpayers — a reason for Schenectady individuals and merchants to buy bits of Glenville property to avoid the toll. It was not until about 1920 that the Washington Avenue Bridge, as it came to be called, became toll free.

The steel bridge became important in local public transportation when the Schenectady Railway Co. used it for the Scotia trolley line opened in April, 1902. A year later, both the SRC and the Fonda, Johnstown & Gloversville Railroad also used the steel bridge for the interurban trolleys which went west to Amsterdam.

When the first Great Western Gateway Bridge opened in December, 1925, the Washington Avenue bridge was used mostly by the trolleys and pedestrians. In the mid-1930s, buses began to replace the electric cars on the Scotia run so that now the old bridge was looked upon by city and village officials as more of a hazard than a necessity. Its upkeep in later years had been sadly neglected, so much so that on the public thoroughfare (separated from the trolley tracks) loose and rotted deck boards could give one an uneasy glimpse of the river flowing below.

It was closed in 1939 and taken down shortly thereafter. The stone piers in the main river channel were removed about 20 years ago. However, both on the Schenectady and Scotia side, traces of the old bridge can still be seen.

During its demolition in the summer of 1874, the old Burr (or Mohawk) Bridge was once more exposed in its original glory — the graceful lines of the laminated Norway spruce cables showing what architect Theodore Burr had intended when it was erected 66 years before. It was among the first suspension bridges built in America and was considered an engineering marvel at the time. A metal bridge, used until 1939 between Schenectady and Scotia, was erected on the same piers shortly after.

Index